Lifestyle Media in Asia

Across Asia, consumer culture is increasingly shaping everyday life, with neoliberal economic and social policies being adopted by more and more governments who have come to see their citizens as individualized, sovereign consumers with choices about their lifestyles and identities. One aspect of this development is the emergence of new wealthy middle classes with lifestyle aspirations shaped by national, regional and global media – especially by a range of new popular lifestyle media, which include magazines, television, and mobile and social media. This book explores how everyday conceptions and experiences of identity are being transformed by media cultures across the region. It considers a range of different media across various Asian contexts, reflecting on how the shaping of lifestyles in Asia differs from similar processes in Western countries, and assessing how the new lifestyle media not only represent an emergent media culture, but also illustrate wider cultural and social changes in the Asian region.

Fran Martin is an Associate Professor and Reader in Cultural Studies at the University of Melbourne, Australia and an Australian Research Council Future Fellow.

Tania Lewis is an Associate Professor in the School of Media and Communication at RMIT University, Melbourne, Australia.

Media, Culture and Social Change in Asia Series

Series Editor: Stephanie Hemelryk Donald

The aim of this series is to publish original, high-quality work by both new and established scholars in the West and the East, on all aspects of media, culture and social change in Asia.

1 Television Across Asia
Television industries, programme formats and globalisation
Edited by Albert Moran and Michael Keane

2 Journalism and Democracy in Asia
Edited by Angela Romano and Michael Bromley

3 Cultural Control and Globalization in Asia
Copyright, piracy and cinema
Laikwan Pang

4 Conflict, Terrorism and the Media in Asia
Edited by Benjamin Cole

5 Media and the Chinese Diaspora
Community, communications and commerce
Edited by Wanning Sun

6 Hong Kong Film, Hollywood and the New Global Cinema
No film is an island
Edited by Gina Marchetti and Tan See Kam

7 Media in Hong Kong
Press freedom and political change 1967–2005
Carol P. Lai

8 Chinese Documentaries
From dogma to polyphony
Yingchi Chu

9 Japanese Popular Music
Culture, authenticity and power
Carolyn S. Stevens

10 The Origins of the Modern Chinese Press
The influence of the Protestant missionary press in late Qing China
Xiantao Zhang

11 Created in China
The great new leap forward
Michael Keane

12 Political Regimes and the Media in Asia
Edited by Krishna Sen and Terence Lee

13 Television in Post-Reform China
Serial dramas, Confucian leadership and the global television market
Ying Zhu

14 Tamil Cinema
The cultural politics of India's other film industry
Edited by Selvaraj Velayutham

15 Popular Culture in Indonesia
Fluid identities in post-authoritarian politics
Edited by Ariel Heryanto

16 Television in India
Satellites, politics and cultural change
Edited by Nalin Mehta

17 Media and Cultural Transformation in China
Haiqing Yu

18 Global Chinese Cinema
The culture and politics of hero
Edited by Gary D. Rawnsley and Ming-Yeh T. Rawnsley

19 Youth, Society and Mobile Media in Asia
Edited by Stephanie Hemelryk Donald, Theresa Dirndorfer Anderson and Damien Spry

20 The Media, Cultural Control and Government in Singapore
Terence Lee

21 Politics and the Media in Twenty-First Century Indonesia
Edited by Krishna Sen and David T. Hill

22 Media, Social Mobilization and Mass Protests in Post-colonial Hong Kong
The power of a critical event
Francis L. F. Lee and Joseph M. Chan

23 HIV/AIDS, Health and the Media in China
Imagined immunity through racialized disease
Johanna Hood

24 Islam and Popular Culture in Indonesia and Malaysia
Edited by Andrew N. Weintraub

25 Online Society in China
Creating, celebrating, and instrumentalising the online carnival
Edited by David Kurt Herold and Peter Marolt

26 Rethinking Transnational Chinese Cinemas
The Amoy-dialect film industry in Cold War Asia
Jeremy E. Taylor

27 Film in Contemporary Southeast Asia
Cultural interpretation and social intervention
Edited by David C. L. Lim and Hiroyuki Yamamoto

28 China's New Creative Clusters
Governance, human capital, and investment
Michael Keane

29 Media and Democratic Transition in South Korea
Ki-Sung Kwak

30 The Asian Cinema Experience
Styles, spaces, theory
Stephen Teo

31 Asian Popular Culture
Edited by Anthony Y. H. Fung

32 Rumor and Communication in Asia in the Internet Age
Edited by Greg Dalziel

33 Genders and Sexualities in Indonesian Cinema
Constructing gay, lesbi and waria identities on screen
Ben Murtagh

34 Contemporary Chinese Print Media
Cultivating middle class taste
Yi Zheng

35 Culture, Aesthetics and Affect in Ubiquitous Media
The prosaic image
Helen Grace

36 Democracy, Media and Law in Malaysia and Singapore
A space for speech
Edited by Andrew T. Kenyon, Tim Marjoribanks and Amanda Whiting

37 Indonesia-Malaysia Relations
Cultural heritage, politics and labour migration
Marshall Clark and Juliet Pietsch

38 Chinese and Japanese Films on the Second World War
Edited by King-fai Tam, Timothy Y. Tsu and Sandra Wilson

39 New Chinese-Language Documentaries
Ethics, subject and place
Kuei-fen Chiu and Yingjin Zhang

40 K-pop – The International Rise of the Korean Music Industry
Edited by JungBong Choi and Roald Maliangkay

41 China Online
Locating society in online spaces
Edited by Peter Marolt and David Kurt Herold

42 Multimedia Stardom in Hong Kong
Image, performance and identity
Leung Wing-Fai

43 Television Histories in Asia
Issues and contexts
Edited by Jinna Tay and Graeme Turner

44 Media and Communication in the Chinese Diaspora
Rethinking transnationalism
Edited by Wanning Sun and John Sinclair

45 Lifestyle Media in Asia
Consumption, aspiration and identity
Edited by Fran Martin and Tania Lewis

Lifestyle Media in Asia

Consumption, aspiration and identity

Edited by
Fran Martin and Tania Lewis

Routledge
Taylor & Francis Group
LONDON AND NEW YORK

First published 2016 by Routledge

2 Park Square, Milton Park, Abingdon, Oxfordshire OX14 4RN
711 Third Avenue, New York, NY 10017

Routledge is an imprint of the Taylor & Francis Group, an informa business

First issued in paperback 2017

British Library Cataloguing in Publication Data
A catalogue record for this book is available from the British Library

Library of Congress Cataloging in Publication Data
Names: Martin, Fran, 1971- editor. | Lewis, Tania, editor.
Title: Lifestyle media : consumption, aspiration and identity / edited by Fran Martin and Tania Lewis.
Description: Abingdon, Oxon ; New York, NY : Routledge, 2016. | Series: Media, culture and social change in Asia ; 45 | Includes bibliographical references and index.
Identifiers: LCCN 2015041237| ISBN 9781138831452 (hardback) | ISBN 9781315736563 (ebook)
Subjects: LCSH: Lifestyles–Asia. | Consumers–Asia. | Identity (Psychology) and mass media–Asia. | Mass media–Social aspects–Asia.
Classification: LCC HQ2044.A78 L54 2016 | DDC 302.23095–dc23
LC record available at http://lccn.loc.gov/2015041237

ISBN: 978-1-138-83145-2 (hbk)
ISBN: 978-1-138-47741-4 (pbk)

Typeset in Times New Roman
by Taylor & Francis Books

Contents

List of figures

Contributors

Bart Barendregt is an anthropologist at the Leiden Institute of Cultural Anthropology and Development Sociology, the Netherlands. He has an interest in popular and digital culture, and has published on and made films about Southeast Asian performing arts, new and mobile media, and (Islamic) pop music. His publications include the edited volumes *Recollecting Resonance: Indonesian Dutch Musical Encounters* (2013) and *Green Consumption: The Global Emergence of Eco Chic* (2014). He is currently working on a book dealing with Islamic boy band music and the mixing of religion, youth culture and politics that has become popular among Malaysian and Indonesian student activists.

Genevieve Bell is an anthropologist and research fellow at Intel, USA. Her expertise in ubiquitous computing is displayed in her co-authored book (with Paul Dourish), *Divining a Digital Future: Mess and Mythology in Ubiquitous Computing* (2011).

Chua Beng Huat is concurrently Convener of Cultural Studies Programs in the Faculty of Arts and Social Sciences, and Research Leader of Cultural Studies in the Asia Research Cluster, Asia Research Institute, National University of Singapore (NUS). Before joining the NUS, he was Director of Research at the Housing and Development Board. His research areas include housing and urban studies, cultural studies in Asia, East Asian pop culture, and comparative politics in Southeast Asia. He is a founding co-editor of *Inter-Asia Cultural Studies.*

Yue Gao is a PhD candidate in the China Research Centre, University of Technology Sydney (UTS). Yue's research interest is in sociocultural representation of diseases, media and health reform in China. Prior to arriving at the UTS, she graduated with both Bachelor's and Master's degrees in journalism from Fudan University, Shanghai, China.

Larissa Hjorth is Professor in the Games Programs at RMIT University, Australia. She is an artist and digital ethnographer who researches gendered customizing of mobile, social and gaming communities in the Asia-Pacific. She is the author of *Mobile Media in the Asia-Pacific* (Routledge, 2009), and

Games & Gaming (2010). Hjorth has co-edited three Routledge anthologies, *Gaming Cultures and Place in the Asia-Pacific Region* (2009), *Mobile Technologies: From Telecommunication to Media* (2009), and *Studying the iPhone: Cultural Technologies, Mobile Communication, and the iPhone* (2012).

Heather Horst is a Vice Chancellor's Senior Research Fellow in the School of Media and Communication at RMIT University, Australia. She has been researching mobile communication, transnational migration and digital media practices, and has published widely in anthropology, media and communication journals. Her books include *The Cell Phone: An Anthropology of Communication* (2006), *Hanging Out, Messing Around, and Geeking Out: Living and Learning with New Media* (2009), and an edited volume with Daniel Miller, *Digital Anthropology* (2012). She is currently carrying out research on mobile media and communication in the global South on three projects.

Chris Hudson is Associate Professor of Asian Media and Culture in the School of Media and Communication, RMIT University, Australia. She has published widely on cultural politics in Singapore, including *Beyond the Singapore Girl: Discourses of Gender and Nation in Singapore* (2013), a study of the politics of fertility, narrative control and resistance in Singapore. She is a co-author of *Theatre and Performance in the Asia-Pacific: Regional Modernities in the Global Era*, funded by the Australian Research Council Discovery Project Scheme, which examines the diverse theatre and performance traditions in the Asia-Pacific region.

Sun Jung is a research fellow in the Asia Research Institute at the NUS. She has published broadly on South Korean popular cultures, lifestyles and transnational media flows, including the monograph *Korean Masculinities and Transcultural Consumption:* Yonsama*, Rain,* Oldboy *and K-pop Idols* (2011). Her current projects include social media and cross-border cultural transmission; K-pop: art of cultural capital; neoliberal capitalism, sustainable lifestyles and media representations; participatory public space: a right to the networked city; and sexuality and gender in Asian pop cultures.

Fumitoshi Kato is a Professor in the Faculty of Environment and Information Studies, Keio University, Japan. His areas of specialty are communication theory, media theory and qualitative research methods. Professor Kato's major publications include, as co-author, *Gemingu shimuleshon* (Gaming simulation) (1998), and as author, *Kyampuron: atarashii firudowaku* (Camp theory: A new fieldwork) (2009). His most recent work involves conducting field research in various local communities in Japan, with a focus on the notion of "mobile learning."

Youna Kim is Professor of Global Communications at the American University of Paris, France, joined from the London School of Economics and Political Science where she had taught since 2004, after completing her

PhD at Goldsmiths, University of London. Her books include *Women, Television and Everyday Life in Korea: Journeys of Hope* (Routledge, 2005), *Media Consumption and Everyday Life in Asia* (Routledge, 2008), *Transnational Migration, Media and Identity of Asian Women: Diasporic Daughters* (Routledge, 2011), and *The Korean Wave: Korean Media Go Global* (Routledge, 2013).

Tania Lewis is Deputy Dean of Research and Innovation and an Associate Professor in the School of Media and Communication at RMIT University. Her research focuses broadly on questions of lifestyle, sustainability and consumption, and on global media cultures. Her books include *Smart Living: Lifestyle Media and Popular Expertise* and *Telemodernities: Television and Transforming Lives in Asia* (forthcoming with Duke University Press and co-authored with Fran Martin and Wanning Sun). She is also a co-author (with Sarah Pink et al) of *Digital Ethnography: Principles and Practices* and editor and co-editor of 3 other collections with Routledge, *TV Transformations*, *Ethical Consumption*, and *Green Asia* (forthcoming). She is a chief investigator on the Australian Research Council discovery project, "Ethical Consumption: From the Margins to the Mainstream".

Chris Malmo has a PhD from RMIT University, Australia. He is co-founder of Paper Giant.

Fran Martin is an Associate Professor and Reader in Cultural Studies at the University of Melbourne, Australia and an Australian Research Council Future Fellow. Her research focuses on television, film, literature, Internet culture and other forms of cultural production in contemporary transnational China (the People's Republic of China, Taiwan and Hong Kong), with a specialization in representations and cultures of gender and sexuality. Her publications include *Backward Glances: Contemporary Chinese Cultures and the Female Homoerotic Imaginary* (2010), *Mobile Cultures: New Media in Queer Asia* (2003, co-edited with Chris Berry and Audrey Yue), *Situating Sexualities: Queer Representation in Taiwanese Fiction, Film and Public Culture* (2003), and *Angelwings: Contemporary Queer Fiction from Taiwan* (2003).

Kana Ohashi is a visiting researcher at the Keio Research Institute at the Shonan Fujisawa Campus, Japan. She graduated from Keio University with a BA in Policy Management and completed a documentary filmmaking program at MET Film School.

Sarah Pink is a Professor at the Design Research Institute and the School of Media and Communication, RMIT University, Australia. She is a global authority on digital visual and sensory ethnographic methodologies and has published over a dozen monographs on the topic.

Wanning Sun is a Professor of Media and Cultural Studies at China Research Centre, UTS, Australia. Sun researches and supervises research students in a number of areas, including Chinese media and cultural studies, gender, migration and social change in contemporary China, and diasporic Chinese media. Sun's current research interests include the cultural politics of class and inequality, regional media cultures, consumption and everyday life, and grassroots media activism in urban China.

Wu Jing is a Professor in the School of Journalism and Communication at Peking University, China. Her research areas are media and cultural studies, social theories of mass communication, media and the public sphere, identity and ideology, media and modernity. She has published articles both in Chinese and English on topics concerning various aspects of media and society. Her most recent book is entitled *Visual Expressions of Cultural Modernity: Ways of Seeing and Communication*. She has guest lectured at the University of Oxford, Columbia University and the Royal Institute of Technology among others.

Miao Xiao graduated from the School of Journalism, Fudan University, China. She now works at Tencent, one of China's largest Internet companies.

Fang-chih Irene Yang is a Professor in the Department of Taiwanese Literature, National Cheng Kung University, Taiwan. Her research addresses the intersection of gender, class, ethnicity and national politics in popular culture in East Asia. Her objects of study include women's magazines, TV dramas, variety shows and popular music. Her most recent publications appear in *The Journal of Popular Culture*, *International Journal of Cultural Studies*, and *The Korea Observer*.

Baohua Zhou is a Professor and Director of the new media communication Master's program at the School of Journalism, Fudan University, China. He is also a research fellow of the Center for Information and Communication Studies and Associate Director of the Media and Public Opinion Research Centre of Fudan University. His research focuses on new media, media effects and public opinion, and has been published in the *Asian Journal of Communication*, *Chinese Journal of Communication*, and various communications journals in China.

Acknowledgements

This book is the product of a research project funded by a grant from the Australian Research Council (DP 1094355).

The editors extend special thanks to Professor Eric Kit-wai Ma, Professor Meaghan Morris, Professor Graeme Turner, Professor Koichi Iwabuchi, Associate Professor Audrey Yue, Dr Tripta Chandola, Dr Jolynna Sinanan, Dr John Postill and our outstanding group of postgraduate students, Marie Kim, Wilfred Wang, Crystal Abidin and Christin Cornell, for their contributions to the conference in Melbourne in 2013 on which this collection is based. Our thanks, too, are due to Jacinthe Flore, without whose assiduous research assistance this volume could not have been prepared, and to Professor Stephanie Hemelryk Donald for her support for this book project.

Foreword

Rethinking consumption in economic recessionary East Asia

Chua Beng Huat

Looking back, I could say the period between the late 1980s and the end of the 1990s were the triumphal days of consumption internationally: both actual material consumption and academic interest in consumption. However, from the early 2000s onward, with the intensification of global finance capitalism, asset ownership began to be associated with disproportionately higher returns than wage work. Middle-class wages have now stagnated or rolled back for more than decade, and the working classes have suffered real wage loss. Income inequalities have intensified in all East Asian countries.

In cities like Taipei, Singapore, Hong Kong and Shanghai, there has been a re-focusing of the middle class on the necessities of housing, healthcare and social security for an aging population. In all these societies, the social safety net is weak. Concern with employment stability has resulted in an emerging xenophobia in Hong Kong and Singapore, two global cities that have previously always been comfortable with strangers. In Taipei, young professionals are unable to afford basic housing. Marriage is delayed. So too is the arrival of first children, due to concerns about the cost of bringing up children in a way that "ensures" that children do not drop out of the middle class. In rapidly aging societies like Japan, Taiwan, South Korea, Singapore and China, funding the costs of prolonged sickness and other retirement needs is a constant source of anxiety, especially since the first line of payment is family members rather than a welfare state. Gone are the days in which double-digit annual economic growth raised the standard of material life for all. The re-focusing of daily life to basic necessities has severely curbed consumption, even if the construction of shopping centers continues as newspapers and magazines get fatter with advertisements and the TV screen continues to project a cornucopia of lifestyle consumption.

Consumption in Asia: after the new rich generation

Setting the scene

Capitalism experienced a long period of global expansion from the early 1950s until, arguably, the end of the 1990s, engendering consumerism as everyday culture, first in Europe, the USA and Australasia, and immediately after the Second World War and before the early 1980s, in the newly industrialized export-oriented economies of East Asia – namely Japan, Korea, Taiwan, Hong Kong and Singapore. The newly industrialized economies of East Asia marked, in retrospect, the first wave of the globalization of late capitalism. By the last quarter of the 20th century, almost all Asian nations had embarked on the same industrial development strategy: vying for foreign direct investment and free flowing financial capital. Global capitalism gathered speed with the collapse, in quick succession, of the real socialist economies in Eastern Europe and Asia. Emerging from the multidimensional disaster of the Great Proletarian Cultural Revolution, socialist China began its transformation into a market economy from the end of the 1970s, under Deng Xiaoping, beginning with the market liberalization of agricultural production in the rural areas, and quickly establishing its first economic free trade zone in Shenzhen in 1980. The 1980s saw the dismantling of the Soviet Union and the relative political and economic independence of Eastern European nations, some of which – such as Poland – quickly joined the European Union. Russia followed with *Perestroika* and *Glasnost*, and the restructuring of both the state and the economy. Meanwhile, social welfare provisions – the result of negotiations between unions and government in Britain and of liberal reforms and civil rights movements in the USA – were being dismantled by Margaret Thatcher and Ronald Reagan, in their respective nations. It was the time of the celebration of the final victory of liberal democracy and free market capitalism over its arch rival ideology, communism, and its planned socialist economy. The triumph of liberal democratic capitalism appeared complete, heralding, for Francis Fukuyama, the "end of history" (1992). To this, the intellectual Left, including academic Marxists, appeared to have no adequate response. The intellectual moral critique of capitalism and its necessary social and economic inequalities lost its material and ethical footing, since asceticism had been the attitude and "lifestyle" with which the 1960s American New Left had sought to identify with the working class and their struggles, and with the symbolic emblem of communists in Asia.

Academic research interests were also correspondingly being redirected: analysis of political economy and the sociology of production were practically abandoned while attention was turned towards the globalization of capital and the reorganization of work by new computer-mediated communication systems. Interests in class politics were displaced by interests in minority rights under a reconceptualization of multiculturalism that extended beyond ascribed minorities, such as those based on race and ethnicity, to include self-constituted groups such as feminists, LGBT (lesbian, gay, bisexual, transgendered) people and many other self-proclaimed minorities who felt discriminated against and marginalized. The language of exploitation shifted to the language of rights and, in the process, individual rights and social justice became increasingly indistinguishable. Social justice today is thus often conceptually reduced to the "equality of individuals," while the social or collective is reduced to a statistical aggregation of individuals rather than defined by structurally determined shared material and ideological interests. Instead of collective struggle for liberation from exploitation determined by the modes and social relations of production, the fight for equality of individuals is increasingly framed in terms of the freedom to choose how to live one's "life." In sum, the shift has been towards "identity" politics: the politics of identity may be said to be a collateral effect of a politics of rights.

Meanwhile, against this backdrop we saw the incorporation of Asia and the rest of the developing world, with its huge surplus labor force, as low-cost production sites for consumer goods that flooded the world: cheap imitations of branded commodities for the emerging middle class in developing nations and genuine luxury products for the wealthy in the developed West. There thus occurred a certain "democratization" of consumption and luxury, appearing to prove the efficacy of unfettered capitalism in providing jobs, economic growth and the improvement of material life for those who reside within the circuit of global capitalism.

Academic research shifted its focus in other ways, as well. The flipside of the sociology, anthropology and political economy of production is, of course, the sociology, anthropology and political economy of consumption. Instead of the "making of the working class" through learning to labor, the focus now increasingly falls on the new middle classes learning to consume, and on their social and cultural construction of the self through "lifestyles." For Cultural Studies, this shift was observable in the trajectory of the works of the Birmingham School. The left-Marxist politics of Stuart Hall's work became progressively obscured, while his conceptualization and arguments on "identity" became emphasized, appropriated and embraced. The focus on working-class culture of the early years of the Birmingham School shifted increasingly towards the politics of identity construction, including identity through consumption – from Paul Willis's work on working-class youth (1977) to Dick Hebdige's *Subculture: The Meaning of Style* (1991) and Angela McRobbie (1998) on the self-exploitation of young women fashion designers as entrepreneurs.

Combining the liberal concept of freedom to choose with the politics of identity, one gets the conceptual core for the idea of the "sovereign" consumer and relatedly the idea of "lifestyle" as individual preference. This is the moment of the discovery of the "active" consumer, with its sub-species, the "active" media audience. Analyses of advertising as an instrument for the "psychological manipulation" of consumers for capitalist profit were displaced by an interest in the semiotics of the image and the consumer's appropriation of these meanings for projects of self-construction. Adorno's conceptualization of the manipulated, mindless mass consumer of pop culture was displaced and replaced by the "creative" individual "reworking" the mass commodity into individualized items for the "fashioning" of the self – for example, reading romance novels (Radway 1984) and watching soap operas on TV (Ang 1985) become part of the female audience's repertoire of self-creation. The politics of multiculturalism, minority identity politics, and the concepts of the active audience and active consumers – all discourses that are tied to the construction of sovereign subjects and preferred lifestyles – have traveled globally, including to Asia and Australia, and have shaped the broad conceptual boundaries of a very large portion of research on media and consumption in Cultural Studies.

Consumerism in Asia

In contrast to the mature capitalist economies of Europe and America, the rise of capitalism in Asia was largely a post-1960s phenomenon. The so-called East Asian economic miracle – the successive rapid industrial development of Japan, South Korea, Taiwan, Hong Kong and Singapore – saw economies growing annually at sustained double-digit rates for more than two decades, from the mid-1960s. This was largely the result of the abovementioned global restructuring of capitalism, in which industries in the USA and Europe relocated industrial production to East Asia, where surplus labor was plentiful and cheap, transforming Asia into the "factory" of globally marketed consumer goods. Domestically, export-oriented industrialization resulted in a rapid and massive expansion of employment in these territories, and lifted a very significant proportion of the East Asian population out of poverty, expanding consumption and driving a massive improvement of their material life. By the late 1980s or early 1990s, an emergent middle class and consumer culture were very clearly observable in the region.

In 1978, China began to emulate the export-oriented industrialization of the other East Asian nations and quickly absorbed a very large proportion of the global direct investment industrial capital, leaving the smaller countries struggling to get their share. However, given the size of the population and the low base from which it started, it would take far longer for China to reach the status of a "middle-class country," relative to its East Asian neighbors. Nevertheless, given its 1.3 billion population, even the still relatively small middle class that China now has is already overwhelming in terms of numbers and is making its presence felt globally through its consumption practices. Furthermore, the shift towards consumer modernity has already trickled down to the working class. To illustrate, I recall an occasion when Hong Kong-based Marxist sociologist Pun Ngai professed to being aghast at how young rural-urban migrant Chinese women workers were wasting their hard-earned wages from the sweatshop factories of Shenzhen on cheap cosmetics, and at the excitement they derived from comparing colors of nail polish and lipstick. Pun's moral indignation clearly reflected the Marxist moral critique of capitalist exploitation of workers and their mindless consumption. However, in light of current approaches to consumption within Sociology and Cultural Studies, such a critique not only seems old fashioned but conceptually misses the point that for these new wage earners, whose lives had hitherto been governed by necessity, the availability of a small sum of surplus cash to be spent on cosmetics of their choice signifies a moment of liberation from decades of material deprivation; a moment of liberation from a life of want to one with the freedom to choose from a cornucopia of consumer goods. The liberal politics embedded in the idea of the "sovereign" consumer are learned through the freedom to choose lipstick colors.

Academic recognition of the emergence of the middle class in Asia was very distinctively marked by the New Rich in Asia research project and the book series, organized in the early 1990s by the then newly established Asia Research Centre (ARC) at Murdoch University in the city of Perth in Australia. The original core members of the ARC were leftist political economists. Their interests in the emerging middle class were the economic status, ideological orientation and role in the democratization of former authoritarian regimes of this class fragment, and the future of the labor unions in the developmental state in East and Southeast Asia. Workshops and edited volumes were organized around each of these foci (Robison and Goodman 1996). There were two exceptions to the conventional political economy concerns: *Gender and Power in Affluent Asia* (Sen and Stivens 1998), and *Consumption in Asia: Lifestyles and Identities* (Chua 2000). The latter was definitely an afterthought, as it was not originally planned but was added after I suggested to Richard Robison, after the first workshop in the series, that the analysis of the middle class would not be complete if it did not examine its consumption practices.

It was obvious to me that throughout the region, the improvement of material life for the population – that is, the expansion of consumption – was the driving force behind the frenzy of national economic growth, and was also central to the perceived legitimacy of the authoritarian regimes. At the individual level, the essential motivation behind the work ethic of the emerging and rising middle class was to gain competitive advantage in consumption relative to each other. This was the period of the five Cs (cash, credit card, car, country club and condominium) in Singapore: the so-called Singapore Dream.

The *Consumption in Asia* volume was published almost a decade after my first essay on fashion consumption in Singapore (Chua 1992) was published in an edited volume largely analyzing Anglo-American consumerism: *Lifestyle Shopping: The Subject of Consumption* (Shields 1992). My interest in fashion consumption was an interest in class politics. It was an entry into studying the rich through their consumption, and the fieldwork was conducted entirely in an expensive fashion boutique which carried designer labels such as Issey Miyaki and Yohji Yamamoto.

Looking back, the New Rich project was inherently linked to the heyday of consumerism in Asia, in spite of the fact that the topic of consumption was somewhat peripheral to the original conceptualization of the project. The first volume of the series appeared in 1996 and the final volume in 2001. In between was the 1997 Asian regional financial crisis. The expansion of consumption lingered on for a few years, but its peak was over. The first sign of the decline of the preoccupation with consumption was the disappearance, in the early 1990s, of busloads of Japanese tourists descending on shopping districts in cities all over the world: the economic bubble had burst and Japan went into two decades of deflation. The 1997 Asia regional financial crisis followed, deflating Asian developmental triumphalism. The massive devaluation of some Asian currencies and the high rate of unemployment caused by International Monetary Fund (IMF)-imposed economic restructuring took their toll on the middle class. In Korea, for example, patriarchal culture demanded that employed women give up their jobs to their unemployed husbands in order to salvage the traditional masculine pride of the head of the household. The middle classes in most of the so-called East Asian "miracle" economies have, up until the present day, not fully regained their former financial security. It is not certain that they will ever regain it, ironically, precisely because the once "developing" economies of East Asia are now fully developed economies. In the words of Singapore's Lee Kuan Yew (2000), they have moved "from third world to first."

Entering the era of economic recession or slow growth

The rapid expansion of East Asian economies from the 1960s to the early 1990s was a period not only of easy access to employment but also of rapid career promotion. The term "high flyer" was a commonly heard Singaporean expression throughout that period. It described a smart young university graduate who rose meteorically within a very short period of time to a senior management position in the civil service which had been vacated by the decamping British colonial administration, or in a newly established private enterprise where management positions had to be filled immediately. The period was also one of easy access to assets and rapid capital accumulation, as housing and other assets were relatively affordable for those with steady white-collar employment. Up until the early 1980s, an accountant just out of university might make less than US$1,000 a month, but would be able on that salary to get married, buy a house or an apartment, own a car and raise children. The accumulated properties and other financial assets are now paying greater dividends than monthly wages earned, as that generation faces retirement. However, over the years, as the state administration has stabilized and the economy matured, career paths have become normalized and promotions now entail a step-by-step climb up the career ladder. An entire generation's opportunities for meteoric career progression and capital accumulation was very much an historical anomaly.

A first world economy has some quite specific downsides: the national economic growth rate slows down, reducing employment opportunities and career advancement; economic cycles become routine, temporary layoffs are frequent and structural unemployment inevitable; anxieties over unemployment and career advancement become pervasive in an individual's everyday life; and finally, income and social inequalities become more pronounced, engendering social divisiveness between "winners" and "losers." The uncertainty of long-term or life-long employment has been intensified by the globalization of capitalism and new digital technologies. Many low-end manufacturing jobs and white-collar jobs have disappeared and will continue to do so, due to deskilling and the replacement of human labor by new technologies. The remaining low-end manufacturing jobs keep shifting from location to location, serially in search of the lowest bidder on labor costs, from Vietnam to Indonesia to Bangladesh, extracting blood money along the way. The characteristic condition of advanced capitalist economies is that of increasingly national economic growth without an increase in employment. Returns on assets exceed the return on labor by a wide margin under finance capitalism, resulting in the stagnation of middle-class income and real wage decline for low-wage earners. The aggregate effect is an intensification of income and social inequalities. Such is the condition that is upon many Asian countries, from which the froth of the economic expansions of China and India has diverted our attention.

I will use Singapore as an illustrative case. First, the upward social mobility that had lifted an overwhelming number of people out of poverty and into the middle class during the close to five decades of rapid growth has now slowed down; consequently, so too has the expansion of the middle class. Individuals who were able to capitalize on opportunities during this rapid growth period and who achieved middle-class status are passing on their advantages, as material and social capital, to their children, facilitating the latter's success. Correspondingly, children whose parents "missed the boat" now inherit the disadvantages of their parents, in a cycle that reproduces working-class life chances and, in some cases, poverty. This is the classic social-economic development process associated with liberal capitalism, where social and economic advantages and disadvantages are transferred across generations.

Second, the clamor for the "five Cs" has all but disappeared from public discussions, replaced by anxiety about the affordability of housing – even when the government practically guarantees every citizen-household 99-year ownership of a government-subsidized apartment; about the exorbitant costs of raising children, especially education expenses in a highly competitive education system in which there is no second chance for failures; and about meeting the retirement needs of a rapidly aging population. The most financially and psychologically stressed are middle-class families, now commonly referred to as the "sandwiched" class: sandwiched between the financial demands of a growing family and the need to maintain aging parents in a society without a national pension system, and where social welfare provision is woefully inadequate and available only to the lowest 20 percent of the income strata.

Third, even very low-income jobs are subject to the forces of globalization or regionalization. Not only the so-called 3-D jobs (dirty, dangerous and degrading), but also low-end retail and personal service jobs find ready workers among the legal and/or undocumented migrant laborers of the region. The migrant workers are "able" to take much lower wages than local labor in the host economies because their living costs are borne by employers, and the cash they earn is remitted to their lower-cost-of-living places of origin. Labor exploitation has been regionalized. Due to this competition, the real income of the low-end working class has declined in absolute terms in the past decade, causing hidden unemployment. In "affluent" Singapore, where there is a constant shortage of labor, 20 percent of the households live in relative poverty, well hidden within public housing apartments.

With some minor adjustments, the social and economic conditions that prevail in contemporary Singapore can be generalized to all the East Asian economies that were the envy of developing and developed countries alike not too long ago. However, there is one significant issue from which Singapore has been exempted so far – namely, youth unemployment. Across the region, alongside every long queue at the launch of the latest Apple iPhone, is a parallel queue of unemployed and/or underemployed youth, as national economies grow without expanding employment. The size of the unemployed and underemployed youth population in each country is large enough for them to have acquired a collective generation name in their respective locations. In Japan, they are called "freeter" – a Japanese borrowing of the English word "free" and the German word, "*arbeiter*" for worker – picking up low-paid part-time work whenever and wherever they can. In Korea, they are known as the 880,000 won (approximately US$650) generation, referring to the meager income they glean from low-end, part-time, casual jobs. In China, they are called the "ant tribe," referring to young rural–urban migrants and/or young university graduates who are forced to take temporary and part-time employment at very low pay, while sharing terribly over-congested, tiny spaces as accommodation. Faced with these conditions, many Korean and Japanese youth postpone their graduation, taking time off in the midst of undergraduate studies, prolonging their time at university for as long as they can.

Going forward, in the developed economies of Asia, those who are currently under 35 years of age are unlikely to have the same opportunities as their parents' generation. In the early 1990s, I often heard older Singaporean parents complain about how "spendthrift" their university graduate children were, in comparison with themselves at the same age. Apparently, their children with similar academic qualifications as them were making twice the wages, or more, at the same stage in life, yet had no savings and were afraid of starting a family in view of the apparent cost of raising children and other familial obligations. Such complaints have largely ceased, even though the nominal starting monthly salary of young professionals is now about S$3,000. Conversely, parents are now more inclined to sympathize with their children and complain that the government is not doing enough to protect the job market for their children, as citizens. For the middle class, intergenerational wealth and assets transfers are now likely to be from the old to the young, in reverse of past practice. The once widely held notion that each successive generation should and would do better in terms of quality of life is no longer a promise made by politicians, as it is one that can no longer be delivered, let alone guaranteed.

China and India are two exceptions to the trend I am describing, for now. They are currently going through the economic expansion phase that was experienced between the 1960s and the early 1990s by the now developed East Asian economies. The expansion of the middle class and consumerism in both countries is highly visible. However, as the two most populous nations of the world, the economic growth necessary to lift the bulk of the citizenry out of poverty is a long-term project. After more than three decades of rapid growth, the middle class in both countries remains a thin layer, although numerically large. The per capita income of China is currently around US $10,000, with very uneven income distribution, while over 20 percent of India remains in absolute poverty (IMF 2013). China and India are not going to reach the annual per capita income level of Singapore, currently US$51,000, or the Korean level of US$22,600, for many more years.

In summary, with the exception of China and India, the economic and social conditions of the middle classes in developed Asia are at best in slow growth but more likely stagnant or in decline. Big-ticket items, such as houses and cars, are no longer within easy reach of most young white-collar workers. Social and economic upward mobility for the working classes has slowed radically, and those who are less educated face long-term unemployment and underemployment. Social stratification is already quite rigid and seems likely to ossify further, creating sizeable strata of both relatively and abjectly poor citizens. These new economic conditions will of course have effects on consumption patterns. Not surprisingly, these effects are most observable in the first world economies of developed East Asia.

New dimensions for research in consumption

East Asian societies at the beginning of the 21st century are undoubtedly radically different from those of the last quarter of the 20th century. These changes provide us with opportunities to rethink the broader conceptual boundaries of consumption studies. First, the history of rapid economic growth and the expansion of consumerism over the last three decades or so arguably bears comparison with the development in consumerism in Europe in the immediate postwar years, when it was introduced to American consumer goods and the American way of life (Ross 1995). This raises a series of questions. Could there be a relatively universal history of capitalist consumer modernity? Conversely, how consequential are different trajectories of modernity – for example, the relatively "stretched out" duration of Euro-American modernity versus the "compressed" modernities of many Asian nations, where material and immaterial consumption and industrialism and post-industrialism may be experienced all at once? Do distinct histories of consumerism and trajectories of modernization produce different forms and experiences of consumer capitalist modernity in the present?

Second, we have known for quite some time that incomes in global cities, such as Hong Kong, Singapore, Shanghai and Tokyo, tend to be very dichotomously distributed, with a large, poorly paid service class serving a thin layer of the rich (Sassen 2001). In the global cities in Asia, employment growth is increasingly restricted to the so-called service industries. A very large proportion of the service industries are menial jobs in consumption services, from frontline retail sales to dishwashing in restaurants, where wages are often barely sufficient to cover the necessities of everyday life in the high-cost global city environment. The waiters and waitresses and the designer uniform-clad employees of fashion and cosmetic boutiques who work on commission are constantly reminded of their relative poverty and deprivation compared with the clients they serve. Any analysis of the culture of consumption is surely incomplete without consideration of the consumption practices of these low-end service employees. Yet, they have consistently been left out of studies of consumption because consumerism is conceptualized as diametrically opposed to poverty: consumerism is conceptualized as a culture of aspiration and excess, while necessity and deprivation are associated with a culture of poverty. Conceptually and substantively, how do we incorporate these low-paid workers into our studies of consumerism? Ironically, for example, while to "consume less" as an ethical practice against excess and waste is a virtue for the relatively wealthy, it is a necessity for the relatively poor.

Third, there is definitely a routine structure and a set of cultural practices in the life of the unemployed that is relatively coherent. A Korean pop song about the 880,000 won youth, "Cheap Coffee," by the band Chang Kiha and the Faces draws a succinct picture:

> I drink cheap coffee
> Stomach feels pain from the tepid drink
> The soles of the feet feel the stickiness of the humid linoleum floor
> Now I'm even indifferent to
> A mere cockroach crawling by
> Every heavy morning, light coughing doesn't seem to stop
> I fold the damp bedding, I venture out the squeaky door.[1]

There is also an observable, if hard to define, complexity to the self-presentation of the very poor: a layering of clothes without regard to color or material coordination, that is often necessary because of a persistent chill caused by low-grade infections. Those who are knowledgeable about the fashion scene in China would remember the parody of "Ah Ke" (Brother Sharp), a hobo wearing random layers of probably found, unwashed clothes who was "celebrated" on the Internet for his "astute" fashion sense, and temporarily turned into a fashion icon by the media.[2] What would happen if we included the daily routines of the growing numbers of unemployed and underemployed and their presentation of self into the concept of "lifestyle," which has generally been reserved for the conscious styling of the self, excluding practices engaged in by necessity?

Theoretically, we should, of course, include the downsides of global capitalist development in our imagination of "Asian modernities," but substantively, we seldom do. Meanwhile, new products will continue to be introduced into the market. The weekend national newspaper in Singapore regularly introduces new cafés, restaurants and trendy retail outlets, increasingly established by young entrepreneurs. It less regularly reports on the rapid failure of these "trendy" enterprises. In Asia, consumerism will continue to expand with the complicity of the state because as exports decline in the face of global recession, domestic consumption will have to be counted upon as a source of economic growth. Academic investigation of new consumption trends and their manifold implications and consequences should of course continue apace but, it is hoped, built into such scholarship will be an awareness of the downsides of consumerism as popular culture, and a recognition of the ethical critique that it deserves.

Notes

1 Lyrics reproduced with permission of the artists. The song's video is available at: www.youtube.com/watch?v=kC6VYw6IUi4.
2 See: knowyourmeme.com/memes/brother-sharp-犀利哥.

References

Ang, Ien. 1985. *Watching Dallas: Soap Opera and the Melodramatic Imagination*. London: Methuen.

ChuaBeng Huat. 1992. "Shopping for Women's Fashion in Singapore." In *Lifestyle Shopping: The Subject of Consumption*, edited by Rob Shields, 115–136. London: Routledge.

ChuaBeng Huat. 2000. *Consumption in Asia: Lifestyles and Identities*. London: Routledge.

Fukuyama, Francis. 1992. *The End of History and the Last Man*. New York: Free Press.

Hebdige, Dick. 1991. *Subculture: The Meaning of Style*. London: Routledge.

IMF (International Monetary Fund). 2013. "World Economic Outlook (WEO) Database 2013." www.imf.org/external/pubs/ft/weo/2013/01/weodata/download.aspx (accessed June 5, 2015).

LeeKuan Yew. 2000. *From Third World to First*. Singapore: SPH Press.

McRobbie, Angela. 1998. *British Fashion Design: Rag Trade or Image Industry?* London: Routledge.

Radway, Janice A. 1984. *Reading the Romance: Women, Patriarchy and Popular Literature*. Chapel Hill, NC: University of North Carolina Press.

Robison, Richard, and David Goodman. 1996. *New Rich in Asia: Mobile Phones, McDonalds and Middle Class Revolution*. London: Routledge.

Ross, Kristin. 1995. *Fast Cars, Clean Bodies: Decolonization and the Reordering of French Culture*. Cambridge, MA: MIT Press.

Sassen, Saskia. 2001. *The Global City: New York, London, Tokyo*. Princeton, NJ: Princeton University Press.

Sen, Krishna, and Maila Stivens. 1998. *Gender and Power in Affluent Asia*. London: Routledge.
Shields, Rob. 1992. *Lifestyle Shopping: The Subject of Consumption*. London: Routledge.
Willis, Paul E. 1977. *Learning to Labour: How Working Class Kids Get Working Class Jobs*. London: Saxon House.

1 Lifestyle media in Asia

Consumption, aspiration and identity

Fran Martin and Tania Lewis

This book has grown out of a four-year collaborative research project on lifestyle media in Asia undertaken by Fran Martin, Tania Lewis, Wanning Sun, John Sinclair and Ramaswami Harindranath, and funded by the Australian Research Council (2010–13). The starting point for that project was our observation of the ubiquitous presence, across Asia, of popular media instructing audiences on aspects of "living the good life," from home decoration and healthy eating to guides to workplace etiquette and personal makeover narratives. In Asia, as elsewhere in the world, it seems, lifestyle media are playing a role in teaching audiences how to live a modern life, and potentially shaping people's understandings of identity, culture and citizenship – serving, in a sense, as etiquette manuals for the 21st century. Our aim, then, was to take up lifestyle media as a strategic lens through which to examine broader social and cultural changes in the region, especially the rapid development of new middle classes in some countries, and the consolidation and expansion of urban consumer cultures in most. Rather than speaking simply about the "social impact" of lifestyle media, though, we wanted to see such media not just as reflective but in fact as *constitutive* of social life (Lewis 2011b).

In Western Europe and the Anglophone west, pop-factual lifestyle advice media exhorting audiences to make the best of themselves and optimize their opportunities while minimizing risks in everything from clothing to childrearing have been theorized as connected with historically particular social, economic and cultural developments. These include the rise to dominance of the idea of a psychologized, malleable "DIY self" whose identity is seen as a project to be worked on and invested in (Bonner 2003; Lewis 2008) – a concept that has been understood as linked with late modern social processes of reflexive individualization (Giddens 1991; Beck 1992; Rose 1996), the relentless normalization of a bourgeois model of selfhood in class-inflected guidance on style (Palmer 2003, 2004; Weber 2009), the increasing intertwining of civic and consumer culture leading to media promotions of a form of "consumer citizenship" based on making ethico-aesthetic choices in consumption (Miller 2007), and the promotion of the "self-governing citizen" following the withdrawal of the European-style post-welfare state from healthcare, education and other services (Palmer 2003; Ouellette and Hay 2008). If lifestyle media have been understood as linking in these ways with broader developments in social and economic life in Western Europe, North America and Australasia, then what is the situation in Asia? Are the effects and implications proposed in relation to Euro-American lifestyle media transferrable to contemporary media cultures in Asia? If not, then what are the appropriate alternative conceptual frameworks to help us make sense of lifestyle media in these contexts?

This book is one of three major publications produced out of our research project that sought answers to such questions. Others include the monograph *Telemodernities: Television and Transforming Lives in Asia* (Lewis, Martin and Sun, 2016), which focuses largely on life advice television in China, India and Taiwan; and a special issue of *Media International Australia* on "Lifestyle Media and Social Transformation in Asia" (Martin, Lewis and Sinclair 2013), which includes chapters examining various aspects of lifestyle media and culture in China, Taiwan, Vietnam, Japan and India. Most of the papers gathered in the current volume were originally presented at a symposium organized as part of our research project, in Melbourne in late 2013.

Research in this area clearly needs to remain sensitive to both the potential and the pitfalls of applying ready-made Euro-American theories to diverse Asian contexts. Our own work draws on the insights of the extant Euro-American scholarship, but also significantly extends it by underlining the specificity of Asian inflections of modern culture and selfhood, rather than presuming the universality of Euro-American forms (Ong and Nonini 1997; Lee 1999; Athique 2006; Martin and Heinrich 2006; Rofel 2007). Such an approach leads us, in Aihwa Ong's words, to "consider how non-western societies themselves make modernities after their own fashion, in the remaking of rationality, capitalism and the nation in ways that borrow from but also transform western universalizing forms" (Ong 1995, 64). Thus, rather than assuming from the outset that lifestyle media must be advancing the global spread of Western-style late modern identity, the "multiple modernities" paradigm cues us to pay detailed attention to how such media are actually produced and consumed in specific contexts, and to remain alert to variations from global models in the visions of modern selfhood and citizenship they project. To take the multiple modernities concept seriously by richly contextualizing Asian lifestyle media in relation to the region's middle-class consumer cultures and the forms of aspiration and identity that they afford, it is necessary first to sketch out the basic material conditions attending Asia's various forms of capitalist modernity. To that end, in the next section we offer a thumbnail sketch of the historical emergence and present situation of Asia's "advanced" ex-tiger economies, its newly industrialized countries, and its post-socialist transition societies.

Consumption: compressed modernities, new middle classes, and the "neoliberal" turn

Since the conclusion of the Second World War, the Asian region has undergone successive waves of capitalist development which have resulted in the emergence and consolidation – at different times, at different speeds, via different paths and to widely varying extents – of middle classes and urban consumer cultures in most of the countries in the region today. The development of capitalist modernities and the associated rise of middle-class cultures of consumption in this region can be seen as closely linked to the embedded histories both of colonialism and imperialism, and of Cold War political, economic and military structures.

In Pacific Asia, as has been argued in detail by both Shunya Yoshimi and Kuan-Hsing Chen, following Japan's defeat at the end of the Second World War and the concomitant collapse of the Japanese annexation and military occupation of many territories in the region, the USA effectively stepped in to replace Japan's regional hegemony (Yoshimi 2003; Chen 2010). South Korea, Taiwan, Okinawa and Japan itself were made into US protectorates, while many other non- and anti-communist nations in the region, including the Philippines, Thailand, Malaysia, Singapore and Indonesia, were incorporated less directly into a broad American sphere of influence. Thus, the Japanese imperialist hold on the Asia-Pacific was in effect replaced with a Cold War military and economic structure, in which capitalist industrialization under developmentalist authoritarian governments was carried out with US support as part of an American-led strategy of communist containment. Japan itself was the first to undergo accelerated industrialization, with a strong middle class and urban consumer culture consolidating by the mid-1960s; the "tiger economies" of Taiwan, South Korea, Singapore and colonial Hong Kong followed, with their "economic miracles" of rapid industrialization between the 1960s and the 1990s. As Chua Beng Huat observes in his Foreword to this volume, it is these five developmental-state territories, with their now well-established middle classes and achievement of "advanced" levels of economic development, that now find themselves facing a certain economic and cultural crisis, with slowed or stagnant economic growth, rising social inequality, living standards under pressure, and mounting popular critiques of the downsides of consumerism and late capitalist modernity. Currently Indonesia, the Philippines, Malaysia and Thailand are all undergoing processes of rapid economic growth and middle-class expansion that are broadly comparable to the experience of the tiger economies several decades ago; these can be classified as second-generation newly industrialized countries (Bożyk 2006, 164). Meanwhile, India, Vietnam and China, nations that in the latter half of the 20th century pursued socialist modernization, have become transition societies – arguably, in the case of China, directly inspired by the "neoauthoritarian development" path of the ex-tiger economies (Dirlik 2012). These post-socialist nations' "opening up" to global capital and their gradual shift from planned to market economies from the early 1980s on has, as in the experience of the other countries surveyed above, heralded a burgeoning of urban middle classes and the growing centrality of consumption to social life and identity. Furthermore, notwithstanding their variegated histories and distinctive political, social and cultural present, all of the nations discussed above are today also subject to a common pressure to integrate into, and find ways to prosper within, the global capitalist economy, entailing inducements to restructure their domestic economies and social infrastructures toward marketization, privatization and deregulation.

As this thumbnail sketch of the enfolding of Asian states into the circuits of globalizing capitalism over the past half-odd century suggests, regardless of the multiplicity of Asian modernities and the specificity of individual nation-states' trajectories, compared with Western Europe and the USA, they arguably share in common what we might call, following Chang Kyung-sup, *compressed* experiences of modernization (Chang 1999, 2010). Chang defines compressed modernity as follows:

> a civilizational condition in which economic, political, social and/or cultural changes occur in an extremely condensed manner in respect to both time and space, and in which the dynamic coexistence of mutually disparate historical and social elements leads to the construction and reconstruction of a highly complex and fluid social system. Compressed modernity can be manifested at various levels of human existence – i.e., personhood, family, residential community, secondary organizations, urban spaces, societal units (including civil society, nation, etc.), and, not least importantly, the global society. At each of these levels, people's lives need to be managed intensely, intricately, and flexibly in order to remain normally integrated with the rest of society.[1]
>
> (Chang 2010, 446)

This quote underlines what is, for our purposes, a crucial observation: that the high-order compressed modernities unfolding across much of Asia today entail certain social and cultural effects; in particular, the need for increasingly *intense, intricate, and flexible management of people's lives* in order to make compressed modernity, with its rapid and relentless dislocation of previous systems of social organization, humanly livable. This task of intricately managing the tensions and contradictions of late modern everyday life is increasingly being taken up, in Asia as elsewhere, by the types of popular media that are analyzed in the chapters of this book.

As the following chapters demonstrate, with some exceptions, lifestyle advice delivered to audiences in Asia through commercial media often presupposes the effectiveness of rather individualized solutions to what might more properly be understood as collective problems resulting from specific social, cultural and economic transformations within compressed modernity. When the post-socialist Chinese state withdraws from its commitment to providing healthcare for the citizenry, for example, media audiences are invited to take on responsibility for health maintenance as individual-level, consumption-based projects of self-care (see the chapters here by Sun and Gao); when contradictions emerge between Taiwanese women's increased opportunities for economic independence and their ongoing subjection to cultural expectations that they shoulder the major burden of care work within families, women's TV travel shows propose commercial tourism as a kind of pressure-release valve to allow them the "me time" needed to (temporarily, superficially) resolve that contradiction (see the chapter by Martin). This frequent individualization of contradictions that might more properly be understood as collective points to the fact that despite the plurality of political, social and economic circumstances of the various geo-cultural contexts addressed in this book, there appears often to be a certain commonality in the *cultural processing* of the tensions of the present. The individualization of collective problems; the repeated entreaties to take responsibility for one's own well-being and self-improvement – in health, in the home or in the workplace; the naturalization of market-based competition and self-interest; the idealization of indicatively middle-class tastes and values; the promotion of consumption as a salve for the contradictions of modern living: these constitute a common thread that several contributors to this volume interpret as "neoliberal" ideology, emphasizing especially popular media's naturalization of market rationality, competitive individualism and the self-enterprising subject.

There have been heated debates over the question of "neoliberalism" as a concept and its potential meaning(s) when applied beyond the West (Harvey 2005; Ong 2006, 2007; Lee 2014) – or indeed within the West (Flew 2014). It is therefore worth underlining that in observing forms of "cultural neoliberalism" as a point of central tendency across several of the examples analyzed in this book, contributors are not necessarily advocating a homogenizing, diffusionist view of "neoliberal globalization" that imagines neoliberalism as a unified, hegemonic tide washing imperialistically and implacably from Western Europe and the USA across the globe. Rather, the approaches taken in this book on the whole follow the lead of scholars including Ulrich Beck and Edgar Grande (2010), who balance the observation that, on one hand, late (or "second") modernity sees nations and peoples linked across territorial borders to a hitherto unprecedented extent – including by the intensifying pressures and risks of the globalizing capitalist economy – with, on the other hand, an appreciation of the distinctive "paths to" and varieties of modern structures and processes that are produced from specific geo-cultural contexts. Taking this view, such structures and processes are revealed as emerging through something more like parallel evolution than through diffusion from a central point. Thus, we come to think not simply of "individualization" as an abstract and (falsely) universal process associated with cultural modernization *in general*, but instead, we are able to think, for example, of Chinese, Japanese or South Korean "paths to" and distinctive formations of individualization (Beck and Grande 2010, 420). A similar point can be made with regard to other aspects of broadly "neoliberal" ideology, such as those that we see instantiated in some of the East Asian media examples analyzed in this book (see especially the chapters on South Korea, China and Taiwan by Jung, Wu, Sun, Gao and Yang). In Aihwa Ong's terms, neoliberalism in Asia should thus be seen not as a globally determined, pre-set structure or set of policies, but rather as a "migratory technology of governing that interacts with situated sets of elements and circumstances," which may be selectively utilized for specific populations, and may co-exist with rather than replacing other political rationalities and cultural logics (Ong 2007, 5; Lewis et al. 2012).

Some specific examples will help to make this point. In both Wu Jing's chapter on home makeover TV shows in China, and Fang-chih Irene Yang's chapter on corporate self-help literature in Taiwan, the authors refer to a China-centered ideological structure that they call "authoritarian neoliberalism." If we take European social theory and experience as normative, this expression might appear oxymoronic, since "neoliberalism" has often been understood as definitionally linked with advanced capitalist democracies in the process of restructuring away from a welfare state model (but see Taylor 2002; Bruff 2014). Yet the type of East Asian authoritarian neoliberalism to which both Wu and Yang refer emerges, instead, from a post-socialist transition society with an authoritarian government (China), and from a neo-developmental state under what Yang characterizes as a democratically elected authoritarian government (Taiwan). In his study of authoritarian neoliberalism in post-socialist China, Arif Dirlik observes:

> What characterizes the Chinese economy is a successful combination of authoritarian management internally with effective activity in the neoliberal market. The combination was not of its invention, as it was characteristic of the neoauthoritarian economies [of Japan, Taiwan, Singapore, South Korea and colonial Hong Kong]. But the communist regime in China has been particularly successful in managing globalization while at the same time retaining strict control over the national market.
>
> (Dirlik 2012, 258)

In this definition, authoritarian neoliberalism as an economic and political system is characterized by market economics combined with autocratic politics (see also Harvey 2005; Ong and Zhang 2008). If, as Wu and Yang argue, cultural expressions of this form of political rationality can be observed in certain Chinese and Taiwanese media examples, then clearly enough, in analyzing such examples we should assume neither that we are dealing with a formation that is identical to Euro-American forms of "neoliberalism," nor that we are encountering something that has emerged in China and Taiwan through a simple geographic diffusion of Euro-American forms. What we see, rather, is a distinctive "path to" authoritarian neoliberalism as a regionally exceptional form, represented in the cultural sphere (Beck and Grande 2010): a type of parallel evolution.

Aspiration: middle-class imaginaries

The liberalization of economies and, to a certain extent, state formations across the region have seen significant shifts in the identities and aspirations of so-called ordinary people. As states have moved from developmentalist models toward global enterprise-based approaches, the logics of national economies have become increasingly tied to the fate and fortunes of the new middle classes. The rise of this upwardly mobile echelon across Asia has been accompanied by the expansion of a range of consumption-oriented lifestyles and consumerist aspirations shaped in complex ways by endogenous, regional and global cosmopolitan ethics and aesthetics. For instance, as we see in Lewis's chapter on food television in India, middle-class households in Mumbai, au fait with global lifestyle shows like *MasterChef Australia*, imaginatively aspire to cosmopolitan lifestyles, even while their own everyday food practices are fairly bound by pre-existing cultural habits and conventions. Indeed, this latter point regarding the often significant gap between material and aspirational lifestyles was a recurrent theme in our study of lifestyle TV in China, Taiwan and India, and speaks to some of the limitations of claims that the region has seen the emergence of a consumer "revolution" linked to a "new rich" or at least consumption-oriented middle class whose lives have been thoroughly transformed by a choice-based post-traditional culture (Robison and Goodman 2006). It also foregrounds the revised aspirations and sense of increasing precarity of a whole generation of middle-class citizens across the region (as discussed in Chua's Foreword to this collection) whose lives have been significantly impacted by the global financial crisis and market decline.

Aspirationalism in the region, while increasingly tied to individualized discourses of consumerism and middle-class taste and aesthetics, is distinctively flavored by local economic and social contexts. Take the notion of middle-class identity, for example. As we have argued elsewhere, although there has been a significant broadening of the base of economic and consumer citizenship in many countries, the term "middle class" can be misleading, particularly when it invokes connotations like those it has in the US, British or Australian contexts, where it is often taken to mean a majoritarian or dominant group (Martin et al. 2013). In the ex-tiger economies, there *has* been something of a middle-class "revolution." In Taiwan, for example, business opportunities flowing from state-led industrialization during the 1960s–1990s, coupled with rising levels of education over this period, resulted in over 70 percent of Taiwan's working population, from professionals to lower-level white-collar workers, falling within the middle classes in 2006 (Li 2013; Tsai et al. 2014). Meanwhile, in India extremely uneven economic development has seen the poverty rate reduce much more slowly compared with other parts of Asia: estimated to be anywhere between 70 to 400 million by differing benchmarks, using the measure of a per capita daily income of above US$8–40, the middle class has grown from 5.7 percent of the population in 2001 to only 12.8 percent in 2010 (153 million) (Shukla 2010).

However, while the category of the middle class needs to be used with care across the wide variety of Asian contexts, the *imaginary* of middle-class identity does function as a key aspirational concept in the region. As scholarship on lifestyle media in the West has suggested, the rise of popular lifestyle advice media tends to be associated with social and economic upheaval, times of relative uncertainty and social fluidity where people look to popular forms of advice for guidance and a sense of reassurance (Bell and Hollows 2005; Lewis 2008). The rising popularity of lifestyle media in Asia can be seen as offering people aspirational guides for managing and imagining emergent modernities; guides which – as also in the West – are often strongly class inflected. The emphasis of life advisors like celebrity chef Jamie Oliver, or the fashion gurus Trinny and Susannah (who have made a version of *What Not to Wear* for TLC India), on bringing everyday artistry and style into the wardrobes, homes and kitchens of ordinary men and women has been interpreted by many critical scholars in the West as promoting bourgeois forms of cultural capital and taste (Palmer 2004; Wood and Skeggs 2004; Lewis 2008; Skeggs 2009; Powell and Prasad 2010). While these "expert personalities" invariably frame the acquisition of personal and lifestyle skills in terms of informed consumer choice, their concern with instructing audiences on what constitutes the bounds of "good taste," it is argued, is often underpinned by an implicit set of class-based assumptions that serve to inculcate aspirations toward indicatively middle-class competencies and values (McRobbie 2004).

In the past decade or so, many Asian societies have seen a proliferation of media aimed at instructing the middle classes in matters of consumption, taste and "the good life," with television playing a central role. Alongside the growing penetration and expansion of television in large parts of Asia, audiences are now exposed to a wide range of global, regional and local lifestyle-oriented programming, from competitive cooking shows and home décor makeovers to spiritual well-being formats. However, the uptake of lifestyle shows is highly variable across the region and is shaped by a range of different local TV traditions, the localization of transnational trends, and locally specific audience demographics, with audiences in countries like India, for example, increasingly divided along linguistic, cultural and geographic lines. Further, lifestyle media content across much of the region also continues to be shaped by political forces: the sociocultural and political contexts in which lifestyle media have emerged in Asia, while having certain shared elements with the Anglo-American late capitalist moment that frames much of the Western scholarship on lifestyle and reality TV, also need to be recognized as quite distinct articulations of classed consumerism, aspirationalism and lifestyle.

Singapore provides a productive example here. While outwardly a highly marketized society where people's aspirations would appear to be strongly driven by an entrepreneurial ethic and by global middle-class consumerist sensibilities, Lewis's work on lifestyle TV in Singapore suggests a more complex, culturally embedded picture. Singaporean-made Chinese-language television (the predominant locally produced mode of programming in the island state) carries a range of glossy lifestyle TV formats that may superficially appear to be purely vehicles of Western-style consumerism and individualism.

As Lewis argues, however, these shows need also to be understood "in the context of Singapore's rather distinctive mode of authoritarian capitalism" (Lewis 2011a, 28). The enormously popular home makeover series *Home Décor Survivor*, for instance, brings together a consumerist ethos with a performative cosmopolitan sensibility, teaching audiences to bring together "ethnic" style with a European art and design aesthetic. The show does so, however, within the constraints of a very tight budget (with two teams competing for who can do the best home renovation for under S$6,000), and the focus is on renovating the small, standardized Housing Development Board flats in which most Singaporeans live.

Aspirations here, while middle-class in taste, are extremely modest, with good budgeting considered a particular virtue at a time when the Singaporean government is keen on promoting a thrift and savings mentality in the populace. Likewise, on a range of other lifestyle shows, from food to competitive weight loss, the emphasis on Singaporean lifestyle TV is not just on aspirational consumption per se, but on savvy and virtuous modes of consumption, tied often quite overtly to governmental, civic and national concerns. The responsible model of good consumption and selfhood promoted on such formats is articulated to a rather localized form of authoritarian neoliberalism (compare with our discussion above, on China), here reflecting the close regulatory relationship between the media and the Singaporean government, which often actively pushes agendas such as aspiring to healthy living through popular media including television. The promotion of entrepreneurial, middle-class aspirationalism takes on a very particular set of cultural and political meanings in a context where, as Birch and Phillips point out, civic rather than civil society continues to dominate (Birch and Phillips 2003).

Another generative example is India, a large and extremely diverse nation where we see a highly variegated relationship between lifestyle, lifestyle media, class and aspirationalism. However, while, as we noted above, the country is still marked by a huge gap between the rich and the poor, with only a small minority of Indians falling into the category of middle class in *material* terms, in contemporary India the consuming middle classes have increasingly becoming a symbol of Indian progress and national aspiration. Central to this shift has been the cultural role of television. The deregulation of the industry from the mid-1990s and the rise of satellite networks have seen the huge growth of popular entertainment TV, much of which carries images of consumption-oriented middle-class aspirationalism. While soap operas, drama and Bollywood films continue to play a central role in Indian programming (and are a key space where new fashions are displayed), reality shows have become hugely popular, from home-grown formats such as Indian wedding makeovers to adapted versions of international formats such as *MasterChef India, The Biggest Loser* and *Bigg Boss*, the very popular Indian version of Big Brother, which showcases high-end lifestyles that stand at a far remove from the ways of life of the majority of Indian viewers.

Another key site in India where aspirational lifestyle content is aired on television is on dedicated cable channels aimed at middle- to upper middle-class audiences, such as NDTV Good Times which airs popular shows such as *Highway on my Plate*, a travel-cookery show that, despite its local Indian content, is a recognizably international format in the tradition of *Two Fat Ladies* or *The Hairy Bikers*. While NDTV Good Times is a self-proclaimed aspirational channel, the identities and lifestyles it promotes often involve complex negotiations between the kind of global cosmopolitanism envisaged on *Highway on my Plate* and a range of other more localized values that might also be read as "middle class." A case in point is the Good Times show *Band Baajaa Bride* (*BBB*), a reality makeover-style wedding format that "marries" aspirationalism and consumer spectacle with family values and religious tradition. With the help of various gurus and two young, stylish hosts, the show deftly moves between a celebration of customary marriage traditions and the bride's style makeover "journey," which can incorporate anything from makeup tips to cosmetic intervention. *BBB* thus attempts to weave together and resolve a number of the conflicting concerns facing aspirational families juggling Western-inflected desires for romance and personal freedom with notions of fate and religious faith and tradition.

While makeover shows are usually vehicles for promoting consumption, this complex combination of individual makeover with "suitable" marriage, religion and cultural tradition speaks to the difficulty of making glib generalizations about the new consumer middle classes in India. Shows like *BBB* – and indeed the huge popularity of religious programming in general in India (where many viewers start their day by watching or listening to a religious guru on morning television) – speak to the problem of invoking terms like a "liberalizing consumer middle class" in India (Lakha 1999), and indeed the limitations of Euro-American notions of secular modernity and middle-class lifestyles in Asia more broadly.

Identity: lifestyle media and subject (trans)formation

In addition to the classed dimensions of lifestyle media and its role in social and cultural aspirations, it also plays a key role in mediating and shaping subject formation more broadly, on the one hand foregrounding shifting identities at times of social, economic and cultural flux, and on the other hand often legitimating new normative conceptions of selfhood and "good" citizenship. Again, much of the extant work on lifestyle media in Euro-American contexts has suggested that lifestyle television in particular can be seen to promote a fairly narrow range of consumption-oriented, capitalism-friendly models of identity. Key here is the argument that the growing popularity of lifestyle television around the world is tied to a broader "lifestyling" of contemporary social life (Moseley 2000). While the term *lifestyle* is used in a range of different contexts, from health to marketing, it is essentially underpinned by a conception of identity that foregrounds personal choice and the malleable nature of the self (Bell and Hollows 2005). Rather than seeing selfhood as limited or constrained by class, race or gender, an influential discourse today holds that ordinary people are able to invent (and re-invent) their own life "biographies." Lifestyle programming, and in particular the makeover show, epitomizes this ethos of voluntaristic self-reinvention, focused as it is on transforming every aspect of individual life from home décor to selfhood (Lewis 2009).

However, while this focus on personal development and reinvention is consumption oriented and choice based, lifestyle media are not purely *laissez-faire* in their approach to lifestyle and identity. Jamie Oliver's international role as a food activist tackling obesity and the lack of fresh food in school canteens from the USA to the UK points to the fact that lifestyle TV is not always concerned with simply encouraging consumption and aspirational lifestyles, but also increasingly works to promote particular kinds of lifestyle choices (see Jung's chapter for a related discussion in the South Korean context). As we noted above, Toby Miller (2007) argues that in the West, civic and consumer culture are increasingly intertwined, such that we now witness the growth of a lifestyle-oriented commercial culture focused on bettering the self through "ethico-aesthetic exercises." For Miller, such a shift means that selfhood and citizenship are increasingly equated with or reduced to commoditized cultural practices and lifestyle choices.

The question is, to what extent can such developments be applied to Asian contexts that are marked by distinctive political, social and cultural formations? China provides a particularly interesting example of the complexities of articulations of capitalist-inflected late modern subjectivity with a post-socialist political formation based on centralized government. As Sun's extensive research on lifestyle-oriented television in China suggests, while, in contrast to the discussion of Singapore above, "lifestyle television" does not necessarily function as a genre in quite the same way, there has been a proliferation of what is termed *shenghuo* (or life) television in China, ranging from somewhat Euro-American-style makeover and reality-lifestyle shows to rather more localized advice shows offering tips for managing the growing complexities of daily life from finances and health to optimizing interpersonal relationships (Lewis et al. 2012).

As Sun notes, the rise and rise of life advice needs to be understood in the context of the growing privatization of identity in China, and an emphasis on Chinese subjects as self-governing and potentially enterprising. This has occurred at the same time as China has witnessed the withdrawal of the state from a wide range of social services, including housing, education and healthcare. The retreat of the state means that, more than ever before, consumers find themselves in need of free or affordable information, knowledge and expert advice about how to manage their daily lives and to shape their identities optimally. Despite the devolution of state responsibilities to the individual, as Sun points out in her chapter for this collection, it is the Chinese state that directs the project of *suzhi* (quality) education and improvement in order to elevate the level of "civility" of the population; that is, to shape consumer citizens who are both self-motivated and self-managing but whose identities are intertwined with those of the state. According to the *suzhi* discourse, a citizen with good *suzhi* is one who is both loyal to the Party and useful to the market. Viewed in this way, the emergence of *shenghuo* or life advice programs further extends the discursive space of *suzhi* education, helping to shape Chinese viewers as "responsibilized" selves.

Thus, lifestyle media in the region are not simply about teaching consumers "practical" knowledge. Equally importantly, they teach consumers a new suite of values, and function to transform media consumers into modern, flexible, cosmopolitan persons who are willing to open up to new experiences and new ways of relating to people and the world. Catherine Earl's research on middle-class women's magazines in Ho Chi Minh City as an example of urban lifestyle media considers the ways in which these magazines foreground an apparently post-socialist identity defined by its globalized, cosmopolitan worldview (Earl 2013). However, at the same time she notes that the magazines tend to continue to naturalize women's domestic roles, Earl suggests that the ongoing regulation of middle-class women's identity through such popular magazines serves as a vehicle for conveying the State's view on women's appropriate (familial) roles to a wider population, including working-class women likely to aspire to the middle-class ideal presented in the magazines. Mediated imaginaries of aspiration, individualization and transnational mobility thus often fight for space with the material and ideological constraints of familial, gendered, classed expectations and constraints. In this sense, lifestyle media not only mediate normative identities but can also often involve complex negotiations and contestations between a range of currently available forms of social identity, as well as values and aspirations.

Lifestyle media in Asia

The chapters in this volume engage with the conceptual rubrics of consumption, aspiration and identity that we have discussed above in a variety of ways. The first five chapters consider how lifestyle media articulate ideologies of privatization, marketization, self-responsibilization and competitive individualism: trends that the chapter authors interpret as symptomatic of East Asian cultures of authoritarian neoliberalism (Chapters 2–6). The second group of five chapters critically analyzes the intersections of lifestyle media with gendered, familial, class and religious identities (Chapters 7–11).

Immediately following this introductory chapter, Sun Jung's chapter links very closely with the analysis presented in Chua's Foreword, of middle-class cultures in crisis in the ex-tiger economies. Jung considers two contemporary South Korean television shows, the comedy *Queen of the Office* and the sustainable living reality-competition format *The Human Condition*, as reflections on Korea's current social and cultural crisis resulting from slowed economic growth, rising unemployment and irregular employment, and environmental degradation. Jung proposes that her two examples reflect the public's dissatisfaction both with environmental unsustainability and with the dominant, neoliberal-style corporate ideology embodied in the *jaebeols* (family-owned conglomerates). The former is critiqued through a focus on sustainable living (*The Human Condition*); the latter is subverted through comedy (*Queen of the Office*). For Jung, these programs at once reflect citizens' critiques of the existing order, and encourage them to envision ethical alternatives, including "just sustainability" and social enterprise.

In contrast to Jung's interpretation of Korean popular television's capacities for cultural subversion and critique, Wu Jing argues in Chapter 3 that her televisual example – China's home makeover reality show, *Exchanging Spaces* – directly advances the Chinese state's agenda in its attempts to manage and smooth over the social contradictions arising from economic reform. Wu's premise is that the Chinese state has taken on elements of neoliberal ideology in the cultural and socio-political domains, even if not strictly speaking in its economic development strategies (which are based on the maintenance of a socialist market economy, or state capitalism, rather than free-market capitalism). In the reforms era, "family" – always-already central to modern Chinese public discourses – has correspondingly become redefined in terms of the ideal of the individualized middle-class family. With housing anxieties strongly intensified as a result of the marketization of residential property, *Exchanging Spaces* mediates these developments by promoting a vision of the "family home" to suit the current era. Specifically, Wu argues, this program from China's state broadcaster invokes older-style socialist and traditional family values in order to counterbalance the disintegrative forces of privatization and commercialization. That is, although Wu sees the program's core premise as exemplifying neoliberal-style values in the media-cultural domain, she proposes that the state effectively conceals its own agenda in this regard by "masking" these values with superficial appeals to older value systems.

Extending the focus on privatization and individualization in China's cultural sphere, the next two chapters focus on Chinese media representations of individualized, self-responsibilized healthcare. In Chapter 4, Wanning Sun considers the mediatization of *yangsheng* (health and well-being) discourses and practices. She sees *yangsheng* as mediating between the state and the market, and between expert and lay knowledge, shifting responsibility for public health onto the individual as the post-socialist state divests itself of the onus of the population's medical care. For Sun, *yangsheng*'s promotion through popular media is central to this process, since it exacerbates the internalization of governance at the level of the individual: "it is through the process of mediatization that the technique of governing becomes a technology of the self." In Chapter 5, Yue Gao, too, examines public discourses on health maintenance in Chinese media: her focus is on the Chinese localization of the global Pink Ribbon breast cancer awareness campaign. Gao proposes that the female celebrities selected to represent this cause in the Chinese media are constructed to embody self-responsible subjecthood, against the backdrop of healthcare privatization. Gao's chapter also highlights the ways in which the Pink Ribbon campaign introduces and establishes middle-class tastes and values, such as yoga practice and the consumption of luxury beauty products, in the name of self-responsible healthcare.

Following this group of chapters analyzing various aspects of the neoliberal-style cultural turn in China, in Chapter 6, Fang-chih Irene Yang presents a robust critique of the impact of Taiwan's strengthening political and economic ties with China on Taiwan's media and public culture. She calls this Taiwan's "neoliberalization through China." Yang proposes that neoliberal thought, particularly the economization of culture and the naturalization of competitive individualism, underlies the political rationalities of both the Chinese Communist Party and Taiwan's (then) ruling Kuomintang, and inflects their increasing cooperation across economic, political and cultural arenas. Reflecting this trend in the media sphere, we see in the Taiwanese take-up of Chinese historical drama *Empresses in the Palace* the reinterpretation of traditional Chinese culture to fit cut-throat corporate capitalism. Yang argues that the Taiwanese business culture's embrace of this drama in a spate of popular guides that use the show to frame advice on how to get ahead in corporate life, produces "authoritarian neoliberal subjects" characterized by selfishness, manipulativeness, self-responsibility and subservience to power. For Yang, this combination of illiberal, authoritarian hierarchy with the market logic of economic survival of the fittest naturalizes social inequality, undermining the social collective and damaging Taiwan's fledgling democratic project.

The next cluster of chapters engages articulations of media, gender and kinship, analyzing how popular media texts and technologies are contributing to the reconfiguration of gendered identities and practices of family in East Asia and beyond. In Chapter 7, Youna Kim draws on her extensive prior work on young, middle-class Korean, Japanese and Chinese women's media engagements to illustrate how the mediated ideas of female individualization and transnational mobility provide these women with potent imaginative resources. Through their consumption of Western popular media, young Northeast Asian women come to idealize the concept of "Western freedom," reflecting an implicit critique of the ways in which the cultures and labor markets of their home countries direct them, as women, to embody family- rather than self-focused identities. These young women's mediated idealizations of Western freedom, female individualization and transnational mobility come into stark contrast not only with the gendered limitations on individualization for women in Asia, but also – for those who do travel to the West, like the group of East Asian international students that Kim interviewed in London – with the realities of racism and social exclusion. Like female individualization, then, for these women, cosmopolitanism is revealed to be more an imagined ideal than a fully achievable reality.

Fran Martin's chapter extends Kim's focus on women, imagined mobility and popular media in East Asia with an analysis of television travel shows in Taiwan that are targeted to or popular with female audiences. Like Kim, Martin finds a tension between the idealized imagination of women's mobility and the gendered limitations on actual mobility that women experience. This tension, she argues, is highlighted by her two central TV examples: young, urban, middle-class Taiwanese women's reception of the US-owned lifestyle cable channel TLC (Travel & Living), and locally produced international travelogue *Miss Traveler*, targeted at the unmarried solo woman traveler. Martin finds that both in responses from TLC viewers and in the content of *Miss Traveler*, transnational mobility is associated mostly with unmarried, middle-class women, thus revealing class-based and familial constraints on the imaginability of women's mobility in Taiwan. Like that by Kim, Martin's chapter highlights the ways in which the idea of transnational mobility as "freedom," transmitted through popular media, functions as an imaginative resource for East Asian women in the face of the actual gendered social constraints they experience.

In Chapter 9, Larissa Hjorth, Heather Horst, Sarah Pink, Baohua Zhou, Fumitoshi Kato, Genevieve Bell, Kana Ohashi, Chris Malmo and Miao Xiao report on their collaborative research project mapping intergenerational locative media practices in Tokyo, Shanghai and East Asian immigrant families in Melbourne. Their analysis highlights a tension between the tenacity of kinship ties on the one hand, and the transformation of practices of intimacy through digital media interactions on the other. This chapter picks up the thematic thread on female individualization that also underlies Kim's and Martin's chapters: the authors note that while some discussions of lifestyle and consumer culture in Asia focus on individualization as a *break* with older cultural values, they are interested instead in the *reproduction* of kinship through media rituals: "these quotidian media practices both re-enact older familial rituals and give birth to new ones."

Chapters 10 and 11 extend the focus on lifestyle media and identity through investigations of how popular media represent class and religious identities in India and Malaysia. Tania Lewis analyzes how both the textual content and the viewer reception of food shows in India articulate contemporary discourses and practices of selfhood, lifestyle and modernity. She focuses particularly on how representations of taste and aspirationalism in these shows reflect – as well as problematize – the idealization of the middle classes as the embodiment of India's modernization and liberalization. The chapter highlights a central dialectic around the normalizing rhetoric of the new middle class on the one hand, and the social realities of a nation characterized by immense social diversity and fragmentation and multiple registers, scales, speeds and experiences of modernity on the other. Lewis's emphasis on the complexity of the Indian case – reflected in the extreme diversity of the cultures of TV viewership seen in her audience study – not only complicates over-generalizing invocations of a rising, aspirational Indian middle class, but also warns us against assuming that some homogeneous, global lifestyle and consumer culture is now spreading transnationally through popular media.

In this volume's final chapter, Bart Barendregt and Chris Hudson address emergent mediated performances of Malay-Muslim identity by "ordinary celebrities" on Malaysian television – in particular, in the Malaysian version of a transnational talent format, *Akademi Fantasia*, and *Young Imam*, a Malaysian reality-competition show. The authors argue that such examples represent a reimagining of Islam in the public sphere, and a new Islamic social imaginary enabled by popular media. Engaging explicitly with the conceptual framework of "multiple modernities" – one that, as we noted above, implicitly underpins much of the work in this volume – Barendregt and Hudson frame "Islamotainment" and its TV celebrities as exemplary of both the modernizing of the Islamic public sphere, and the re-scripting of local tradition in the framework of commercialization.

As a whole, this collection illustrates the role of popular media in both *mediating* and *managing* diverse experiences of compressed modernity. Chang observes in the quote cited earlier in this introduction that the compressed modernities that typify many Asian societies today – necessitating new, ever more intricate and flexible strategies of life management, which we argue are exemplified in popular media – manifest across multiple levels of human experience, from the micro (personhood, family, residential community, urban space) to the macro (civil society, the nation, global culture) (Chang 2010, 446). This book's focus on concepts, representations and practices of "lifestyle" means that the primary interest of the chapters is in media interventions at the micro-level of social and subjective experience: family and kinship, gender relations, work practices, health maintenance, food and eating, housing practices, leisure travel and religious faith. However, far from seeing these small-scale, often personal domains as merely trivial in comparison with "big ideas" like civil society, nationhood and globalization, the chapters demonstrate that it is precisely within these micro-territories of everyday experience that modern social life is made, in the intricate cross-linking of consumption practices, aspirational imaginaries and identity formation.

While it may be tempting to view the emergence of certain globally recognizable forms of lifestyle media in these Asian sites as evidence of the widening spread of Euro-American norms, nevertheless, as we argued above, the examples analyzed in the chapters as often represent the "parallel evolution" of cultural imaginaries and social norms within locally prevalent conditions as they do a straightforward diffusion from a putative Western center. Indeed, in light of the ever more complex entanglement of elements of transnationally mobile media cultures with diverse localities, a clear distinction between "global" and "local" elements becomes difficult to sustain. Under these conditions, as Arjun Appadurai has argued, "localities [...] are temporary negotiations between various globally circulating forms. They are not subordinate instances of the global, but in fact the main evidence of its reality"

(Appadurai 2013, 69). Each of the examples considered in the chapters that follow – from Korean television's critiques of the culture of *jaebeol*-based late capitalism, to the Taiwanese media's reflection of "neoliberalization through China," to the elaboration of Islamic modernity in Malaysian reality-competition formats – illustrates precisely that co-constitution of global-level forces and local contexts, histories and applications, entwined in a mutually transformative dialectic.

Note

1 While Chang originally developed the theory of compressed modernity to describe the historical experience of the ex-tiger economies, especially South Korea (Chang 1999), he has more recently argued that as a result of globalization, compressed modernity can now be seen as a globally shared condition (Chang 2010). Thus, both early modernizing (Western; "autonomous") and late modernizing (non-Western; "dependent") societies are subject to compressed modernity, but "relatively autonomous second modern societies can be characterized by low-order compressed modernity," since modernization evolved mostly from their own internal processes, whereas "dependent second modern societies can be characterized by high-order compressed modernity," since modernization was generally imposed, borrowed or adapted from elsewhere (Chang 2010, 449–50).

References

Appadurai, Arjun. 2013. *The Future as Cultural Fact: Essays on the Global Condition.* London and New York: Verso.

Athique, A.M. 2006. *Transnational Audiences For Indian Films' Media and Identity in Asia.* Miri: Media Asia Research Group.

Beck, Ulrick. 1992. *Risk Society: Towards a New Modernity.* London: Sage Publications.

Beck, Ulrick, and Edgar Grande. 2010. "Varieties of Second Modernity: The Cosmopolitan Turn in Social and Political Theory and Research." *The British Journal of Sociology* 61(3): 409–443.

Bell, David, and Joanne Hollows, eds. 2005. *Ordinary Lifestyles: Popular Media, Consumption and Taste.* Maidenhead: Open University Press.

Birch, David, and Marianne Phillips. 2003. "Civic or Civil Contingencies? Regulating Television and Society in Singapore." In *Television, Regulation and Civil Society in Asia*, edited by Philip Kitley, 115–130. London and New York: RoutledgeCurzon.

Bonner, Frances. 2003. *Ordinary Television: Analyzing Popular TV.* London and Thousand Oaks, CA: Sage.

Bożyk, Paweł. 2006. *Globalization and the Transformation of Foreign Economic Policy.* Aldershot and Burlington: Ashgate.

Bruff, Ian. 2014. "The Rise of Authoritarian Neoliberalism." *Rethinking Marxism* 26(1): 113–128.

Chang, Kyung-sup. 1999. "Compressed Modernity and its Discontents: South Korean Society in Transition." *Economy and Society* 28(1): 30–55.

Chang, Kyung-sup. 2010. "The Second Modern Condition? Compressed Modernity as Internalized Reflexive Cosmopolitanization." *The British Journal of Sociology* 61(3): 444–464.

Chen, Kuan-Hsing. 2010. *Asia as Method: Towards Deimperialization*. Durham, NC and London: Duke University Press.

Dirlik, Arif. 2012. "The Idea of a 'Chinese Model': A Critical Discussion." *China Information* 26(3): 277–302.

Earl, Catherine. 2013. "Saigon Style: Middle-Class Culture and Transformations of Urban Lifestyling in Post-Reform Vietnamese Media." *Media International Australia* 147: 85–97.

Flew, Terry. 2014. "Six Theories of Neoliberalism." *Thesis Eleven* 122(1): 49–71.

Giddens, Anthony. 1991. *Modernity and Self-identity: Self and Society in the Late Modern Age*. Cambridge: Polity Press.

Harvey, David. 2005. *A Brief History of Neoliberalism*. Oxford: Oxford University Press.

Lakha, Salim. 1999. "The State, Globalisation and Indian Middle-Class Identity." In *Culture and Privilege in Capitalist Asia*, edited by Michael Pinches, 252–274. London and New York: Routledge.

Lee, C.K. 2014. "A Chinese Developmental State: Miracle or Mirage?" In *The End of the Development State?*, edited by Michelle Williams, 230–276. New York: Routledge.

Lee, Leo Ou-Fan. 1999. *Shanghai Modern: The Flowering of a New Urban Culture in China, 1930–1945*. Cambridge, MA: Harvard University Press.

Lewis, Tania. 2008. *Smart Living: Lifestyle Media and Popular Expertise*. New York: Peter Lang.

Lewis, Tania, ed. 2009. *TV Transformations: Revealing the Makeover Show*. London: Routledge.

Lewis, Tania. 2011a. "Making over Culture? Lifestyle Television and Contemporary Pedagogies of Selfhood in Singapore." *Communication, Politics & Culture* 44(1): 21–32.

Lewis, Tania. 2011b. "'You've Put Yourselves on a Plate': The Labours of Selfhood on MasterChef Australia." In *Real Class: Ordinary People and Reality Television across National Spaces*, edited by Beverley Skeggs and Helen Wood, 104–116. London: BFI.

Lewis, Tania, Fran Martin, and Wanning Sun. 2012. "Lifestyling Asia? Shaping Modernity and Selfhood on Life Advice Programming." *International Journal of Cultural Studies* 15(6): 537–566.

Lewis, Tania, Fran Martin, and Wanning Sun. 2016 *Telemodernities: Television and Transforming Lives in Asia*. Duke University Press.

Li, Chunling. 2013. "Sociopolitical Attitudes of the Middle Class and the Implications for Political Transition." In *Middle Class China: Identity and Behaviour*, edited by Minglu Chen and David S.G. Goodman, 12–33. Cheltenham: Edward Elgar Publishing.

Martin, Fran, and Larissa Heinrich, eds. 2006. *Embodied Modernities: Corporeality, Representation, and Chinese Cultures*. Honolulu, HI: University of Hawaii Press.

Martin, Fran, Tania Lewis, and John Sinclair, eds. 2013. "Lifestyle Media and Social Transformation in Asia." Special issue, *Media International Australia* 147.

McRobbie, Angela. 2004. "Notes on 'What Not To Wear' and Post-Feminist Symbolic Violence." *The Sociological Review* 52(2): 97–109.

Miller, Toby. 2007. *Cultural Citizenship: Cosmopolitanism, Consumerism and Television in a Neoliberal Age*. Philadelphia, PA: Temple University Press.

Moseley, Rachel. 2000. "Makeover Takeover on British Television." *Screen* 41(3): 299–314.

Ong, Aihwa. 1995. "Anthropology, China, and Modernities: The Geopolitics of Cultural Knowledge." In *The Future of Anthropological Knowledge*, edited by Henrietta L. Moore, 60–92. London and New York: Routledge.

Ong, Aihwa. 2006. *Neoliberalism as Exception: Mutations in Citizenship and Sovereignty.* Durham, NC: Duke University Press.

Ong, Aihwa. 2007. "Neoliberalism as a Mobile Technology." *Transactions of the Institute of British Geographers* 32(1): 3–8.

Ong, Aihwa, and Donald Nonini, eds. 1997. *Ungrounded Empires: The Cultural Politics of Modern Chinese Transnationalism.* London and New York: Routledge.

Ong, Aihwa, and Li Zhang. 2008. "Introduction: Privatizing China: Powers of the Self, Socialism from Afar." In *Privatizing China: Socialism from Afar*, edited by Li Zhang and Aihwa Ong, 1–19. Ithaca and London: Cornell University.

Ouellette, Laurie, and James Hay. 2008. *Better Living through Reality TV: Television and Post-Welfare Citizenship.* Chichester: Wiley-Blackwell.

Palmer, Gareth. 2003. *Discipline and Liberty: Television and Governance.* Manchester: Manchester University Press.

Palmer, Gareth. 2004. "'The New You': Class and Transformation in Lifestyle Television." In *Understanding Reality Television*, edited by Susan Holmes and Deborah Jermyn, 173–190. London and New York: Routledge.

Powell, Helen, and Sylvie Prasad. 2010. "'As Seen On TV.' The Celebrity Expert: How Taste is Shaped by Lifestyle Media." *Cultural Politics* 6(1): 111–124.

Robison, Richard, and David S.G. Goodman, eds. 2006. *The New Rich in Asia: Mobile Phones, McDonald's and Middle-Class Revolution.* London: Routledge.

Rofel, Lisa. 1999. *Other Modernities: Gendered Yearnings in China After Socialism.* Berkeley, Los Angeles and London: University of California Press.

Rofel, Lisa. 2007. *Desiring China: Experiments in Neoliberalism, Sexuality, and Public Culture.* Durham, NC: Duke University Press.

Rose, Nikolas. 1996. *Inventing Our Selves: Psychology, Power, and Personhood.* Cambridge and New York: Cambridge University Press.

Shukla, Rajesh. 2010. *How India Earns, Spends and Saves – Unmasking the Real India.* New Delhi: SAGE and NCAERCMCR.

Skeggs, Beverley. 2009. "The Moral Economy of Person Production: The Class Relations of Self-Performance on 'Reality' Television." *Sociological Review* 57(4): 626–644.

Taylor, Marcus. 2002. "Success for Whom? An Historical-Materialist Critique of Neoliberalism in Chile." *Historical Materialism* 10(2): 45–75.

Tsai, Ming-Chang, Gang-Hua Fan, Hsin-Huang Michael Hsiao, and Hong-Zen Wang. 2014. "Profiling the Middle Class in Taiwan Today." In *Chinese Middle Classes: Taiwan, Hong Kong, Macao and China*, edited by Hsin-Huang Michael Hsiao, 17–35. London and New York: Routledge.

Weber, Brenda. 2009. *Makeover TV: Selfhood, Citizenship and Celebrity.* Durham, NC and London: Duke University Press.

Wood, Helen, and Beverley Skeggs. 2004. "Notes on Ethical Scenarios of Self on British Reality TV." *Feminist Media Studies* 4(2): 205–208.

Yoshimi, Shunya. 2003. "'America' as Desire and Violence: Americanization in Postwar Japan and Asia during the Cold War." *Inter-Asia Cultural Studies* 4(3): 433–450.

2 Neoliberal capitalism and media representation in Korean television series

Subversion and sustainability

Sun Jung

"This is the era when the number of non-regular contract workers has reached 8 million," says the voiceover narration of the Korean television drama *Queen of the Office* (on KBS in 2013).[1] It continues, "Koreans no longer aspire to national unification but to attaining a full-time regular position." *Queen of the Office* is a satirical comedy that portrays the unfair treatment and other problems facing contract-based temporary employees in the neoliberal capitalist corporate environment of contemporary South Korea. Additionally, the popular Korean "real-variety" program *Infinite Challenge* (on MBC) recently included an episode on "Muhan Trading Company" which also focused on redundancy as a central theme. These examples demonstrate that current affairs and news programs are not the only places on Korean television where the negative consequences of a neoliberal market economy have become a source of interest: this theme is now also visible in entertainment programs. This reflects a growing dissatisfaction amongst the Korean public, who are unhappy with the current socioeconomic environment that has seen a polarization of wealth, an increase in youth unemployment, and the increasing collapse of small and medium-sized business enterprises. This chapter examines the television drama *Queen of the Office* and the reality show *The Human Condition* (on KBS in 2013), and explores their representations of the dissatisfaction of many Korean people with the current socioeconomic order. Emphasizing the close connections between the themes of these programs and current public debates around social and environmental equity in Korea, I argue that these shows represent people's collective dissatisfaction with the status quo by subverting the dominant corporate ideology through comedy (*Queen of the Office*), and by focusing on social and environmental sustainability in a reality-competition format (*The Human Condition*).

Queen of the Office emphasizes the absurdity of the corporate neoliberal capitalist system by highlighting the inequalities between regular and irregular employees. The female lead, Ms. Kim (played by Kim Hye-Soo), subverts this politics by voluntarily choosing to be a contract worker, defying corporate workplace conventions: she believes that she does not have to follow such conventions as she is not a regular employee and thus, in her own terms, is not "a slave of a company." The reality show *The Human Condition* also addresses this situation by raising concerns about neoliberal market economies and investigating sustainable remedies to the socioeconomic crisis. In this show, six comedians occupy a house for one week and adopt one sustainable lifestyle action, such as living without waste or without a car. One of their missions was to consume local food, where they had to both locate and then confirm who was producing the food, a project that speaks to the current boom in living cooperative associations (생활협동조합, 生活協同組合, せいかつきょうどうくみあ). The booming co-ops and the ways they encourage direct "green trading" between producers and consumers reflects their members' beliefs that the co-op-led social economy can replace the current corporate-led neoliberal economic system.

Based on analysis of these programs, this chapter identifies two important societal symptoms: collective accumulated fatigue with neoliberal capitalism, and public desires for sustainable living, which have arisen as a response. These symptoms are evident in the contemporaneous public discourse focused on anti-*jaebeol* (family-owned conglomerates) and pro-social-enterprise sentiments. This indicates that ordinary citizens are seeking a new socioeconomic paradigm where social equity and economic development are equally valued and respond to each other within the framework of a newly emerging social economy. Such an interaction between social equity and economic development discourses calls into question current entrepreneurial strategies (mainly practiced by major *jaebeols*) and opens the door to exploring how sustainability and social justice can be integrated within anti-*jaebeol* and anti-neoliberalism discourses. This chapter examines how the shows examined present an alternative, along these lines, to the existing socioeconomic order. I also identify these programs as making a call for implementing "just sustainability" (Agyeman 2008), as emblematized in civic cooperative movements, media representations of green lifestyles and emerging social enterprises.

Defining terms: just sustainability and social enterprises

The idea that we should live "sustainably" was first used by the World Council of Churches in 1974 (Dresner 2002, 1). More than a decade later, sustainable development came to prominence when the World Commission on Environment and Development published the report "Our Common Future" (usually known as the Brundtland Report) in 1987. In this report, sustainable development was defined as development that "meets the needs of the present without compromising the ability of future generations to meet their own needs" (WCED 1987). The Brundtland Report suggested sustainable development was needed to meet the demands of both environmental protection and economic development, an approach to development that supports both equity between generations and equity within generations.

The sustainability discourse is therefore not only about environmental well-being but also social equity. As the Brundtland Report argued, the need for a new global development path that transcended older development-first ideologies arose due to both the increasing number of poor and vulnerable, as well as the growth in environmental degradation (WCED 1987). The Commission attempted to reconcile concerns for "environmental protection with the desires for economic development in the South and economic growth in the North" (Dresner 2002, 35). Environmental degradation often affected the poorest groups in society most severely, as they were unable to protect themselves from the environmentally destructive activities of richer and more powerful individuals or groups (ibid.), and often practice environmentally destructive activities as a desperate means of ensuring short-term survival (WCED 1987).

Regarding the inseparability of environmental quality from human equality, Julian Agyeman suggested his "Just Sustainability Paradigm." He wrote:

> From global to local, human inequality is bad for environmental quality … If sustainability is to become a process with the power to transform, as opposed to its current environmental, stewardship or reform focus, justice and equity issues need to be incorporated in its very core … The dominant wilderness, greening and natural resource focus [of the existing notion of "environment"] now includes urban disinvestment, racism, homes, jobs, neighborhoods and communities. The "environment" became discursively different: it became "where we live where we work and where we play" (Alston 1991) … [This new way of conceptual framework is what I call] the *Just Sustainability Paradigm.*
>
> (Agyeman 2008, 752)

The dichotomy between an (older-style) environmental paradigm and an environmental justice paradigm is amplified in debates between the richer countries of the global North that concern a "green" agenda more (e.g. environmental protection, biodiversity and the protection of the ozone layer), and the poorer ones in the South that support a "brown" agenda (e.g. poverty alleviation, infrastructural development, health and education) (McGranahan and Satterthwaite 2000). Agyeman argues that the "just sustainability paradigm" is an emergent middle ground between the dichotomized green environmental paradigm and the brown/environmental justice paradigm. The boom in social enterprise and social economy discourse in Korea mirrors this philosophy of just sustainability.

The term "social enterprise" was first coined by Joseph Banks (1972), who proposed business organizations needed to use managerial skills to resolve social problems. In recent years, the social enterprise has become a global phenomenon as a result of the growing needs of expanding marginalized communities, the increased dominance of multinational corporations, and the withdrawal of the State from public service and provision (Drayton and Greiner, cited in Yue 2012). Many individuals or groups with similar interests, driven largely by passion and a strong vision to challenge the existing economic system, have established their own companies or organizations to provide products and services that bring positive social impacts. Their efforts often take the form of non-profit or low-profit companies that employ new technologies and creative solutions to leverage resources and supply markets faster, better or at lower cost than traditional corporations (Mainwaring 2011, 166; Yue 2012). Social entrepreneurship is characterized by market orientation, innovation and sociality (Nicholls 2006). According to Geoff Mulgan, "social entrepreneurship is part of the much broader story of democratization: of how people have begun to take control over their own lives, over the economy, and over society. It is, in some respects [...] inseparable from the rise of social movements" (Mulgan 2006, 94).

As Mulgan observes, the boom in social enterprises in Korea, in particular, is closely connected to democratization and related social movements. This reflects civil society's rejection of the old order and its demand for greater democratic participation in various local and regional movements linking economic, environmental and social concerns. Such social entrepreneurial efforts reflect a powerful trend in Korea back towards community-based, grassroots-driven small enterprises, where people seek creativity, cooperation, justice, sociality and sustainability rather than the commercial competition that is emblematic of the existing neoliberal capitalist order, led by large multinational corporations.

In the next two sections this chapter explores how the powerful trend toward just sustainability and social enterprises is reflected in Korean popular television, demonstrating subversive civic desires to deconstruct neoliberal market systems and to build sustainable living structures in their place.

Subversive desires and *Queen of the Office*

In Korea, television dramas are one of the most popular modes of mass communication and as such wield enormous social influence (Ha 1999, 147). Locally produced television dramas signify either macro- or micro-histories of Korean people and society. They demonstrate universally accepted social norms and the collective imagination of the realities that construct the public unconsciousness (Yoon So-Young, cited in Ha 1999, 147). In the case of *Queen of the Office*, Korea's collective imagination is revealed through the subversion of the female lead, Ms. Kim, and the program in turn may reinforce the public's unconscious desire for socioeconomic subversion. Ms. Kim is described as "Korea's first voluntary irregular worker" and she wields enormous power based on her extraordinary work skills and competence. She chose to be an irregular worker to live freely an uninterrupted independent life rather than succumbing to the corporate machine, and by so doing, she represents the subversive desires harbored by many ordinary people in contemporary Korea.

The rise of these subversive desires in large part stems from an oppressive local economic environment that favors gigantic conglomerates (*jaebeol*) and has often been seen to be a destructive force in the lives of many middle- to working-class Koreans. During the past five years of the conservative Lee Myung-Bak regime (2008–13), the government implemented pro-*jaebeol* economic policies by eliminating various regulations against *jaebeol* such as "the equity investment limit" (출자총액제한), which allows unlimited growth of *jaebeol* through mergers and acquisitions and "the separation of financial and industrial capital" (금산분리). Within such a *jaebeol*-friendly economic environment, it has become a serious social issue that big conglomerates intrude on small local businesses. For example, *jaebeol*-owned bakeries encroach into neighborhood districts where smaller local merchants are clustered and in many cases those existing local bakeries lose competitiveness and have to shut down. The pro-*jaebeol* policies of the Lee regime intensify the polarization of wealth while depriving small to medium-sized companies and the working class of economic benefits.

Lee's pro-*jaebeol* inclinations are also evident in the media sector. The Lee government enacted the General Service Cable Television Channel Policy which granted the right to launch integrated cable channels to four conservative newspaper companies, Chosun Ilbo, Joong-ang Ilbo, Dong-a Ilbo and Maeil Gyungje Shinmoon, often referred to as *jaebeol* media.[2] The four channels immediately became mouthpieces of the Lee government and the ruling Saenuri Party (along with the existing state-controlled terrestrial stations, KBS and MBC). In addition, the Lee government attempted to control the media through parachuting in presidential cronies to run the country's most prominent media outlets and to implement increased censorship (The Economist 2012). Television news and current affairs program producers have cowered from criticism of the government, particularly after the producer and the writers of *PD Note* – a current affairs show – were dismissed.[3] In line with such a changed media atmosphere, the number of pro-government and pro-*jaebeol* news reports visibly increased (Chae 2009), and according to Freedom House in the USA, "South Korea declined from Free to Partly Free to reflect an increase in official censorship" (Freedom House 2011).

Within such an oppressive environment, many current affairs programs either were forcefully shut down or lost their critical edge.[4] Consequently, general television viewers tend to receive limited and biased information about the contemporary economic system. In this sense, *Queen of the Office* is one of the few programs directly speaking for neglected social minority groups on a mainstream media channel. As a satirical comedy, *Queen of the Office* portrays various levels of workers in a corporate environment. They are mainly identified by their contractual status, i.e. whether they are regular (permanent) or irregular (temporary) employees. As one aspect of its inequitable *jaebeol*-based economic structure, Korea has one of the highest rates of temporary employment among members of the Organisation for Economic Co-operation and Development (OECD), at 32.3 percent of the total workforce compared with the OECD average of 25 percent (cited in Song 2013). The *jaebeol*s prefer to hire temporary workers, who are paid less, have no welfare benefits and are easier to sack than regular workers. "Companies have hired more temporary workers because protection for permanent workers is so strong that it is hard to adjust their workforce in times of difficulties" (Yoo Kyung-Joon, cited in Song 2013). In the same workplace with the same job requirements, irregular employees often get paid only 50 percent of the salary of regular employees. After one or two years on contracts, the majority either do not have their contracts renewed (effectively sacking them) or may get an extension of a couple more years, but even in these cases they continue to suffer from ongoing job insecurity. *Queen of the Office* represents and critiques this discriminatory work practice in Korea's current neoliberal capitalist environment.

The drama presents two main characters who represent each employment category. Ms. Kim represents irregular employees while Jang Gyu-Jik (Oh Ji-Ho) represents both regular employees and the general corporate culture where succeeding in corporate competition is a virtue prized above all others. With his MBA from the USA, he wins at all costs and, as a consequence, has attained the level of upper management even though still at an early stage of his career. Supporting characters also represent each group, including the recent graduate Jeong Ju-Ri (Jeong Yoo-Mi), a clumsy and inexperienced worker on a three-month contract. Ju-Ri is a significant character: while Ms. Kim represents the subversive hopes and desires of many Korean workers, it is Ju-Ri who in fact is probably much closer to their reality. Ju-Ri represents one of Korea's most critical social problems: youth unemployment. People like her are often called the "880,000 won generation" because these young university graduates live in fear of being financially stranded below the 880,000 won per month pay scale (approximately US$650). This figure is "what a temporary staff or contract worker makes a month in net pay and is also a sign of the crushed dreams of the country's youth who bet an elite education would lead to a rewarding career" (Seo and Kim 2009). Mu Jeong-Han (Lee Hee-Joon) is another supporting character who, like the competitive and assertive Gyu-Jik, is a regular employee, but Jeong-Han is considerate and cooperative and considers the company as a community based on friendship and kinship, and as such reflects the values of many Korean people, a sentiment he views as forgotten in the contemporary corporate climate. From this perspective, Jeong-Han can be understood as representing pre-neoliberal capitalist Korea.

At the center of the show's satirical treatment of workplace inequity is Ms. Kim. She is employed on a three-month temporary contract with Y-Jang (a leading food company), and although an irregular employee, she holds an impressive array of 124 professional qualifications. These include certificates in Russian, Spanish, hairdressing, piloting airplanes, midwifery, Japanese and Chinese cooking, and lifesaving. Whether it be making coffee or operating heavy machinery, she is capable of doing the work of three regular employees. Impressed by her abilities, the company desires to convert her contract to that of a regular employee, but she refuses because, as she says, "I don't want to be a slave restrained by the company." Ms. Kim is a so-called "super *gap*".

Figure 2.1 Ms. Kim, holding a certificate of midwifery, assists at a birth, *Queen of the Office*, KBS, 2013

Figure 2.2 Status of Jeong Ju-Ri: "Looking for a job, student loan debt of 17,000,000 won", *Queen of the Office*, KBS, 2013

The "*gap* and *eul* relationship" (갑을관계) has become a buzzword in Korea in recent years. *Gap* and *eul* refer to the two parties in this type of contractual situation, where a *gap* refers to someone who is in the dominant position in the contract while an *eul* is the subordinate. Thus the terms are often used to describe unfair relationships in work situations, where the *gap* wields enormous power over the *eul*. [5] In most cases, companies (and those in high-profile management positions) fulfill this role of *gap* while their employees are *eul* and contract-based workers can be understood as super *eul*. Yet in the case of Ms. Kim, despite being an irregular employee, she is a super *gap*.

Several episodes portray the mistreatment of irregular super *eul* workers by the company. In episode 12, for example, Ju-Ri's business proposal is selected as a team project, but she is told to submit it under her boss's name because she is only a temporary employee. Episode nine, meanwhile, follows the story of a female temporary employee who finds out she is pregnant and tries to hide it from her colleagues, especially her boss. As contract-based workers do not receive maternity leave under current Korean labor laws, the majority of pregnant women are forced to quit their jobs before giving birth. In *Queen of the Office*, no one out speaks against such discriminatory practices because they are afraid they will be disadvantaged when it is time to have their own contracts extended. Except for Ms. Kim: she takes assertive action against such irrational and unjust requests by the company and her boss. For example, at one point Ms. Kim refuses to go to a departmental dinner. When Gyu-Jik forces her to go, she says, "a temporary contract worker like me has no reason to socialize with others and to flatter the boss. I do not see the point of participating in get-together drinks, which is almost like a suicide-bombing where you both harm your health and waste your time." As a compromise, she demands overtime pay in return for her attendance. According to her, every activity beyond the nine-to-six working hours must be paid because she is a contract-based temporary worker, and her contract does not include these extra activities. Her demand reveals the irony that the company is willing to discriminate against irregular workers in terms of benefits and salaries, yet still demands the same kind of duties and commitments as regular workers.

Ms. Kim's subversive actions – gestures that in reality would possibly cause fractures in the institutionalized imbalances between regular and irregular employees' working conditions – have been celebrated by many bloggers and in online community forums. Over 4,000 blog posts and almost 800 Naver café (online community forum) posts appeared citing the terms *Queen of the Office* and "irregular employee."[6] Many posts demonstrate how the bloggers identify with the absurd but at the same time reality-based situations the series addresses. Blogger "ZummaRella" states "that this 'bad employment' situation which causes discrimination and unfair sacking and does not offer job security to individual employees is not one single person's problem, but rather an issue about the entire social system" (ZummaRella 2013). She then points out that KBS (the network that broadcast the program) is also guilty of the same irregular employment problems (ibid.). Another blogger, "Shain," mentions the scene where Gyu-Jik's mother is accidentally killed during a protest to amend irregular employee protection laws, explaining that the law that is supposed to protect irregular workers is actually often used to sack them (Shain 2013). In the program, this law is both the reason for the protest and the cause of the subsequent death of the mother, and it signifies the oppressive system of neoliberal capitalism and its power to destroy ordinary working-class households (like Gyu-Jik's). "Shain" describes how this law gives many corporations reasons to lay off irregular employees and to create a new employment arrangement called a "permanent irregular employment scheme," where companies can exploit well-trained, experienced workers by paying them the same low wage for many years (Shain 2013). In blogging and commenting online, netizens discuss their concerns provoked by the issues highlighted in the drama, enabling a broader arena for public discussion of the very topic the drama seeks to address.

In another episode, Ju-Ri is late to work because she has a hangover after her team's evening of social drinking, and explains that senior colleagues have told her that such events are crucial because networking like this is essential to building a good career. Ms. Kim reacts strongly against this, saying, "for contract workers like us who don't have good backgrounds, connections and 'real' workmates, our body and certificates are all we have. We can work for any other company as long as we have this damn body and certificates." What is crucial here is that she exposes the absurdities that riddle Korea's corporate culture which privileges collectivity, so that individual workers are expected to follow collectively decided (primarily top-down) decisions. This feature of collectiveness is a signature characteristic of Korean society, and can be considered both a constructive and destructive traditional virtue depending on the context. In corporate culture, this virtue of collectiveness is often evoked to oppress individual choice. Ms. Kim articulates that it is an individual's abilities and their capable physical individual body (rather than intangible networking connections vaguely garnered through forced socialization) that will truly enable liberation from such oppression.

Episode 10 concerns the middle-aged regular employee Go Jeong-Do (Kim Gi-Cheon) who has worked for Y-Jang for 28 years and is advised to resign. It is felt that Jeong-Do is a relic from a pre-digital technology-empowered era. He was unable to cope with new digitized business processes, and needed the assistance of his colleagues to do computer-related tasks. He is slow and often dozes in the office. He lacks both the physical strength and the intellectual rigor to perform fieldwork successfully. He is therefore treated badly, and even called "a broken watch" by his colleagues. Jeong-Do is considered a useless part in this fast-paced corporate machine. However, the episode shows that his experience and skill set would be in high demand if his tech-savvy colleagues were faced with challenges beyond their familiar digital environment in an unfamiliar analogue world. This is the scenario that occurs just before the company is about to sign an important contract: when the electricity goes out, no one knows how to prepare a contract form without computers. Suddenly, in this context, Jeong-Do's professional experience is valued and he prepares the form using a pen and a ruler, meaning his team can successfully sign the contract. At the end of the episode, Jeong-Do compares himself to a broken watch while he sees Ms. Kim as a new one; he says: "no one can go alone. The minute and hour hands and other parts of the watch all should go together. Then a broken watch like me can go along with others. It is too lonely if you turn all the hands all by yourself." Although in this fictional instance Jeong-Do retains his job, in reality this would be unlikely, but his comment addresses very real issues concerning contemporary corporate life in Korea, where values around community spirit and cooperation pale next to the dominant attributes of success and competition.

In its representation of super *gap* contract worker heroine Ms. Kim, *Queen of the Office* reflects the subversive desires held by many ordinary workers who feel oppressed by what they perceive as their undervalued role in the corporate machine. In episode 14, Jeong-Han is about to lose his current position and be forced to move to a regional branch, allowing Gyu-Jik to take his job. While sad about his friend's misfortunes, Gyu-Jik tries to justify it by saying, "to keep our seat, sometimes we have to step on somebody else's seat." Ms. Kim responds: "losing your friend is much more unbearable than losing your seat." While Ms. Kim may be the most cartoony and unrealistic character on the show, she still demonstrates the subversive possibilities beyond the current *gap* and *eul* relationship, particularly in regard to reclaiming forgotten values in Korea's contemporary corporate environment that has sought to bury them. The recent boom in co-ops in Korea, discussed below, further demonstrates how many Koreans are enthusiastically seeking to return to these values in another way.

The co-op boom and sustainable living: *The Human Condition*

The three major candidates for the 2012 Korean presidential election promised a "welfare nation" and a "sustainable society," along with a focus on developing a "social economy." Even before the election campaign, there had been a series of citizen campaigns on- and offline reinforcing these significant sociopolitical directions, which stood in opposition to the conglomerate (*jaebeol*)-led neoliberal market economy, the polarization of wealth, increasing youth unemployment and collapsing small and medium-size enterprises. There has been a strong and urgent demand by Korean citizens for a higher quality of life, encapsulated in the notion of sustainable living and a social economy. The boom in cooperative associations is one of the most visible social changes reflecting these civic demands. According to the International Co-operative Alliance (ICA), "a co-operative is an autonomous association of persons united voluntarily to meet their common economic, social, and cultural needs and aspirations through a jointly-owned and democratically-controlled enterprise" (ICA 2013).[7] Its basic philosophy resonates with the concerns of many Koreans over recent years who have reinvigorated the cooperative association movement as it swept the nation.

On December 1, 2012, The Cooperative Association Fundamental Law took effect, and within the next 100 days, 137 cooperative associations registered in Seoul and more than 500 nationwide. To encourage cooperative associations (or co-ops), the city of Seoul announced that it would increase its number of co-ops to 8,000 by 2022, making up 5 percent of the gross regional domestic product (GRDP). This reflected the influence of Mayor Park Won-Soon, founder and director of the Hope Institute, a think tank designed to promote grassroots-led solutions to social, educational, environmental and political problems. Living co-ops are at the center of the phenomenon that mirrors the desires of Korea's contemporary middle class for sustainable, green lifestyles. Middle-class urban consumers who voluntarily participate in direct trading with rural producers have become a driving force in this alternative food supply chain. Modeled on Western co-ops (particularly the Legacoop in Bologna, Italy), these local co-ops seek to join a global movement that fights rural poverty, respects the environment and practices food safety. Korea's living co-ops embody the rising social economy as a consequence of rapid globalization and technological developments.

In the past, most traditional village or neighborhood organizations in Korea had a hierarchical structure where patriarchal chiefs were steered by political patrons into predominantly conservative trajectories. This is also true of the contemporary Korean corporate environment, where higher-level management wields enormous power over lower-level employees within a hierarchical corporate structure. Nevertheless, in recent years it has become evident that new forms of association have arisen, growing from ordinary citizens who are voluntarily drawn together by mutual interests. The current boom in co-ops provides a good example. In contrast to older-style community organizations, these new co-ops are composed of individuals who are willing to pursue their shared sociopolitico-economic interests within a largely horizontal structure of trust-based relationships with persons outside their immediate social circle. In particular, with the growth of an urban, well-educated and prosperous middle class as well as emerging social media networks, social movements have been active on the local political front and constantly address concerns about sustainable living, social well-being, equity, consumer interests, consumer rights, education issues and environmental well-being.

The reality program *The Human Condition* depicts these emerging desires for sustainable living and environmental well-being within the Korean middle class. The program follows six comedians (Park Seong-Ho, Kim Joon-Ho, Jeong Tae-Ho, Kim Joon-Hyeon, Heo Gyeong-Hwan and Yang Sang-Gook), who are given one sustainable lifestyle mission a week as they all live together in the same house. By mid-September 2013, ten missions had been broadcast.

- First mission
  To live without television, computer and mobile phone
- Second mission
  To live without waste
- Third mission
  To live without a car
- Fourth mission
  To live without money
- Fifth mission
  To live on only locally produced food
- Sixth mission
  To live for true friends
- Seventh mission
  To live with a very limited supply of water
- Eighth mission
  To live without electricity
- Ninth mission
  To spend a holiday in a clean environment
- Tenth mission
  To live on the recommended calorie intake

Their fifth mission was to consume local food, where they had to both locate and confirm where food came from, reflecting the fundamental sensibility of living co-ops.[8] The main purpose of this mission was to trace the journey of the food on one's dining table, and the influence of its production on the broader environment. As members could only consume locally produced food, the idea of a safe food supply chain was also introduced during their search. The key factor of this mission was that participants must know who produced the food, leading them to visit farms and food manufacturing factories. In one sequence, Kim Joon-Ho was trying to figure out whether he could consume his favorite food, instant ramen. After spending a few minutes online, he found out that most of the ingredients were foreign, including the main ingredient, flour, which came from the USA. In another scene, after picking strawberries at a farm, Joon-Ho wanted to make strawberry jam using sugar. He soon discovered, however, that all sugar consumed in Korea is from tropical regions such as the Philippines. The strawberry farm owner said that sugar has very high "food mileage." The audience is then shown the definition of "food mileage" on screen: "food mileage (or food miles) is a term which refers to the distance that food is traveled from the time of its production through transport, distribution to the consumer's dining table." Through Kim Joon-Ho's investigation into making strawberry jam, the program introduces the concept of food mileage and how it affects the environment.

When participants visit farms to purchase vegetables, eggs and meat, the program specifies the food mileage (tkm) for each item, calculated as the sum

Figure 2.3 The Human Condition's fifth mission: "consuming local food", *The Human Condition*, KBS, 2013

of the amount of transported food (t) times the transported distance (km). According to the National Institute of Environmental Research, Korea's average food mileage per person is 7,085tkm, almost ten times higher than France (cited in Cho 2013). *The Human Condition* emphasized the significance of this figure, and its social impact was immediately visible: after the episode was broadcast, the term "food mileage" was ranked as the top real-time search word on Naver, the top portal website in Korea. Additionally, various news articles and blog posts appeared that elaborated on food mileage and local food consumption. Almost 400 blog posts appeared with the keywords *The Human Condition* and "local food," while 90 posts were found with the alternative keyword "food mileage."[9]

Blogger "hsback2000" identifies as a housewife, and her blog is dedicated to the various food she prepares (hsback2000 2013). She uploaded a post in response to this episode, confessing that she had previously been purchasing groceries mainly based on their price without concern for where they came from. She remarked that the episode had taught her the importance of consuming local food and low-carbon green products to protect the environment. She concluded her post by introducing the related "Namyangju Slow Food International Festival" event. Another blogger, "lar928," said that she found

Figure 2.4 Food collected by the members, with the location of its origin confirmed, *The Human Condition*, KBS, 2013

out about "food mileage" through Kim Joon-Ho who introduced the concept in the episode (lar928 2013). She then posted a diagram of food mileage per person in each country, showing that Korea (7,085) is ten times higher France (735), and emphasized the significance of consuming local food. She concluded her post by introducing various local food direct outlets in Seoul, as well as the "local food consumer workshop" organized by Local Food Korea.

Major news media also highlighted the issue of local food and food mileage after the episode was broadcast. A major daily newspaper, *JoongAng Ilbo*, publicized that reducing food mileage significantly affects the consumer price by using the example of radish distribution (Han 2013). According to the Korea Agro-Fisheries & Food Trade Corporation, through the existing distribution channel with major supermarket chains, consumers pay five times more for a radish compared with its primary cost (cited in Han 2013). A current affairs website, *Media Today*, noted in their review of the episode that food mileage is also closely related to national self-sufficiency, observing that Korea's grain self-sufficiency is only 22.6 percent (2011), the lowest among the OECD countries (and it had dropped to half compared with the 1990s, at 43.1 percent) (Cho 2013). It also indicated that a decrease in food mileage impacts direct trading between producers and consumers, meaning consumers pay the correct price for products: for example, the Hansallim living co-op has a 76 percent return of its profit price back to the producer (Cho 2013). This presents a strikingly different scenario from the one that currently stands with large supermarket chains, which take anywhere from 50–70 percent of the producers' profits (Cho 2013).

As elsewhere in capitalist Asia, it is now common for urban middle-class Koreans to consume seasonal food products from overseas producers through the international distribution networks associated with hypermarkets and SSMs (super supermarkets).[10] According to Statistics Korea, the total revenue of hypermarkets reached US$33.7 billion in 2013, a figure that has tripled over the past ten years (Statistics Korea 2013). These *jaebeol*-owned market chains aggressively target local consumers who once used private-owned small marts or traditional neighborhood markets. A variety of products from across the world and competitive prices have attracted consumers, eventually driving small markets and shop owners out of business. Such vicious business practices see consumers paying overblown distribution costs to conglomerates, while producers earn less profit. Public awareness of the need to rebuild the economic ecosystem and consumer demand for sustainable living has triggered the current boom in living co-ops, and this spike in public awareness is reflected in episode five of *The Human Condition*.

Here, members visit various farms and factories where consumers directly trade with the producers. Heo Gyeong-Hwan visits a beef farm to identify the producer of organic Korean beef (*hanwoo*) which he purchased through a farmers' direct outlet. Yang Sang-Gook visits a *kimchi* factory where all the organic ingredients are supplied by approved local producers, authenticated by their photos and signatures. This process addresses the significance of understanding how the food we consume is produced, and how it is eventually delivered to our table. It also emphasizes how consuming local food by known producers through direct trading rejuvenates the local food industry and eventually enhances social sustainability, allowing both farmers and small neighborhood shop owners to survive.

Local food and the local food consumption movement can be explained through the conceptual paradigm of a "collaborative effort to build more locally based, self-reliant food economies – one in which sustainable food production, processing, distribution, and consumption is integrated to enhance the economic, environmental and social health of a particular place" (SAREP, cited in Feenstra 2002, 100).[11] In the contemporary Korean middle-class consumer market, such collaborative efforts are realized through the emergence of living co-ops through which producers earn equitable profits and consumers acquire fresher food direct from the source. By tracing the journey of food, *The Human Condition* reflects this contemporary middle-class consumer desire for sustainable living, as well as for rebuilding the financial ecosystem of the food supply chain. As an alternative to the all-or-nothing, success-obsessed neoliberal market system, these Korean citizens are attempting to rebuild a cooperative market environment where farmers and small neighborhood marts can exist alongside *jaebeol*-owned hypermarkets, reinvigorating a spirit of both social justice and social and environmental sustainability.

Conclusion

Justice and equity issues must be incorporated into the core of Korean social sustainability practices where social minority groups must be addressed. The social inequalities experienced by many irregular contract workers and farmers in rural areas demonstrate how these groups suffer from social exclusion, uneven wealth redistribution and inequitable access to environmental values. Clarke and Agyeman (2011) have noted how low-income earners living in inner urban areas often encounter a range of environmental and social problems such as poor housing, lack of green open space, air pollution, racism and unemployment. The case of irregular workers in Korea's corporate system may support a related taxonomy, as they too often suffer social exclusion and economic pressures based on similar demographic positioning. Small neighborhood shop owners whose businesses were shut down due to the invasion of *jaebeol*-owned hypermarkets and farmers unable to garner their due profits because of the tyranny of conglomerate distributors could also be categorized in similar ways. In this situation, seeking subversion and sustainability might offer alternative ways to remedy the current system.

The two television programs that provided case studies in this chapter have demonstrated these possibilities. These programs demonstrate the symptoms of neoliberal fatigue and offer possible remedies. In *Queen of the Office*, this chapter has explored how this fatigue has been satirically represented in the subversive stance of Ms. Kim, a woman who challenges Korea's neoliberal capitalist-driven corporate practices. Through Ms. Kim's subversive voice, the program reinforces re/constructing social equity between regular (mainstream) and irregular (minority) workers and rebuilding community values. The second case study, *The Human Condition*, reveals the ways in which this fatigue can be remedied through sustainable living. By focusing on local food consumption as a method of rebuilding community values that benefit both producers and consumers, it aroused widespread public discussion regarding social justice and social sustainability. The public desires and possible remedies articulated in these programs are further developed and consolidated by viewers and citizens online, activities which at their best can potentially lead to offline practices.

This chapter does not seek to celebrate the constructive visions and optimistic effects of television media in raising public awareness or driving social change, but rather focuses on the contextual background of transformations in Korean society and the possible choices media audiences could make that would propel both the deconstruction of the current climate and the (re)construction of sustainable living. Any discussion of these sociocultural issues cannot be separated from the particular contexts in which they are located and the related sociopolitical mechanisms that underpin them (Grossberg 2010). Apart from social context, individual choice is another significant factor to be considered. Anthony Giddens (1991) identifies that an increasing number of areas of daily life have become subject to human agency as a result of individualization and modernization, such that individuals are able to take control of problems that occur in the environment by exercising personal choice and responsibility. This chapter has addressed how the television media portray those changes and the possible choices available to today's citizens, as well as television's role in mediating the relationship between the decisions made by individuals and the particular sociopolitical context of contemporary Korea. Televisual examples like the ones discussed here encourage citizens to seek social inclusion, equity and justice actively through the delivery of sustainable development and/or subversion of the existing social and economic order.

Notes

1. The show is based on the 2007 Japanese TV series, *Pride of the Temp* (*Haken no Hinkaku*).
2. Prior to this policy, all cable channels had to specialize in certain categories such as comedy, drama, music, fashion and lifestyle.
3. *PD Note* is one of the top current affairs programs broadcast on MBC (Munhwa Broadcasting Corporation), which was once famous for its broad and open-minded critique of power.
4. As a result of government interference in the existing mainstream media, during 2011 and 2012 countless social media-driven current affairs podcasts were launched.
5. In 2010, a salesperson at Namyang Dairy Products made abusive comments to force a retail distributor to purchase and stock their products. The retail distributor recorded the abusive tirade and went public with the recording in May 2013. This

caused the general public to take notice of the unfair and widespread business practices that have occurred for many years in the industry and shed light on the fundamental problem of the *gap* and *eul* relationship, where Namyang Dairy Products (and the salesperson) is the *gap* and the retail distributor is the *eul*.

6 As of December 1, 2013.

7 The values that cooperatives uphold are self-help, self-responsibility, democracy, equality, equity and solidarity, while the seven principles include voluntary and open membership, democratic member control, member economic participation, autonomy and independence, education, training and information, cooperation among cooperatives, and concern for community (ICA 2013). Witnessing growing sociopolitical turmoil, economic stagnation and the social insecurity that future generations face in terms of jobs, essential social services and even just meeting their basic needs, the ICA has identified four key issues that cooperatives could help to address: environmental degradation and resource depletion; an unstable financial sector and increasing income inequality; a growing global governance gap; and a seemingly disenfranchised younger generation (ibid.).

8 Aired on May 4, 11 and 18, 2013.

9 As of December 1, 2013.

10 "Hypermarket" refers to large supermarkets which are mostly *jaebeol*-owned chains, e.g. E Mart, Lotte Mart and Home Plus. "Super supermarket" (SSM) refers to those corporate-owned supermarkets that are bigger than private-owned local marts or convenience stores and smaller than hypermarkets, which includes GS Supermarket, Lotte Mart, Kim's Club Mart, Home Plus Express and E Mart Everyday.

11 SAREP is the Sustainable Agriculture Research and Education Program at the University of California.

References

Agyeman, Julian. 2008. "Toward a 'Just' Sustainability?" *Continuum: Journal of Media & Cultural Studies* 22(6): 751–756.

Banks, Joseph. 1972. *The Sociology of Movements.* London: Macmillan.

Chae, Eun-Ha. 2009. "Lee Myung-Bak's Utopia, Press's Dystopia [이명박의 유토피아, 언론인의 디스토피아]." *Pressian*, March 30. www.pressian.com/article/article.asp?article_num=40090330011804 (accessed May 23, 2013).

Cho, Soo-Gyeong. 2013. "Have Thought of Food Mileage of Your Dinner Tonight? [오늘 저녁 밥상, 푸드 마일리지 따져보셨습니까?]" *Media Today*, May 5. images.mediatoday.co.kr/news/articleView.html?idxno=109232 (accessed June 23, 2013).

Clarke, Lisa, and Julian Agyeman. 2011. "Shifting the Balance in Environmental Governance: Ethnicity, Environmental Citizenship and Discourses of Responsibility." *Antipode* 43(5): 1773–1800.

Dresner, Simon. 2002. *The Principles of Sustainability.* London and Sterlin, VA: Earthscan.

The Economist. 2012. "No News is Bad News." March 3. www.economist.com/node/21549008 (accessed June 23, 2013).

Feenstra, Gail. 2002. "Creating Space for Sustainable Food Systems: Lessons from the Field." *Agriculture and Human Values* 19(2): 99–106.

Freedom House. 2011. "Freedom of the Press: South Korea." www.freedomhouse.org/report/freedom-press/2011/south-korea (accessed May 23, 2013).

Giddens, Anthony. 1991. *Modernity and Self-Identity: Self and Society in the Late Modern Age.* Cambridge: Polity Press.

Grossberg, Laurence. 2010. *Cultural Studies in the Future Tense*. Durham, NC: Duke University Press.

Ha, Yun-Geum. 1999. "Representation of Female Household Heads in Television Dramas Post-IMF [IMF 사태 이후 드라마에 나타난 여성가장의 표상]." In *Mass Media and Politics of Gender* [대중 매체와 성의 정치학], edited by Kim Myeong-Hye, Jeong Gi-Hyeon, and Yoo Se-Gyeong, 145–168. Seoul: Nanam Publishing.

Han, Jin. 2013. "Preparing Chuseok Dinner Table with Healthy Food [건강한 먹거리로 추석 차례상 차리기]." *JoongAng Ilbo*, September 10. article.joins.com/news/article/article.asp?total_id=12567487&cloc=olink|article|default (accessed October 23, 2013).

hsback2000. 2013. "The Human Condition and Local Food [인간의조건 '산지음식만먹고살기'편으로본로컬푸드]." *Naver*, June 12. hsback2000.blog.me/80191859236 (accessed October 27, 2013).

ICA (International Co-operative Alliance). 2013. "Co-operative Identity, Values and Principles." ica.coop/en/what-co-op/co-operative-identity-values-principles (accessed October 27, 2013).

lar928. 2013. "The Human Condition and Food Mileage [인간의조건, 푸드마일리]." *Naver*, June 12. blog.naver.com/lar928?Redirect=Log&logNo=120194740022 (accessed June 28, 2013).

Mainwaring, Simon. 2011. *We First: How Brands and Consumers Use Social Media to Build a Better World*. New York: Palgrave Macmillan.

McGranahan, Gorden, and David Satterthwaite. 2000. "Environmental Health or Ecological Sustainability? Reconciling the Brown and Green Agendas in Urban Development." In *Sustainable Cities in Developing Countries: Theory and Practice at the Millennium*, edited by Cedric Pugh, 73–90. London: Earthscan.

Mulgan, Geoff. 2006. "Cultivating Invisible Hand of Social Entrepreneurship." In *Social Entrepreneurship: New Models of Sustainable Social Change*, edited by Alex Nicholls, 74–95. Oxford: Oxford University Press.

Nicholls, Alex. 2006. *Social Entrepreneurship: New Models of Sustainable Social Change*. Oxford: Oxford University Press.

Seo, Eun-Kyung, and Junghun Kim. 2009. "Young South Koreans become the '880,000 Won Generation'." *Taipei Times*, April 12. www.taipeitimes.com/News/biz focus/archives/2009/04/12/2003440846 (accessed October 27, 2013).

Shain. 2013. "Queen of the Office, Irregular Employee Protection Laws that Cause Miss Kim and Jang Gyu-Jik's Tragedy [직장의 신, 미스김과 장규직의 비극을 낳은 비정규직 보호법]." *Tistory*, May 22. shain.tistory.com/1540 (accessed June 3, 2013).

Song, Jung-A. 2013. "South Korean Contract Workers Struggle for Rights." *Financial Times*, July 13. www.ft.com/intl/cms/s/0/810c6612-e954-11e2-9f11-00144feabdc0.html#axzz2djF31HI3 (accessed November 7, 2013).

Statistics Korea. 2013. *Revenues of Big Markets in 16 Cities*. kosis.kr/wnsearch/totalSearch.jsp (accessed November 7, 2013).

World Commission on Environment and Development (WCED). 1987. *Our Common Future*. WCED. www.un-documents.net/wced-ocf.htm (accessed November 7, 2013).

Yue, Audrey. 2012. "We're the Gay Company, as Gay as it Gets." In *Queer Singapore*, edited by Audrey Yue and Jun Zubillaga-Pow, 197–212. Hong Kong: Hong Kong University Press.

ZummaRella. 2013. "Irregular Employment, Bad Employment [나쁜일자리인비정규직]." *Naver*, June 17. blog.naver.com/bigmama30/189382901 (accessed November 7, 2013).

3 Family, aesthetic authority and class identity in the shadow of neoliberal modernity

The cultural politics of China's *Exchanging Spaces*

Wu Jing

It is a widely acknowledged proposition that the world in the past 30 years has seen a hegemonic socioeconomic and political complex of governance called neoliberalism spreading its influence from the center to peripheries of the capitalist global system, and causing major upheavals and uncertainties in the economic, social and cultural life of the world's population (Brenner and Theodore 2002). The core of the neoliberal doctrine, as described by its critical researchers, is the assertion that private property rights, the free market and free trade will bring the best results for economic production as well as social well-being, and that government intervention should be limited to providing legal protection of the monetary system, property rights and national defense, leaving social welfare, education, healthcare, culture, environmental protection and other previously public domains to the competition and allocation of the free market. In North America and Western Europe, this involves a huge overhaul of a well-established consensus about social justice since the Second World War; for example, Keynesian economic policy, government investment in public projects, strong labor unions, government intervention in enforcing ethical labor and environmental standards, public provision for platforms of cultural production like public broadcasting, fine arts and education, and so on. Therefore, the rise to power of neoliberal policy is not merely a political maneuver, but entails a complicated re-evaluation of foundational modern beliefs around social justice, progress and ethical relationships among human beings, communities, nations, as well as between humans and the earth (Gore 2000; Harvey 2000). As David Harvey observes, the success of the neoliberal way of thinking is not accidental, but is underpinned by its advocates' occupation of positions of considerable influence, such as in universities, think tanks, the media, corporate boards and financial institutions, key state institutions like treasury departments and central banks, and also international institutions like the International Monetary Fund, the World Bank and the World Trade Organization (WTO) (Harvey 2005).

The understanding that neoliberalism is not only a set of political and administrative strategies and policies, but also a comprehensive system of ideology and cultural beliefs, leads to critical studies of public and media culture where ideas about society, self and the good life are imagined and formulated discursively. Many have noticed the correlation between the rise of consumer-oriented entertainment content in the mass media and the increasingly dominant neoliberal reorganizations of society (Andrejevic 2004; Miller 2007). In the field of Euro-American television, against the background of traditional public service broadcasting, a significant change in programming has taken place in the past two decades – namely, the coming to prominence of the reality TV genre, especially in so-called lifestyle television. The form and style of the reality TV genre originally grew out of news and documentary programming, focusing on various social issues and exploring the conditions and behaviors of ordinary people in real life. With structural changes in the TV industry, which have placed more economic pressure on previously public service programs such as news magazines and documentaries, the reality TV genre has become more dramatic, sensational and commercially driven, to the extent that the genre's previous preoccupation with public issues, national narratives and social affairs has transformed into a documentary style of exhibiting people's private lives and secret emotions, or educating audiences to be better consumers, turning product placement into legitimate TV content. With low production costs, the convenience of product placement and targeted merchandising, chances of audience participation and the appearance of realism, the reality TV genre combines the economic, social and aesthetic aspirations of the era of neoliberal globalization so well that it has become one of the major genres of network and cable TV, as well as new forms of interactive TV (Raphael 2009). In its celebration of consumption, competition, personal makeover and self-improvement, the genre holds up a value system that places market logic at the center of social life, emphasizing individualism in the sense of ownership of particular commodities or property, and advocating an ethic of constant self-improvement and competition in order to seize the best position and limited resources. In effect, scholars argue, the genre serves to alleviate ideological resistance to the neoliberal overhaul of social policy by distracting public attention from the field of politics and institutions, toward private life and consumerism, at the same time cultivating an ethic of success through constant self-improvement, discipline and transformation to meet the requirements of the market. Along these lines, Nick Couldry calls reality TV the secret theater of neoliberalism (Couldry 2008, 3) Others argue that the lifestyle reality TV genre redefines social values from social binding to individualism, from equality to getting ahead of others, from community contribution to consumerism, and from a stable vision of self and society to one that celebrates the uncertainty of change (Ouellette 2009; Hollows and Jones 2010; Lewis 2011).

In light of these socioeconomic and cultural transformations in mostly Anglo-American countries, a question arises as to how the rest of the world is dealing with the globalizing hegemony of neoliberalism. It is already obvious that both neoliberal economic policies and reality TV genres have become increasingly dominant institutional phenomena in many parts of world over the past ten years. With the economic and cultural hegemony of the West in global capitalism, it is not surprising to see replicas or simulations of Western economic and cultural patterns in the rest of the world. However, it would be unwise and erroneous to think that social and cultural formations can simply be planted into any society without (mis)recognition, negation, negotiation, intermingling, reconstitution and even (re)creation. China is an interesting case in this respect. Ostensibly, there exist developments in both China's economic policies and its cultural landscape that parallel the Western neoliberal turn. Yet when looked at carefully, China has been taking a fairly idiosyncratic route since the institution of the reform and opening up policy 30 years ago that has turned a poor socialist country into the second largest economy in the world. China's hard-to-define socioeconomic regime mixes elements of state capitalism, Confucian patriarchy, authoritarian socialism, and neoliberalism. The cultural discourses are no less perplexing: cosmopolitan imagination, rejuvenation of traditional cultural ideals, socialist legacy and new subjectivities fostered in the market society all strive for audience and recognition on the platforms of mass culture.

The remainder of this chapter will focus on one of China's lifestyle programs, *Exchanging Spaces*, as an example through which to extrapolate the everyday cultural politics of constructing modernity with Chinese characteristics, and producing modern identities that negotiate with their socio-economic conditions. Both taking on influences from Western television and maintaining certain traditions of Chinese TV culture, lifestyle programs in China are predominantly aimed at a family audience. Taken together, both the older-style content of cooking, home decoration and health advice, and the more commercialized versions of contests, weight control and psychological therapy form a symbolic environment where dominant ideas about individual subjectivity, family, society and the interrelationships between these are formulated. The pedagogical overtones of most lifestyle programs mean that modern selfhood is constantly shaped and reshaped through the watching of, or participation in, these programs. It is therefore interesting to look at the raw materials of such identity formation work, and seek to understand how exactly they are mingled to develop the project of cultural and subjective modernity in contemporary China. By looking at the identities, social imaginaries, aesthetic pursuits and class aspirations that are formulated and promoted in *Exchanging Spaces*, I hope to provide a nuanced and dialectical description of the cultural and ideological formations of everyday life in China in the shadow of hegemonic neoliberal modernity. Although there are disputes as to whether China's *developmental strategies* can really be categorized as neoliberal, I will argue in the next section that because of the coincidence between China's opening up to Western political and economic systems and the neoliberal turn in Anglo-American societies, it is safe to say that neoliberalism serves as the dominant *ideology* for a China that is eager to learn from capitalist societies (Lee 2014).

Economic reform and the commercialization of everyday life

Starting from late 1970s, China's economic reform coincided with the neoliberal turn in the West during the Regan-Thatcher era (Harvey 2005). At the beginning, economic reform may well have been an independent decision of the Chinese leadership to solve problems of inefficiency and lack of initiative in the socialist planned economy. Yet with the introduction of Western capital and management style, and increasing cultural and educational exchanges with the capitalist world, the discussions of socioeconomic policies and cultural enlightenment in China increasingly became dominated by elite intellectuals and government officials who think mostly within the framework of modernization, the market economy, rational individualism and the celebration of capital as a progressive force in world history. Some (in)famous propaganda slogans during this era, such as "to get rich is glorious," "knowledge is power," "the good cat is the one who can catch mice, no matter whether it is a white or black cat," etc., communicate very well the idea of instrumental rationality and market individualism. In contrast, traditional and socialist cultural ethics such as collectivism, suspicion of commerce, obedience to authority, family values, etc., came to be considered backward and obstructive to China's modernization drive. With China's active pursuit of membership of the WTO during the 1990s, legal frameworks and institutional arrangements were drastically changed to meet the requirements of the WTO in order to be considered a market economy. Further integration into the global capitalist economy meant that the official ideology has by and large given up any serious attempt to define a socialist economic model different from the dominant neoliberal package. Depoliticized terms like modernization, reform, scientific management, rule of law and market mechanism are used to phrase government socioeconomic visions, in place of terms like capitalism, privatization and deregulation – terms that would cause immediate uproar in a society that is still officially socialist and culturally sympathetic to socialism.

Though proceeding with the careful disguise of official propaganda that still echoes the familiar discourse of socialism, the sweeping marketization of production, privatization of public institutions, and commercialization of everyday life within a short decade have proven too drastic for many individuals to cope with smoothly. Many have noticed the cultural backlash against China's dramatic turn toward capitalism in the new century: labor unrest, popular hatred of the rich and powerful, nostalgia for Maoism, rising nationalist sentiments, and the rejuvenation of patriarchy and conservatism in gender and social relations (Wu 2006; Lee and Yang 2007). It is the latter phenomenon – the regeneration of patriarchy, mingled with cosmopolitan ideas of family, success and gender relations – to which this chapter will now turn, in order to provide insight into the ideological formation of everyday life in contemporary China and the role of lifestyle television within it.

Family has always been a central idea in Chinese society. Confucian teaching lays down a four-layered process of social building: cultivating the self, managing the family, ruling the state and appeasing the world. Family is represented not only as the basic unit of society, but as a miniature society; that is, the law and ethics that apply to maintaining a good society derive from family life, as opposed to the modern idea of the separation between private and public life. Ideas of the sacredness of the patriarchic family and related moral teachings like filial piety, respect for social hierarchy, conformism and the virtue of loyalty to one's community, lie at the root of China's traditional social order (Fei 2013). Individual life or social practice can only be meaningful in light of one's conformity to family values. Modern cultural reformist and revolutionary movements since the early 20th century have targeted the family as the key element to be changed. Most significant of all was the introduction of the concept of the independent individual as antithetical to the centrality of family value. The individual's pursuit of happiness, true love and self-determination has been promoted as higher values than following the family tradition, arranged marriage and sacrificing self-interest to shoulder family responsibility. At each of the three most significant social transformative events of modern Chinese history – the May Fourth Movement, the socialist revolution and the post-socialist reform – there have been different ways proposed to uphold the individual against the supposedly repressive structure of family. In the first decades of the 20th century, the May Fourth cultural reform movement stressed the right of the individual to make decisions over their own life, especially against the institution of arranged marriage. The socialist revolution of the mid-century inherited the modern pursuit of individuality, and above it put forward the imagery of class solidarity and national collectivism against the exclusive and self-sustaining bourgeois family. The reform ideology of the late 20th and early 21st centuries, while acknowledging the fruits of all previous revolutions, introduces the market as an increasingly important mediator and regulator of different aspects of social life. Thus, individual and family gradually become defined as legal units that have rights and responsibilities in the market. In the end, this cultural modernization drive ultimately means a reconstruction of family in the ideal image of the modern middle-class nuclear family. Thus, family is no longer considered a miniature society, but a private sphere based on individual interests and rights, laying the ground for a family (private life)–society (public life) divide. Wu (2011) argues that both the traditional Chinese family and traditional Christian family are value-laden social units, whereas the modern secular family contract is based on individual interest and instrumental reason. Thus the individual-centered nuclear family model becomes the keystone of a neoliberal and market-centered imagination of society. Although the socialist revolution tried to bridge the divide between blood-family and the social collectivity through the socialization of production, social welfare, education and family management, thus projecting a larger "socialist family" on top of the "small family" of the clan, it is the individualized middle-class family that has gradually gained legal and institutional hegemony during the post-1979 era of modernization and marketization.

Further consolidating an understanding of the family as a separate, self-reliant unit of society in the contemporary period has been China's series of marketization reforms in the areas of everyday life toward the end of the 1990s. The privatization of housing and the commercialization of education and healthcare shake the fundamental belief in a collective vision of social life, and introduce commodification and individualism into the most common life experiences of housing, going to school and seeking medical service. The marketization of housing has not only created a prosperous real estate industry and a group of *nouveau riche* developers, but also made an apartment the most important and, of course, pricey consumer product of all. With sky-rocketing housing prices in big and small cities alike, buying a house or investing in real estate has all of a sudden been turned into the most significant thing a person or a family should and must do. A house has become the most significant materialization of "family" and the happiness of individual and family life in an era when all social values have to be re-evaluated according to their performance on the market. Commercial media and the marketing arm of the real estate industry have wasted no time in churning out media content that urges people to "own residential property," and public discussions of housing prices and news about disputes concerning newly developed commercial housing communities fill the mass media and the Internet. It is no exaggeration to say that owning and decorating one's own apartment has become a central topic of life, the media and associated social institutions. Many have noticed that the central concept underlying real estate advertising in contemporary China is the privatization and individualization of land, space, social capital and success, instead of community life or the ethics of caring and sharing (Wu and Wang 2007; Wang 2008). It is not surprising, therefore, that housing and issues over housing, such as ownership, decoration, marriage, family values, inheritance disputes, etc., have become central topics, creating value-laden discourses about love, social status, legal rights, individualism, identity and so on. It is in this context that we now turn to the discussion of the lifestyle program *Exchanging Spaces*, created and broadcast on the Financial Channel of China's Central Television Station (CCTV2), which thrives on the popularity of housing-related topics.

From at your service to lifestyle TV

Many have described the transformation of China's mass media from state-owned propaganda organs to state-owned commercial institutions during the reform era (Zhao 1998, 2003; Lewis et al. 2012). Besides maintaining political safety, the biggest task facing China's mass media transforms from that of building a socialist culture into that of running a cultural business. As Zhao Yuezhi argues, both the party line and the bottom line have to be constantly negotiated (Zhao 1998). However, as the party line changes inexorably from socialist politics to pragmatic economic development, and the government defines its legitimacy increasingly through economic performance, the party line comes more and more to coincide with the bottom line.

Lifestyle programming on television can illustrate this trend vividly. On Chinese television, the kind of programming most similar to lifestyle genres in the West is so-called service programs, providing practical information about product choice, product safety, and household issues such as energy saving, home decoration, cooking tips, health suggestions and, increasingly in recent years, fashion advice. In the old socialist vocabulary, the term "service" (*fuwu*) was widely used to describe the Party's relationship with the people. The famous slogan written by Mao, "serving the people heart and soul," as the mission statement of the Chinese Communist Party, is still highly visible in many public spaces, especially government buildings and public institutions like schools and state-owned enterprises. Thus, when the earliest lifestyle show, CCTV's *At Your Service* (*Wei Nin Fuwu*) appeared in 1982, it was no accident that the word "service" was used in the title. It was an unequivocal reminder to the audience of this new kind of soft programming's consistency with party policy. Its content, providing various suggestions and information for everyday life, sent the message that individual happiness is now also a major concern of the party.

With the increasing commercialization of everyday life and mass media in China, lifestyle and service-oriented TV genres have become a convenient platform for merchandising, product placement and the socialization of audiences into a cosmopolitan consumer culture. *Exchanging Spaces*, a program created in 2005 as the weekend version of *At Your Service*, is currently aired on CCTV2. Its creators claim that it is a service program "close to the ordinary audience, advocating DIY and thrifty home decoration." The booming real estate and home decoration markets are obviously the main drivers behind the creation of this program. Yet against the hyperbolic propaganda of the high-end real estate industry, which inundates the cultural landscape with images of luxurious housing styles modeled after Western mansions and traditional Chinese palaces, *Exchanging Spaces* targets urban middle-class families living in apartments. In the newly commercialized housing market, many middle-class families face the problem of choosing, decorating and installing basic functions in their own apartments purchased through the commercial real estate market, in contrast to the old reliance on the socialist housing allocation mechanism, which more or less standardized space design, home decoration and functions.

Exchanging Spaces is a reality TV format. In each episode, two families chosen from a pool of volunteers swap apartments with each other. With the guidance of a professional designer and a fund of ¥18,000 (about US$3,000) sponsored by an interior design company, each group has 48 hours to makeover the other family's designated room decor.

At the end, each group returns to their own home, sees the results and gives comments. Each episode starts with the two families introducing their concerns and wishes for the room to be redecorated, and the designer articulating

Figure 3.1 Host, designers and two families together, *Exchanging Spaces*, CCTV2, March 7, 2015

his or her thoughts and plans. The 48 hours of decoration work on both sides are recorded and an edited version is shown to reveal the choices, negotiations and processes involved. A short video is also inserted to introduce a famous artist or designer and his or her home decoration ideas and works. This part is supposed to be educational, introducing the latest trends in home design. In this part, the examples used are mostly big mansions in the suburbs, and they serve as perfect models of ideal homes rather than realistic representations of middle-class households. Among the episodes the author watched, most of these soft commercial parts are promoting design aesthetics that could be called postmodern, i.e. ideas of closeness to nature, using natural and environmentally friendly materials, pursuing exotic, foreign or traditional and primitive styles, etc. This part actually presents a sharp contrast between the artistic mansions and the middle-class apartments to be reshaped. The two families, besides helping the designers to finish the home decoration work, must also participate in a small creativity competition, making something out of ordinary materials designated by the host – for example, mineral water bottles or old boxes. Some 50 audience representatives vote for their favorite transformation piece. Stylistically, the program does not pursue the spectacular or confrontational strategies of most reality TV genres. Its presentation of things and people can be described as plain, friendly and educational. According to its producers, the program's mission is to serve, inform and entertain its audience at the same time, with information about the latest home design trends, choices of new materials, and demonstration of individuality as well as community spirit and mutual help.[1] As a matter of fact, the conservative construction of visual representations makes this program more informational and educational than entertaining.

Although bearing a name that reminds people of the old-style socialist public service programming, all the imagery and content design in *Exchanging Spaces* serves the interests of sponsors who target a very particular audience stratum. The program asks families who have redecoration needs to register for the chance to take part in the competition, and in each episode,

Figure 3.2 Designer and family discussing decorating style during the project, *Exchanging Spaces*, CCTV2, March 7, 2015

two families with similar concerns and backgrounds are paired up. As CCTV is a national network, the production team goes to different cities of China to shoot episodes, showing a variety of cultural backgrounds as well as an image of national unity. The amazing thing is that after watching many episodes, viewers will realize that no matter what cultural and natural differences you might expect of a nation as large as China, the apartments, families and issues that appear on the program all seem very similar. Since it is a program to promote commercial home decoration, those who are eligible are limited to families who own apartments, rather than those who live in rented houses or workers' and students' dorms. The so-called encouragement to DIY boils down to the small part where the families have to make a small object out of designated materials. The majority of the redecoration work is led and managed by the designer, who will introduce their plans, take the participants to markets that sell home improvement materials, and educate the families and audience alike on new materials and styles. The families chosen are mostly nuclear families, sometimes extended families living with elders. To fit the requirement of redecoration, apartments have to have been lived in for a while and require some change for particular reasons, such as the recent birth of a baby, to host a newly married couple, or just to change the decoration style. The majority of the families featured are young, urban, middle-class couples, with stable jobs and moderate income, some with small children, and some living in parents' apartments.

Filtered through the selection process of the program, the family norm presented on the TV screen thus covers the urban, young, upwardly mobile sector in Chinese society: exactly the sector targeted by the new real estate and home decoration industries. The rural population, the urban poor who cannot afford to renovate their housing, those who live in socialist-era workers' housing, and people who do not own their own apartments are of course left completely invisible. Yet it seems that this does not stop them from watching the program and aspiring to the possibility of buying and decorating their own house in the future, with the aesthetic norm of commercial housing

Figure 3.3 Family awaiting the revelation of their transformed living room, *Exchanging Spaces*, CCTV2, March 7, 2015

ingrained, as the program's rating reports show that the program is welcomed by all strata of society except the very upper class who do not watch television at all.[2]

Family values and modern aesthetics: the negotiations among authority, community and neoliberal individualism

The norm prescribed by the show for the housing conditions of this social stratum and age group is that they have at least one moderate apartment under their name. Sometimes, the apartment is shared by parents and their married children. In these cases, it is almost certain that the parents are using their savings gained during the socialist era to help out children who have to buy commercial housing, as the parents' generation secured their own housing and pension through socialist allocation. In other cases, it is the children who work and marry in another city from their hometown, and bring their parents to live with them in order to be together or help alleviate the pressure of childcare. This normalized family pattern reveals how Chinese cultural tradition is reshaping the cosmopolitan model of individualism and nuclear family. Parents and their adult children, even after marriage, may share the financial burden of buying a home, and also the social and monetary burden of childcare. Thus, the rapid commercialization of housing and education for the new generation is partly cushioned by the traditional family value and the socialist legacy achieved by the older generation.

This partial reinstitution of the extended family is taken cordially by the program host. In cases where such extended families occur, the wish of the participants is usually to have the designer consider and reconcile the needs and tastes of both generations. The designers most often interpret this request as reconciling traditional Chinese with modernist styles of home decoration. One thing worth notice is that in the families presented, there is no attention drawn to which individual has more property rights vis-à-vis the apartment, and no clear description of the division of labor in family life. Couples always appear equally to share a common home and both have their own jobs. In families with small children but with no grandparents, there is also no visual description of how housework and childcare are shared. This shows that for this program, the return of traditional family values only involves the parent-children relationship (at least among the middle-class families it represents). The representation of gender relations within the family, however, maintains a socialist gender-equality façade. Patriarchy and tradition, in this case, are considered a good thing when they mean caring parents, filial children and shared economic duty. Mixing socialist and traditional family values to hold back the disintegrative forces of the privatization and commercialization of everyday life is the cultural strategy proposed by this mainstream program aimed at "serving the people."

Meanwhile, in the real world, social disintegration is not so easily buttressed by reinstalling traditional values. In 2010, the People's Supreme Court issued a detailed judiciary interpretation about items in the Marriage Law on the division of residential property in divorce cases. This is a response to increasing disputes over newly established property rights in divorce cases, which are rapidly on the rise in China's big cities. Zhao Xiaoli argues that the key to this judiciary interpretation is the change of definition of property rights from a socialist common property framework to one that allocates property rights to individuals. The old law emphasizes the "right to have a dwelling space" and the "right of the victim" in considering the way to divide up housing in divorce cases, whereas the new one emphasizes the "right to property" (Zhao 2011). Qiang Shigong also observes that the old law is conservative in the sense that by defining individual property as common family property, the law is biased toward preserving family and discouraging divorce. On the other hand, the new law has separated family from property rights and stipulates that even in a family there is individual property that cannot be considered common property at the time of divorce. The change promotes the idea that marriage is merely a legally binding and economic cooperative, rather than an ethical promise, thus reducing the moral burden and social pressure against divorce (Qiang 2011). These discussions, of course, are not present on a family-centered program like *Exchanging Spaces*. The subjects are so preoccupied with the prospect of having a more beautiful and fashionable living room for the family that they appear to have not the slightest intention of thinking about the whole process as a market exchange that involves rights, duties and debts, although it is increasingly taken as so by the legal establishment. In this sense, the program can be seen as a diversion from the questions and anxieties aroused by these legal developments.

The ideal family life is not only defined by ownership of housing, but more importantly it is shaped by a symbolic environment that connects everyday life with a global cultural imaginary. Modernity is both a lived and a discursive experience. The task of home decoration is precisely to bring these two together, and to realize the ideal of a modern lifestyle in the materiality of the spaces used to eat, sleep and watch TV. In China's real estate market, it has become a norm that new apartments sold are not ready to live in, especially cheaper houses for the middle class. People have to paint the walls, lay down floors, and install a kitchen and bathroom. With the decline of standardized housing and functional working-class aesthetics, home decoration has become one area that can demonstrate individuality, aesthetic taste and social identity for the aspiring middle class. The booming home decoration market is at the same time a kaleidoscope that absorbs homeowners' dreams and imaginations, and a trap that may exhaust people in endless choices of unfamiliar materials, gadgets and designs. *Exchanging Spaces* comes along to offer help. It claims to provide a service that mere money cannot buy: taste, rational space planning and social status, and to ease the anxiety of having to make decisions in a market of competing persuasions. Because of the limitation of the funding, the program only offers to redecorate one room which the family proposes. It is not surprising that most of the rooms proposed are living rooms, a place where the entire family has to meet and spends a lot of time together, and also the place that is most open to visitors. The living room, rather than the bedroom, is considered more in need of a narrative and a cultural façade. This suggests that family or home in China is still seen as a social unit, which has a social role to play and a social identity to sustain, instead of a pure site of intimacy and privacy.

So the job of the professional designers on the program is to offer the dual service of effective space arrangement and fashionable decoration on the one hand, and on the other to help realize the family's special wishes and requests. In the program, the designers usually re-phrase the participants' wishes in professional terms when the hopes are articulated as vaguely as, "we want the room to have more taste." The designer will throw in terms like "Moroccan style," "spring dreams," "coffee time," "seaside holiday," etc., to explain the rationale behind the use of color, lighting, paint and other décor. Most of the time, families express marvel and excitement when witnessing the changes made to their room, and unlike their Western counterparts, Chinese reality TV programs, especially this one shown on the official network, are not very keen on dramatizations of private emotions or insidious evil. The shots are static mid-shots, and participants are not good at showing off; they appear to be joining the program mostly for the sake of having their homes renovated. When there is dispute, usually concerning the use of color and materials, it is most often the family that retreats from its original idea and acknowledges the aesthetic authority of the designer. The articulation of disagreement by participants against designers is very mild most of the time. Families often pose doubts over certain decisions by a designer in the form of a self-reflexive question, like that posed by a student to a teacher: not challenging, but asking for further explanation. It is a very rare case that participants go back to their transformed home and claim that they are not satisfied. Even if they have some doubts, the way they express these on camera is that they need some time to digest the professional decisions of the designer, but they thank him or her for the beautiful job done. So all in all, this is a program that sells

Figure 3.4 After renovation, the combination of professional and popular taste, *Exchanging Spaces*, CCTV2, March 7, 2015

modernity from the top down, and socializes people into the market of home decoration, rather than one that encourages people to express creativity or individuality through changing their living environment.

The combination and careful balance among traditional values, commercial demands and the pursuit of individuality as an ideal by the new middle class makes the program rather conservative in both form and content. Formally, the program structure emphasizes the performance of professional designers, whereas family participants only serve as on-screen students to learn the lesson of modern aesthetics and space rationale. Their role is mostly to reflect on what they have done wrong before rather than exert their own will about decorating their home. In terms of content, the styles and materials introduced are all available on the market and consonant with an emerging middle-class taste, with only a very few "surprising" or "shocking" elements such as bright colors, exotic references or abstract modernist shapes. If we study this cultural construction in light of its coherence with neoliberal thinking and policies, it amounts to what we might call *authoritarian neoliberalism*. Privatization is forcibly pushed forward while the burden of accommodating this trend ideologically is laid onto mythical family values and the good will of the authorities, such as big media and experts, to lend a helping hand. Marketing maneuvers are thus clothed in the warm, soft façade of (post-)socialist "service."

Neoliberalism with Chinese characteristics? Family values as mediator between old and new models of modernization

The commercialization of housing and the development of the real estate market can be understood as a quintessential symbol of the neoliberalization of China's economic and social life. The place where family life and social organization intersect, when commoditized, privatized and individualized serves as a disintegrative force for both traditional and socialist-era social values such as family first, community sharing and caring for the weak. In a society where most people still understand capitalism through media representations and grand generalizations rather than first-hand social experience, the concept of housing as expensive property or an item of speculation, rather than as a public service, is directly pedagogical to the majority of city dwellers, instructing them on what capitalism means and how it operates. As both a cultural intermediary and the state's propaganda organ, lifestyle television on CCTV is undertaking the difficult job of legitimizing the neoliberal turn in economic and social policies while framing these changes in the façade of maintaining traditional values of sharing, collectivism and benign patriarchy in order to reduce anxiety and uncertainty caused by social change.

Exchanging Spaces is a program created to extend and modernize the public service tradition of socialist-era television by borrowing formats from commercial reality TV genres. This peculiar combination results in some extraordinary representations and mixed cultural messages. For example, even though the setup of the program – two families swapping apartments – indicates elements of competition, the actual process is very peaceful and friendly. The family with the other family's apartment in their care demonstrates more a sense of responsibility and care than an impulse to show off their own individuality and creativity. This communitarian rather than competitive approach to the task is shared by all families, so that everyone is sure that their own apartments are in the hands of helpful people with good intentions. Even though the neoliberal values preached by commercial media such as real estate advertising stress getting ahead of others and the desirability of one's exclusive occupation of space and environment, the program projects a scenario of shared progress in the form of helping each other to transform interior décor. The appearance of equality and sharing, in presenting the prospect of a commercial system of housing, attempts to bridge the gap between neoliberal and socialist agendas, with the state providing a necessary service to people who are trying to achieve success in the competitive market. Individualism, in this case, as the central doctrine in neoliberal thinking, is not presented as antithetical to the collective good or as something that must be achieved through aggression or independent of authoritarian intervention. It is coated in the image of a better living space and a happier family life, which is achieved through mutual help, and especially the help of benign authorities.

This respect for authority also shows itself in the families' attitudes toward the professional designers, who do the actual job of redesigning the apartments. The participants simply follow the plans and suggestions of the professionals and take up their lessons about home decoration aesthetics, strategies and skills. The newly rising home decoration market can be very threatening and unsettling to people, with the lack of regulation on production, employment and product safety, and with most people's lack of knowledge or experience in this field. Instead of presenting the process of designing, selecting and buying materials, and executing the project as a potentially risky process full of traps, the program turns it into a relaxing and educational tour guided by experts. The program presents very little trace of anxiety or uncertainty, either over design quality or taste competition. Most families seem assured from the very beginning that their apartments will be significantly improved. The only sense of suspense concerns what the old room will become in the hands of the other group. The families have to focus on decorating their counterparts' room and can only look at their own house after it is finished. In trying to fulfill the impossible task of both promoting the neoliberal commercialization of housing and maintaining people's trust in socialism, lifestyle reality shows in China have to sacrifice one of the key elements that contribute to the success of reality TV genres worldwide: anxiety and desire, which lead to overt performances of aggression and self-aggrandizement. The socialist state still proposes to patronize and guide the population even when it decides to hand over many of its social responsibilities to the market.

Karl Polanyi argues that the development of capitalism involves a great transformation of a society's economic mentality from reciprocity and redistribution to rational maximization of self-interest, and this remolding of the mindset cannot be achieved without the assistance of the modern nation-state, which creates legal, educational and cultural institutions to shape the mentality and practice of the population. In responding to massive social dislocations caused by the market, the society rises to its own protection (Polanyi 2001). When looking at the neoliberalization of China's previously Third World socialist economy, Polanyi's argument can be complicated by questioning the state–society divide. In China's case, the "state" is not necessarily a structure accompanying the rise of the market and acting as an external force to reshape "society." "Family" – as biology and/or, more recently, as socialist metaphor – has been the ethical, social and political foundation of China's social organization for most of its recorded history. In the cultural disorientation of economic reform, it seems that family and family values have become the only available stabilizing imaginary that can suture together a range of ideologies as various as socialism, neoliberalism and traditional beliefs. Against the legal institution's aggressive dismantling of the family, the government, the hegemonic cultural institutions such as television, and even the market are clinging to the moral high ground of family values in order to win over "society." Thus, even if both the market and the state hope to introduce modernity in the form of consumption and a commodity system by commercializing housing, they must do so by promoting the family and its associating values, promising the population that family is enhanced rather than diminished by marketization.

Notes

1 See tv.cntv.cn/videoset/C10495.
2 See tieba.baidu.com/p/707261437.

References

Andrejevic, Mark. 2004. *Reality TV: The Work of Being Watched*. Oxford: Rowman & Littlefield.

Brenner, Neil, and Nik Theodore, eds. 2002. *Spaces of Neoliberalism: Urban Restructuring in North America and Western Europe*. Maiden, MA: Blackwell Publishing.

Couldry, Nick. 2008. "Reality TV, or The Secret Theater of Neoliberalism." *The Review of Education, Pedagogy, and Cultural Studies* 30(3): 3–13.

Fei, Xiaotong. 2013. *From the Soil: The Foundations of Chinese Society*. Beijing: Foreign Language Teaching and Research Press (费孝通 《乡土中国》 北京 外语教学与研究出版社 2013).

Gore, Charles. 2000. "The Rise and Fall of the Washington Consensus as a Paradigm for Developing Countries." *World Development* 28(5): 789–804.

Harvey, David. 2000. *Spaces of Hope*. Berkeley and Los Angeles, CA: University of California Press.

Harvey, David. 2005. *A Brief History of Neoliberalism*. New York: Oxford University Press.

Hollows, Joanne, and Steve Jones. 2010. "'At Least He's Doing Something': Moral Entrepreneurship and Individual Responsibility in Jamie's Ministry of Food." *European Journal of Cultural Studies* 13(3): 307–322.

Lee, Ching-Kwan. 2014. "A Chinese Developmental State: Miracle or Mirage?" In *The End of the Development State?*, edited by Michelle Williams, 230–276. New York: Routledge.

Lee, Ching-Kwan, and Guobin Yang, eds. 2007. *Re-Envisioning the Chinese Revolution: The Politics and Poetics of Collective Memories in Reform China*. Stanford, CA: Stanford University Press.

Lewis, Tania. 2011. "Making Over Culture? Lifestyle Television and Contemporary Pedagogies of Selfhood in Singapore." *Communication, Politics & Culture* 44(1): 21–32.

Lewis, Tania, Fran Martin, and Wanning Sun. 2012. "Lifestyling Asia: Shaping Modernity and Selfhood on Life-advice Programming." *International Journal of Cultural Studies* 15(6): 537–566.

Miller, Toby. 2007. *Cultural Citizenship: Cosmopolitanism, Consumerism, and Television in a Neoliberal Age*. Philadelphia, PA: Temple University Press.

Ouellette, Laurie. 2009. "'Take Responsibility for Yourself': Judge Judy and the Neoliberal Citizen." In *Reality TV: Remaking Television Culture*, edited by Susan Murray and Laurie Ouellette, 223–242. New York: New York University Press.

Polanyi, Karl. 2001. *The Great Transformation: The Political and Economic Origins of Our Time*. Boston, MA: Beacon Press.

Qiang, Shigong. 2011. "Chinese Family under the Initiative of Law." *Beijing Cultural Review*2 强世功 《司法能动下的中国家庭》 《文化纵横》 2011年2月刊.

Raphael, Chad. 2009. "The Political Economic Origins of Reali-TV." In *Reality TV: Remaking Television Culture*, edited by Susan Murray and Laurie Ouellette, 123–140. New York: New York University Press.

Wang, Xiaoming. 2008. "From Architecture to Advertising: The Changes of Shanghai's Cosmopolitan Space in Recent Fifteen Years." In *Hot Wind Scholarship (Re Feng Xue Shu)*, edited by Wang Xiaoming and Cai Xiang, 3–23. Guangxi: Guangxi Normal University Press 王晓明 《从建筑到广告 – – 最近十五年上海城市空间的变化》 出自《热风学术》 王晓明 蔡翔主编。广西 广西师范大学出版社2008年3月 第3–23页.

Wu, Fei. 2011. "The Value Deficiency of Contemporary Chinese Marriage." *Beijing Cultural Review* 1. 吴飞 《当代中国婚姻的价值缺位》 《文化纵横》 2011年1月刊.

Wu, Jing. 2006. "Nostalgia as Content Creativity: Cultural Industries and the Popular Sentiment." *International Journal of Cultural Studies* 9(3): 359–368.

Wu, Jing, and Yingyao Wang. 2007. "Visible Real-estate, Invisible Home: The Analysis of the Cultural Politics of Real-estate Advertising." *Advertising Research (Guang Gao Yan Jiu)*6 吴靖 王颖曜 《可见的地产、不可见的家 房地产广告的文化政治》 《广告研究》 2007年第六期.

Zhao, Xiaoli. 2011. "A Strong Move toward Capitalism for Chinese Family," *Beijing Cultural Review*2 赵晓力 《中国家庭资本主义化的号角》 《文化纵横》2011年2月刊.

Zhao, Yuezhi. 1998. *Media, Market and Democracy in China, between the Party Line and the Bottom Line*. Chicago, IL: University of Illinois Press.

Zhao, Yuezhi. 2003. "Transnational Capital and Market Tensions in Chinese Communications." *Media Development* 3: 8–11.

4 Mediatization of *yangsheng*

The political and cultural economy of health education through media in China

Wanning Sun

Yangsheng, usually translated as "life nurturance," "health cultivation" or "wellness promotion," has become a catch-all phrase in China which encompasses just about everything one can do to improve one's health, including what tonic to take, what to eat and drink, how to take care of one's body, how to relate to time and space, and how to relate to other people and the environment. While middle aged and older people have more time for *yangsheng* than young people, just about everyone seems to know a thing or two about it. More importantly, just about everyone will tell you that they learn most of their *yangsheng* tips from television. In one of the few scholarly Chinese-language books on the topic of *shenghuo* or life advice television programs, health programs are defined in both a broad sense and a narrow sense. The former refers to a wide range of programs that are concerned with healthy living and nurturance of good health, whereas the latter refers to those programs that invite experts to give advice on how to treat and prevent specific diseases and health problems (Han and Zheng 2005, 92). One does not have to live in urban China for very long to get the impression that just about everyone is a *yangsheng* expert. Housewives have *yangsheng* in mind when they decide what to buy for dinner, retirees think of the benefit of *yangsheng* when they join their friends for a round of *tai chi* in the morning, restaurant waiters recommend their dishes based on their special *yangsheng* benefits, and real estate agents try to sell apartments in remote locations by pointing out their *yangsheng* potential.

What one can and should do to strengthen one's body and improve one's well-being is a question that has occupied the Chinese for many centuries. The tradition of "repairing", "nourishing" and balancing the *yin* and *yang* of the body through the consumption of food and herbal medicine has always been part of *yangsheng* practice (Farquhar 2002, 50), and its cultivation is always considered distinctively Chinese and, as such, has a long history. Indeed, that *yangsheng* is an essential part of China's cultural tradition has become a more or less default explanation for its contemporary popularity. However, Farquhar and Zhang are not prepared to take this explanation on board wholesale. To them, a number of reasons, including the aging population, the privatization of healthcare and the ensuing climate of anxiety, all conspire to the reinvention of the tradition (Farquhar and Zhang 2012, 28). However, even though they repeatedly point to the emergence of the publishing industry and the proliferation of health information in the media, Farquhar and Zhang, focusing on the anthropological and philosophical dimensions of the *yangsheng* practice, do not make it their core business to consider *yangsheng* as an intensely mediatized domain of social life, nor do they examine the political and cultural economy of *yangsheng* as a media form and discourse. In other words, what is still largely missing from the existing scholarship is an explicit articulation of cultural expressions of *yangsheng* as a category for analysis. Yet, a picture of *yangsheng* as a mostly grassroots and everyday social practice in China is not complete unless we consider it as at once a social artifact, a body of knowledge and a set of consumption practices. Furthermore, the central question of how *yangsheng* mediates between the state and the market, and between expert and lay knowledge, needs to be addressed.

The concept of mediatization is central to this discussion. Mediatization is considered a "meta-process," which like other meta-processes such as globalization, commercialization and individualization, has gripped the world (Krotz 2009). In critical media and communication studies, mediatization not only refers to the ubiquitous presence of media in every domain of our social life, but more importantly, it refers to the fact that the operation of each domain of our social life is profoundly changed due to the increased power of media. Understanding media and communication in this way has analytic and methodological implications. As Sonia Livingstone (2009) observes, it is no longer adequate just to study media effects, media impact or media influence. Mediatization affects all social institutions. As a result, we can no longer study politics or the family or religion alone. Instead, questions have to be asked about how the characteristics and nature of each of these institutions is subject to change due to their growing dependency on and interaction with media (Hjavard 2014).

Central to the concept of mediatization is the relationship between media logic and political logic (Strömbäck and Esser 2009). "Media logic" refers to the tripartite combination of a commercial logic, a technological logic and a cultural logic (Mazzoleni 2008). Often, media "operate according to their own logic" (Lundby 2009, 8), and this logic can be compatible with or in contradiction to the logic of political actors. Studying the process by which the tension between political logic and media logic is negotiated provides clues to the dynamics of interplay between political, economic and cultural forces in a given society. Mediatization, conceptualized this way, is important to study, as it alerts us to media's capacity for agenda setting and producing spectacles that shape public imagination (Mazzoleni 2008). Given that *yangsheng* is an age-old cultural tradition which has experienced a dramatic comeback in the era of increasing mediatization and globalization, it presents itself as an ideal place to study mediatization as a "richly contextualized, strongly historical process" (Livingstone 2009, xi). The questions therefore naturally follow: what shape and form does the mediatization of *yangsheng* take, and to what extent has mediatization reshaped and reconstituted *yangsheng* practice as we know it today? In what follows, I will first consider a number of ways in which political logic and media logic intersect to produce *yangsheng*-related media content. I will then look at the most popular genres, enduring themes and dominant discourses related to the topic of *yangsheng*, paying particular attention to the role of media in normalizing certain languages and ethical positions in *yangsheng*-related television programs.

Celebrity gurus and gullible consumers: *yangsheng* as a media phenomenon

To anyone in China who is interested in practicing *yangsheng*, the mere mention of the name Zhang Wuben would open a floodgate of strong views and opinions. In early 2011, Zhang was the biggest health guru in China, with his newly published *Eating Yourselves Out of Diseases* having become the most popular book in the country. Espousing the magical health benefits of a few simple and affordable foods, such as mung beans, eggplant (aubergine) and white radish, Zhang argued that these simple foods could treat all diseases, significantly improve the health of everyone, and cure terminal diseases such as breast cancer. Zhang was hailed as a "magical doctor" (*sheng yi*) in possession of the power and knowledge to heal. His promotion of mung beans led this humble food to become a sought after consumer item, causing havoc in the grocery market which led to wide-ranging practices of price fixing among mung bean merchants and vendors. Zhang became a household name following his appearance on *Encyclopedia* (*Baike jiangtan*), a very entertaining lifestyle show on Hunan Satellite Television that enjoyed a huge national following for its advice on health issues. Zhang's celebrity guru status was fortified subsequently through his appearance on China Central Television's 30-episode program, *Medicine of the Big Nation* (*Daguo yidao*). It is said that Zhang was the most expensive doctor in Beijing, and patients could expect to wait for up to one year for an appointment with him.

Zhang's fame did not last long. By the end of the same year, he was in disgrace. His claim to be one of the first health specialists and dieticians officially consecrated by the Department of Health had been debunked. A former factory worker who had a smattering of informal medical education and dabbled in pyramid sales of Amway, health tonics and calcium tablets, Zhang was found to have fabricated numerous certificates, diplomas and professional accreditations. His clinic, once an almost mythical place in the public imagination, closed down and the building housing it was demolished. Hunan Satellite's lifestyle television program that made Zhang famous in the first place was cancelled, and Zhang's bestselling book was taken off the shelves of bookstores. Mung beans returned to their normal price. Master Zhang was now seen as a "fake," a con artist, a sham.

Figure 4.1 Shenzhen TV, April 14, 2011, "The rise and fall of Chinese medicine guru Zhang Wuben"

However, the Zhang Wuben phenomenon is not an isolated incident. As early as 2006, a book titled *Dr Liu Talks About Health* caught the imagination of the nation with its bold claim that its author, Dr Liu, in Tangshan City, Hebei Province, possessed the secret formula of Chinese herbs to cure various kinds of cancer. Liu was later exposed as a self-promoted trickster who had fabricated a range of fancy accolades. Similarly, in 2007 Ma Yuanlin from Nanjing shot to national stardom with her book *The Wisdom of Not Getting Sick* (*bu shengbing de zhihui*), claiming that she had cured more than 100 breast cancer patients. Instead of mung beans, as Zhang Wuben promoted, Ma's magical food was potato as well as a much less appetizing recipe: raw loach (a kind of fish that lives in muddy water) eaten with *dongkuai*, a common Chinese herbal medicine. Previously a nurse, a health product salesperson and eventually a host of one of the Jiangsu Provincial Television's health and lifestyle programs, Ma's 2007 book saw her going from provincial to national fame, and resulted in a number of readers trying out her raw loach recipe and ending up in the emergency rooms of local hospitals in various Chinese cities. In 2010, CCTV 1's *Enter the World of Science* (*zou jin kexue*) told the story of a number of people in Sichuan Province falling seriously ill following the ingestion of raw loach, having followed the advice of Ma.

Parallel to the frequent comings and goings of these *yangsheng* teachers, masters and magical doctors is the vibrant growth of *yangsheng* publications as one of the biggest industries in China. Statistics show that 80 percent of the books published each year in China are health related, and around 6,000 publications can be found on the shelves of various bookstores across the country, in addition to a plethora of media formats such as talk radio shows and health-oriented magazines. *Yangsheng* and the related healthcare industry is primed to become the fifth biggest sector in China's economy, following real estate, IT, automobiles and tourism (Wen 2012). Contributing to the aggressive development of the *yangsheng* industry are more than 1,300 television programs throughout the country, mostly broadcast at prime time, all claiming to specialize in the cultivation of health (Guo 2011). In fact, health and well-being-related lifestyle shows are the backbone of Chinese television's lifestyle programming, exceeding food and cooking shows as well as travel programs, which are also popular.

Not surprisingly, the media came under attack for being enthusiastic promoters of unscrupulous individuals like Zhang Wuben. Overnight, the lifestyle advice shows that had promoted these figures came under scrutiny and looked suspiciously untrustworthy, as criticism of *yangsheng* shows as "socially irresponsible and morally questionable" gained ground (Chen 2010). Journalists and well-known bloggers like Zhang Yegang called for the cancellation of all health-related television programs on all channels. Health-related programs across the board were told to adhere strictly to regulations and standards or face being shut down. However, it is not just the *yangsheng* gurus who end up being condemned in these public debates. Consumer citizens are also chastised for their low health literacy and gullibility. After Zhang Wuben's downfall, the media, including both press and television, in a 180-degree turnaround, cited examples of individuals who became seriously ill after drinking excessive quantities of mung bean juice, uncooked eggplant and white radishes, all of which Zhang claimed to have magical curing powers. Although adopting a sympathetic stance towards gullible consumers, media stories of these individuals are intended to tell the population that people should believe in nothing but science, and engage in self-education that enables them to differentiate science from pseudoscience, hearsay and superstition.

Although many *yangsheng* programs have little science underpinning them, they are immensely popular, given that their health and well-being theme makes sense in terms of both political and media logic. In terms of political logic, the imperative is to avoid producing media content that is capable of triggering social unrest and conflict, and hence is threatening to social and political stability. This imperative is all the more pertinent in the era of economic reforms. Widespread privatization, marked by the rise of private property ownership and the state's retreat from a wide range of social services, including housing, education and healthcare, has given rise to anxiety, disorientation and insecurity in both material and psychological terms (Ong and Zhang 2008). Having transformed themselves from a "work-unit" person into a "social person" (Farquhar and Zhang 2012), individuals in China, more than ever before, are searching for solutions to a wide range of ethical, moral and practical challenges. If deepening social inequality has given rise to a widespread sense of injustice, discontent or even anger among underprivileged social groups, then a pervasive sense of loss, fear and insecurity is seen to be an equally potent trigger for social unrest.

To be politically safe and useful, television has stepped in to provide this much-needed guidance. Nowadays, most local and provincial stations as well as the national broadcaster CCTV have a number of designated channels and programs offering so-called Life TV (*shenghuo dianshi*). Also, many popular entertainment programs, especially those in the genre of lifestyle programs, combine practical knowledge and information with entertainment (Xu 2007, 2009). While they appear to be non-political on the surface, they are centrally concerned with teaching people a wide range of skills – in the realms of healthcare and *yangsheng*, mental, psychological and emotional well-being, familial and interpersonal relationships, personal finance, travel and everyday living – which are necessary to survive the turbulence caused by the transition from socialism to a neoliberal market economy. In doing so, these shows perform a profoundly ideological role on behalf of both the Party-state and capital (Lewis et al. 2012).

In response to the political imperative of ensuring stability and defusing social tension, commercial media in China can in effect do more effective "thought work," since audiences, while they may be skeptical of the state media, nevertheless have an implicit trust in the commercial media outlets (Stockmann and Gallagher 2011). The great majority of *yangsheng* programs have served the twin master of the Party-state and the market most effectively by busily turning social issues such as poverty, poor health and lack of opportunities for individuals from disenfranchised groups into positive stories of diligent individuals achieving personal growth and self-cultivation, be it in the domain of health or mental and psychological well-being. These programs give viewers the illusion – camouflaged as hope – that as long as one tries hard enough, these problems can be overcome. This is most clearly evidenced in the more than 1,300 lifestyle programs on Chinese television that are devoted to teaching the nation how to engage in health improvement and *yangsheng* practices (Zhou 2011). In other words, a nation of individuals who are excessively preoccupied with and actively involved in the activities of maintaining and improving their own health is deemed patently more conducive to stability than a population that is politically subversive and socially discontented. This is especially the case in China, given that health problems are the most immediate concerns of its rapidly growing aging population. As early as 2003, China's population over the age of 60 was 11 percent of the total population, and this proportion is expected to grow to 31.27 percent by 2050 (Bai and Liu 2008). In other words, like Japan, South Korea, Taiwan and Singapore, China is quickly becoming one of the largest aging populations in Asia. China's aging population makes up half of the total aging population in Asia, and one-fifth of the world's aging population. One key area of interface between the issues of aging and healthcare is the health and well-being of individual senior citizens. While the didactic instructions from Party leaders and government officials are often viewed with skepticism, the televisual advice on a range of "life matters" comes from doctors, psychologists, scientists and experts, and the public often sees no reason to suspect that these shows have any agenda other than transmitting practical and useful knowledge, especially for elderly citizens.

Similarly, industry economics of television production can go some way towards explaining the dominance of *yangsheng* programs on Chinese television. After all, ordinary people are mostly willing to appear on TV without much payment, and even if a medical expert requests a large sum of money to appear on the program, the production cost is still miniscule from the point of view of income to be generated from the programs. For this reason, health and well-being topics make a logical choice to fill television airtime. According to the production staff of Hunan TV, *yangsheng* programs are cheap to make, involving only an expert and some basic studio setup. Furthermore, they are highly lucrative in terms of ratings and advertising income. For instance, the *yangsheng* program *Encyclopedia*, Hunan TV's most well-known entertainment program, rated exceptionally well. "From the point of the view of both television station and medical experts, it is a win-win situation," according to Hunan TV's producers (Lin 2010).

Yangsheng as a field of contestation

The nationwide celebrity status of Zhang Wuben and other fraudsters would not have been possible without their promotion on television. In the absence of the party leaders at the old-style work units, organized ideological study sessions as part of the work routine, and other forms of moral education one associates with socialism, people in the reform era have to use their own initiative to identify affordable and accessible ways of seeking practical advice on how to live their life. Television is a logical place to look for this type of information. At the same time, the disgracing of Zhang Wuben and others in 2011 made the Chinese government and its various top health-related bodies realize that the market alone could not be trusted to act responsibly and ethically, and that effective regulatory mechanisms needed to be put in place to ensure that citizens receive reliable scientific information in order to advance health literacy. In other words, the marketization of healthcare and the privatization of health information have led to ongoing tension and contestation over legitimate genres of representation and forms of expertise, and the control of *yangsheng* discourses is as important to the Party-state as it is to the market. As this section will go on to show, a wide range of health and well-being shows, ranging from high-end medical knowledge to everyday dietary advice, draw on and in turn produce various systems of health knowledge. This points to *yangsheng* as an extremely complex and multifactorial phenomenon that is at once political, economic and cultural, and as such, mediates between the state and the market, and between scientific knowledge and alternative health practices. The media do not merely influence or impact on the ways in which people practice *yangsheng*, but in fact set the agenda according to which health issues are to be talked about, imagined and practiced. They shape the very parameters within which certain ways of teaching and practicing *yangsheng* are accepted while others are not.

The government responded to the trend of celebrity gurus by putting in place a number of regulatory measures. In January 2012, 21 offices were set up across the nation aiming to certify the provision of Chinese medicine-based health products, and a document entitled "Methods of Regulation of Professional Standards for Traditional Chinese Medicine" was issued in Beijing (Wen 2012). In June 2010, the State Administration of Press and Publishing issued edicts requiring that future publications on topics of health and health cultivation must pass a review by officially registered and certified specialists before being published, and any publications that failed to do so could be recalled or penalized. While *yangsheng* rides on the enduring strength of tradition to thrive and flourish, the crackdown on its unsavory consequences is carried out in the name of science and truth.

A number of television stations largely responsible for the promotion of *yangsheng* gurus were widely criticized for their tendency to sacrifice science in their pursuit of ratings. Hunan TV's *Encyclopedia*, for instance, is known for its entertainment values and sensationalism. The show is hugely popular on a national scale but it was somewhat tainted by its promotion of the fraudster health guru discussed above. In contrast, more "worthy" *yangsheng* shows are actively promoted. For instance, CCTV's flagship health program, *Chinese Medicine*, is considered to be the most well-researched, authoritative health program in China, and is perceived to set the benchmark for the standard of health and well-being programs on Chinese TV. The show is steeped in erudite medical knowledge and in traditional Chinese medicine, and is widely considered to be the most credible, if not the most lively, health program on Chinese television. In addition to giving the audience advice about how to keep healthy, the show also actively and explicitly promotes certain attitudes and mindsets that are deemed conducive to keeping healthy.

Equally credible but less serious and far more accessible is Beijing TV's *Yangsheng House* (*Yangsheng tang*), which has been touted as a paragon of credibility and trustworthiness. Launched in 2009 on Beijing TV's Science and Education Channel, *Yangsheng House* was moved to Beijing TV's flagship channel in 2011, and has now become the most popular *yangsheng* program on Chinese television, watched by as many as 567 million viewers across the country in 2011 (Wang 2012). *Yangsheng House* targets China's aging population and manages to strike a balance between authoritativeness and accessibility. Its content and style cater to the needs of a predominantly older segment of the Chinese viewership, which constitutes the majority of the audience of health-related programs. The show also attributes its success to its unrivalled status as the most authoritative yet lively and interactive medical program, being able to draw on the expertise of the most respected specialists in Beijing, as well as its consistent practice of privileging accessible knowledge and ensuring audience participation and broader benefit to the community. Speaking of its program, *Yangsheng House*'s producer, Wang, says: "All information and knowledge in our show must withstand the test of science and evidence. Unlike some TV channels, we do not chase ratings at all costs, nor do we invite experts with spurious credentials. Claims such as 'mung beans can cure most diseases' will not appear on our show. Our viewers will not be hoodwinked" (Wang 2012).

Departing from the seriousness and orthodoxy of *Chinese Medicine* on CCTV and *Yangsheng House*'s association with the elderly, *36.7 C*, a health show on Shanghai TV, aims for lightheartedness and targets a younger audience. Speaking the Shanghai dialect, the host invites a *yangsheng* pop-expert (*daren*) to come into the studio to share their ideas for a healthy breakfast menu. The guest's expertise is loosely defined – she is merely a "famous nutritionist." Through lighthearted banter with the host and participants, she recommends a breakfast that includes water with honey, fruit such as apple and kiwi, lotus roots, eggs and wholemeal bread. Viewers are told to drink water, have sufficient intake of vitamins and minerals and to avoid certain breakfast items, including coffee and tea, fried dough and fried rice cake, all of which are popular breakfast foods for Shanghai people (September 3, 2013).

CCTV's *Chinese Medicine* and Beijing TV's *Yangsheng House* are now touted as exemplary health and well-being programs which are endowed with both scientific authoritativeness and popular appeal. These shows mostly adopt the television-plus-expert format. That is, the shows provide a platform for the experts – doctors, nutritionists and medical specialists – to showcase

Figure 4.2 Beijing TV's *Yangsheng House*, February 12, 2015

their expertise and give advice. In addition to this, throughout China, hundreds of local and regional life advice channels impart a large amount of health-related information and knowledge to viewers who live in mostly semi-rural settings and have lower health literacy than metropolitan audiences. These programs often adopt modes of presentation that privilege quantity of information, clarity of message and effectiveness of communication over veracity, aesthetics and style, and aim to present as much information as possible within the shortest possible time, and with minimal production costs. Bengbu Television, in Bengbu, Anhui Province, is one of the hundreds of third-tier city television stations that produce a large number of terrestrially transmitted health and well-being programs. On May 30, 2011, a randomly chosen day on which the station was recorded for analysis, the program *Zero Distance to Health* featured a story on how to choose antibiotics correctly, in view of a widely held assumption that newer and more expensive antibiotics deliver more effective outcomes. The program quotes doctors who suggest that generic antibiotics, which may be cheaper than new brands, may be more suitable or effective, so patients should learn to discern the appropriate antibiotics based on function rather than branding.

Along with the featured programs of the day, Bengbu TV's Hotline also runs a rolling on-screen banner, which offers endless tips and advice for everyday living. On the same day as *Zero Distance to Health* was aired, the running credits told viewers, without bothering to identify the source of the information, that kiwi fruit, grapes and bananas help with sleep problems, and that beer should not be consumed simultaneously with vinegar. Most of these shows combine the television-plus-expert format, in which the scientific nature of the health-keeping advice is assumed rather than presented. In other words, viewers are asked to assume that this advice must be correct because it is on television.

As an incentive to attract viewers, *Zero Distance to Health* also regularly offers quizzes to selected viewers, who can win prizes of substantial value. For instance, a middle-aged woman viewer is stopped in the street and asked two questions: first, at what times does the show go on air each week, and second, what are the "five highs" that pose a threat to health (answer: high blood pressure, high cholesterol, high blood sugar, high blood viscosity and high urea content in the blood). When she answers both questions correctly, after much assistance from the host, she is presented with a shopping voucher for ¥358 (a lucky number in China).

It is clear from these examples that China's health authorities and media are now actively engaged in improving the health literacy of the population, in order to increase public understanding of science so that citizens become informed and knowledgeable about their bodies and health prospects. Essential to these efforts is the expectation that citizens cannot be allowed to remain passive about their health; they must actively educate themselves, act upon advice and guidance from health experts, and be willing to take responsibility for their actions. This ethos of self-responsibility is tellingly reflected in the title of one regular segment of CCTV's *Chinese Medicine*, which is simply called "Taking Control of Your Own Health." On January 4, 2008, the host of the show starts her program with this preamble:

> Hello dear viewers, welcome to *Chinese Medicine*. Good health and longevity is something we all aspire to, but how can we achieve it? An old man over the age of 90 once said this: "*Yangsheng* relies on science, longevity requires no miracles. If one wants health and longevity, it's 90 percent down to the self." [The Chinese version of this four-line doggerel proceeds in rhyme.] What does it mean when he said it's "down to the self"? He meant acquiring a good attitude and good habits. What is a habit? It is something you stick at consistently and with commitment over a long period of time. Doing something once or twice is not a habit. Adopt a good health routine that suits you and stick to it.

The show then went on to give examples of various individuals, ranging from ancient poets to contemporary figures, who have achieved longevity through sticking to a good habit, be it "drinking goji tea" or "practicing tai chi."

While empowering individuals with information about their health may appear to have democratizing potential, questions must be asked about whether it is also motivated by an authoritarian impulse to govern the biological sphere of the population. Similarly, the question remains as to how the assumption that everyone is in need of improvement in their health and well-being, and that nobody is immune, has come to be so widely accepted.

For the last two decades, the media, especially the advertising sector, have actively engaged in the promotion of the notion of a "sub-healthy population" (*ya jiankang renkou*), as if it were a self-evident scientific truth. This discourse is enthusiastically endorsed and perpetuated by salespeople representing pharmaceutical manufacturers of tonics and herbal medicine supplements. The main thrust of the sub-healthy argument is surprisingly simple, and seems to require no proof or substantiation. For instance, one publication, exploring the emergence of health-related programs, cites the dramatic increase in China's sub-healthy population from 20–28 percent "in the past" to 60–70 percent now (Chen 2012). According to this discourse, the majority of the Chinese population lives in the liminal space between being healthy and ill. The state of "sub-health" is thus described by some writers as the "third state of being," where people are neither healthy (the first state of being) nor diseased (the third state of being), but somewhere in between. Children fall into this category because of the undue stress related to study; youths fall into this category due to the lack of disciplined and regular routine in life; middle-aged professionals are the prime victims of sub-health because they work long hours under pressure; old people are by definition the inhabitants of the sub-health zone since their bodies are in progressive decline. Anyone who self-diagnoses against the long list of symptoms usually associated with sub-health is bound to be found wanting, since all of us are likely to experience, say, lethargy, lack of appetite, insomnia and feelings of stress and anxiety at some point. However, according to this widespread discourse, if they do heed these warning signs, they have chances of becoming healthy again. Mobilizing a potent cocktail of emotions such as fear, desire, anxiety and hope, "sub-health" discourses thus assume the appearance of the most unquestionable common sense.

The discourse of a sub-healthy nation provides both collective and individual motivation for the nation's excessive preoccupation with how to maintain and improve its health. The implication of the "sub-healthy nation" discourse seems painfully obvious at the particular juncture of privatization and marketization of the health sector: unless you start to take action to take care of your health, you may progress from "sub-health" to disease – or even worse, death. In the same way that you are in the best position to decide if you need improvement, you are also solely responsible for the decisions you might make to improve your health. The willingness to take responsibility for one's own health – or lack of it – has both economic and moral dimensions. Clearly, investing in one's health now in terms of time and money is key to safeguarding one's current level of health and warding off major health problems in the future: a preventative measure that is crucial to the maintenance of the financial and economic viability of the individual and the household. However, equally important, a person who refuses to engage in self-care is implicitly deemed a socially irresponsible citizen.

Considering the discourse of sub-health in conjunction with the range of *yangsheng* practices outlined, it becomes clear to us that *yangsheng* not only embodies "ten thousand things" about China (Farquhar and Zhang 2012), but equally significantly, it helps demonstrate how a preferred way of life is taught, promoted, justified and perpetuated through a particular set of cultural forms, discursive categories and media practices.

Conclusion

As mentioned above, the privatization of public goods, services and properties has taken place in tandem with the privatization of the self, giving rise to the need to create self-governing subjects who will "enrich and strengthen Chinese authoritarian rule" (Ong and Zhang 2008, 10). The shift of responsibility from the state to the individual has taken place in the moral and ethical as well as the material domains. In contrast to the Maoist decades, when the state determined what proper life would be, leaving little room for individuals to make their own decisions (Farquhar and Zhang 2012), people are now actively pursuing a wide range of self-governing and self-enterprising activities which shape and optimize their life chances (Rofel 2007; Ong and Zhang 2008; Yan 2008; Hoffman 2010). This shift occurs simultaneously with the process of "depoliticization" (Wang 2009), whereby topics connected with social, political and ideological concerns are recast as natural and neutral, mostly within technical, scientific, legal and medical frameworks (Ong 2006).

This body of knowledge forms the new common sense, the "survival kit" necessary to stay on top of the "new regime of living" (Collier and Lakoff 2005). As well, individuals are compelled to make choices and decisions about a range of things – the meaning and value of work, career, money, love, happiness, beauty, success – on their own.

The reinvention of cultural traditions such as *yangsheng* has taken place at the intersection of these larger social processes. In fact, this discussion has shown that *yangsheng* has engendered crucial spaces in contemporary social life in China whereby political logic and media logic dovetail to produce new normative citizen subjects. We now know that *yangsheng* has a strong discursive as well as a material dimension, and that there is a complex and symbiotic relationship between the knowledge casually trotted out by people in the street about *yangsheng*, and the health-related information and advice provided by scientific authorities. I have argued that rather than simply an "everyday life activism" which is "little commodified" (Farquhar and Zhang 2012, 16), *yangsheng* has been significantly shaped by market forces and has, in fact, become a key site of debate and contestation surrounding issues of citizenship, governmentality and the making of the ethical self. We now know that *yangsheng* mediates between the state and the market, and between expert and lay knowledge.

Among other factors, *yangsheng* owes its popularity to its infinite capacity for mediatization, a process that involves the effective working out of the tension between political logic and media logic in media and cultural production. More than ever before, *yangsheng* is not just what people do in everyday lives, but is also what the media teach people to do, and what people choose to believe in the media. In this sense, the media are an integral part of the *yangsheng* industry. Like tonic medicine that supposedly promotes the well-being of the body, media products in the form of visual and narrative material promoting a healthy lifestyle are an integral part of the *yangsheng* industry. In other words, we are not talking about how *yangsheng* as a cultural tradition has been changed or reinvented due to the presence of the media; we are talking about how its mediatization has become an essential, defining aspect of the very practice that we know today.

Taking this discussion of health education through the media to a more general level, we can say that television, and the media in general, is an integral part of a process by which the neoliberal "technique of governing" turns into an everyday "technology of the self" (Couldry 2010). Exploring *yangsheng* by focusing on its mediatization, we are able to lay bare a number of key questions regarding citizenship, governmentality and the making of the ethical self. As this discussion shows, it is through the process of mediatization that the technique of governing becomes a technology of the self. The widespread and systematic legitimation and communication of expert knowledge would not be achievable without ubiquitous media reliably lending a helping hand. The ideology of self-responsibility and individual choice could hardly be expected to be widely promulgated to and internalized by consumers, if *yangsheng* and health education did not become key sites for the logic of the media to work its magic.

References

Bai, Haiyan (白海燕), and LiuZhicai (刘志财). 2008. "A Preliminary Analysis of the Problem of Ageing in China and Possible Solutions" 浅析我国人口老龄化问题对策. *Shanxi Dadong University Journal: Social Sciences Edition*, 《山西大同大学学报 社会科学版 4. www.cqvip.com/qk/88773x/200804/28488433.html (accessed February 15, 2015).

Chen, Pei (陈佩). 2012. "A Cool-head Look at the Popular Health and Yangsheng Television Programs." [健康养生类电视节目热播的冷思考]. *Media Age* [媒体时代] 12: 15–7.

Chen, Yongjie (陈永杰). 2010. "Erroneous Information is Inundating Yangsheng Programs; Who is in Charge of my Health?" [养生节目谬误流传 我的健康谁做主]. *Beijing Science and Technology* 《北京科技报》, May 25. scitech.people.com.cn/GB/11686002.html (accessed December 7, 2013).

Collier, Stephen J., and Andrew Lakoff. 2005. "On Regimes of Living." In *Global Assemblages: Technology, Politics, and Ethics as Anthropological Problems*, edited by Aihwa Ong and Stephen J. Collier, 22–39. Malden, MA: Blackwell.

Couldry, Nick. 2010. *Why Voice Matters: Culture and Politics after Neoliberalism*. London: SAGE.

Farquhar, Judith. 2002. *Appetites: Food and Sex in Post-Socialist China*. Durham: Duke University Press.

Farquhar, Judith, and Qicheng Zhang. 2012. *Ten Thousand Things: Nurturing Life in Contemporary Beijing*. New York: Zone Books.

Guo, Xin (郭欣). 2011. "A Study of Formats in Life-Themed Programs on China's Television" [我国生活类电视节目类型研究]. MA thesis, Northeast Normal University, China.

Han, Qing (韩青), and Wei Zheng (郑蔚). 2005. *A New Study of Service-Oriented Television Programs* [电视服务节目新论]. Beijing: China Broadcasting and Television Press.

Hjavard, Stig. 2014. *Handbook of Mediatization*, edited by Knut Lundby, 199–206. Berlin: de Gruyter Mouton.

Hoffman, Lisa M. 2010. *Patriotic Professionalism in Urban China: Fostering Talent*. Philadelphia, PA: Temple University Press.

Krotz, Friedrich. 2009. "Mediatization: A Concept with which to Grasp Media and Societal Change." In *Mediatization: Concept, Changes, Consequences*, edited by Knut Lundby, 21–40. New York: Peter Lang.

Lewis, Tania, Fran Martin, and Wanning Sun. 2012. "Lifestyling Asia: Shaping Modernity and Selfhood on Life Advice Programming." *International Journal of Cultural Studies* 25(5). doi: 10.1177/1367877912451693.

Lin, Yanwen (林艳雯). 2010. "The Low Cost of Producing Yangsheng Programs" [养生节目成本低 做容易]. *Shanghai Youth Daily*上海青年报, June 4. youthdaily.why.com.cn/epublish/node4/node30837/node30845/userobject7ai225649.html (accessed July 15, 2014).

Livingstone, Sonia. 2009. "Forward: Coming to Terms with 'Mediatization.'" In *Mediatization: Concepts, Changes, Consequences*, edited by Knut Lundby, iv–xiii. New York: Peter Lang.

Lundby, Knut. 2009. "Introduction: 'Mediatization' as Key." In *Mediatization: Concepts, Changes, Consequences*, edited by Knut Lundby, 1–20. New York: Peter Lang.

Mazzoleni, Gianpietro. 2008. "Media Logic." In *The International Encyclopedia of Communication*, edited by Wolfgang Donsbach, 2930–2932. Malden, MA: Blackwell.

Ong, Aihwa. 2006. *Neoliberalism as Exception: Mutations in Citizenship and Sovereignty*. Durham, NC: Duke University Press.

Ong, Aihwa, and Li Zhang. 2008. "Introduction: Privatizing China: Powers of the Self, Socialism from Afar." In *Privatizing China: Socialism from Afar*, edited by Li Zhang and Aihwa Ong, 1–20. Ithaca: Cornell University Press.

Rofel, Lisa. 2007. *Desiring China: Experiments in Neoliberalism, Sexuality, and Public Culture*. Durham, NC: Duke University Press.

Stockmann, Daniela, and Mary E. Gallagher. 2011. "Remote Control: How the Media Sustains Authoritarian Rule in China." *Comparative Political Studies* 44(4): 436–467.

Strömbäck, Jesper, and Frank Esser. 2009. "Shaping Politics: Mediatization and Media Interventionism." In *Mediatization: Concept, Changes, Consequences*, edited by Knut Lundby, 205–223. New York: Peter Lang.

Wang, Hong (王泓). 2012. "The Modus Operandi and Development of Health-Related Television Programs" [健康类节目的经营与发展]. *Modern Communication* [现代传播] 7: 163–164.

Wang, Hui. 2009. *The End of the Revolution: China and the Limits of Modernity*. London: Verso.

Wen, Qi (雯琪). 2012. "Yangsheng Market is in Serious Need of Crackdown and Regulation" [养生保健市场 正待监管部门出拳整顿]. www.138job.com/shtml/Article/18207/71085.shtml (accessed January 20, 2014).

Xu, Janice. 2007. "Brand-New Lifestyle: Consumer-Oriented Programmes on Chinese Television." *Media, Culture & Society* 29(3): 363–376.

Xu, Janice. 2009. "Building a Chinese 'Middle Class': Consumer Education and Identity Construction." In *TV China*, edited by Ying Zhu and Chris Berry, 150–168. Bloomington, Indiana: Indiana University Press.

Yan, Hairong. 2008. *New Masters, New Servants: Development, Migration, and Women Workers*. Durham, NC: Duke University Press.

Zhou, Mi (周蜜). 2011. "Television Programs on Health and Well-being: A Study of Developments and Current Situation 健康类电视节目的发展现状研究." *Television Era* 电视时代 (*Dianshi shidai*) 12: 9–11.

5 The Pink Ribbon Campaign in Chinese fashion magazines

Celebrity, luxury lifestyles and consumerism

Yue Gao

The Pink Ribbon Campaign discussed in this chapter was first initiated in 1992 in the USA by Evelyn Lauder, the chief executive of Estée Lauder, one of the largest skincare and makeup manufacturers in the world. It aimed to raise awareness of breast cancer among women in the USA, and to raise funds for scientific research into preventing and curing the disease (Estée Lauder 2013). The Pink Ribbon concept soon engulfed almost all of the Western, developed countries and regions including Canada, Australia and the European Union. After two decades, the campaign is still popular in the West. The campaign was brought to China in 2003 by *Trends Health* (*shishang jiankang*) magazine, a monthly fashion magazine distributed by the Trends Group, which targets young, urban, middle-class Chinese women.[1] Since 2003, a special issue of the magazine themed "Pink Ribbon Campaign" has been produced and circulated every October, which is also designated as breast cancer awareness month globally (King 2006). Every year, three or four Chinese female celebrities are invited by the magazine to be spokespersons. The campaign includes taking pictures of these celebrities wearing a pink ribbon and recording their stories about their breasts and breast cancer. In this chapter, I examine how these celebrities, their bodies and lifestyles have been constructed in the campaign throughout the years and how their cultural meanings have been presented to readers. Against the backdrop of the ongoing healthcare reform and withdrawal of the state from people's healthcare in China, I will also explore how the campaign potentially shapes the female readers' perceptions of their bodies, living and subjectivities.

Much of the extant literature has confirmed that celebrity endorsement campaigns in Western countries have been used not only to sell specific brand products, but also for philanthropic purposes, promoting exemplary citizenship and "changes to governmental policies on health, youth, the environment, and multiculturalism" (Edwards and Jeffreys 2010, 7). In China, due to the media liberalization and commercialization that followed the economic reforms begun in the 1980s, soft news and entertainment content in the media, including celebrity stories and tabloid-style formats, have been on the increase, with this commercial content aimed at attracting consumers and advertisers alike (ibid.). This has given rise to the flourishing of a celebrity culture in post-socialist China, similar to the production and consumption of celebrity in Western countries. Having examined celebrities in all walks of life in today's China, Edwards and Jeffreys (2010) suggest that both the diversification of Chinese celebrities and the socioeconomic complexities involved in producing and consuming them, are worthy of research as these figures imply broader social and cultural change in today's China. In particular, they contend that it is important to analyze the implications of celebrity culture in contemporary China, tied as it is to the growing role of commodification processes in shaping cultural identity.

Grant McCracken (1989) contends that celebrity endorsement is a special case of a more general process of significatory transference. According to this model, there is a conventional path for the transference of cultural meaning in consumer societies. Celebrity endorsement plays a crucial part in this meaning transfer process. When celebrities advertise products, they bring the meaning that already resides in them, obtained from their dramatic roles, to that product. Therefore, some of the meanings associated with the celebrity become attached to the product itself, and in turn potentially to consumers.

Celebrities also are associated with building desired selves. The self so created is almost always "attractive and accomplished." The constructed self makes the celebrity an exemplary and inspirational figure for consumers to obtain symbolic properties and connect them with their own lives (McCracken 1989). McCracken also suggests a second and more interesting way in which celebrities play the role of a "super consumer" (ibid., 317). The celebrity becomes a kind of experiment in self-construction and an inventor of a new self the consumer can "use." This experimentation, McCracken suggests, makes the celebrity an especially powerful source of meaning for the marketing system and a guide to consumers' self-invention.

The Pink Ribbon Campaign in *Trends Health* magazine has highlighted female celebrities from all walks of life in Chinese society, from sports to the entertainment industry. In this chapter, I explore the Pink Ribbon Campaign in China and these celebrities by: first, examining how the celebrities are constructed and what kind of "selves" are created and epitomized; second, asking what cultural meanings of breast cancer are being constructed by the campaign via the participation of the celebrities; and third, considering how this cultural construction may shape consumers' perceptions and understandings of the disease as well as of their own bodies.

Celebrities as embodiment of self-responsible subjecthood

Since 2005, *Trends Health* magazine has featured a cover photo of three unclothed female celebrities in its October edition, all of whom are TV/movie stars, singers or TV hostesses. In the photos, the three celebrities either sit or stand together, usually gently leaning on each other to help shade each other's private body parts, and to express the idea of support and love for each other. Their hands are delicately posed, indicating love, gentleness and protection of their breasts. Each year, "love" for women is claimed as one important reason for the magazine displaying the pictures of the celebrities, to morally justify the nudity in the photos.

Besides seemingly directing love towards each other, "beautiful" is another key word mentioned repeatedly by the celebrities in the articles in the special issue when asked why they were willing to pose for photos unclothed. They say that in the photos, both their figures and faces look beautiful without any sexual inference. For example, in the cover photo in 2007, the three spokeswomen, Wu Peici, Li Xiaoran and Zhao Yazhi, smiled as they looked at the camera. Their eyes glistened under the spotlight, just as a lake glistens in the moonlight, making them even more goddess-like. Their hair was neatly coiffured and very shiny. Their faces were unblemished. Even Zhao Yazhi, who is 53, looked wrinkle-free, her complexion spotless. The unclothed bodies, as the main elements of the photo, were also spotless; and all three looked fit, free from unnecessary fatty flesh. They opt for comfortable ways of sitting, standing or lying down, looking very natural. Taken together, the sum of these elements makes these photos of highly stylized and idealized female bodies look not only beautiful, but also elegant.

Talking about the role of celebrities in the era of public health reform in post-socialist China, Hood (2010) states that regarding the case of HIV/AIDS prevention in China, Pu Cunxin epitomizes the contemporary "AIDS celebrity" through his HIV/AIDS activism. The activism aims to help the socially vulnerable, and to alleviate the consequences of privatization and insufficient state provision in the health sector during the reform period. I argue that in the current case of the Pink Ribbon Campaign, the use of female celebrities can also be analyzed against the backdrop of the ongoing healthcare system reform and the ensuing privatization of healthcare as an individual responsibility in today's China. In the mid-1990s, public health reform and its associated politics privatized public health provision to meet the demand and provide opportunities for transnational pharmaceutical companies and other medical businesses to prosper in China (Chen 2008, 127). With the retreat of the Party-state from the public health domain, healthcare has become a private issue, and a substantial amount of literature has documented that in China today the new rich are practicing a novel form of self-care following the collapse of socialized medicine (for example, Chen 2008; Zhan 2008). As the central Party leaders, health bureaucrats, local governments and public healthcare units all have strong incentives to shirk their responsibilities regarding the provision of affordable healthcare, the end users have to bear the cost. Out-of-pocket payment as a share of total health expense for end users grew from 20 percent to almost 60 percent between 1978 and 2002 (Smith et al. 2005, 3). In hinterland China, between 60 percent and 80 percent of all patients in rural areas have no option but to die at home, simply because they cannot afford the medical expenses. Healthcare expenses have reportedly become the third largest consumption item for ordinary people in China (Huang 2009).

I argue that in the Chinese Pink Ribbon Campaign, female celebrities (most of whom are singers, movie stars and TV hosts, not professional medical care providers) have been constructed as self-responsible and entrepreneurial subjects in the space of women's health and lifestyles. Their positions as role models on breast cancer prevention and women's healthcare are partly manifested in the almost perfect mediated representation of their physical bodies and beauty. The highly developed techniques of both applying makeup and photo processing help to make the celebrities look almost perfect in the photos: each has a pair of perfect breasts, spotless skin and a very fit body shape, which taken together fulfill the imagination of middle-class aesthetics and tastes vis-à-vis the female body. The celebrities, in this case, are open for construction and optimization as role models for the readers, particularly for those urban young female elites who might attempt to emulate or aspire to their body shapes.

To further highlight these celebrities as embodiments of self-entrepreneurial, lifestyled subjecthood, the celebrities are also constructed in the campaign as constantly working on and optimizing their bodies and health, exercising extreme self-discipline in their daily lives. Celebrities also emphasize their "lifestyles" as healthy, wise and something they have been constantly working on to improve. Almost all of the articles written by these celebrities emphasize that they pay particular attention to taking care of their breasts, and to maintaining their attractive figures and health. Using skincare products like essential oils and body lotions, having a breast massage or doing the massage themselves, and wearing high-quality bras suitable to their individual breast size were the most frequently mentioned methods to take care of their breasts. For example, Wu Peici, a TV hostess, star and model in Taiwan said: "I like buying different kinds and brands of breast care products and often use them in turn, because nutritious elements contained in one product might be very limited. If I use them in turn, my breasts can get all the possible nutrition and also it is fun to do so" (Wu 2007, 67). They also reveal their "secrets," which included drinking nutritious soups and having regular massages in beauty salons to help maintain the shape of their breasts.

By juxtaposing their almost perfect bodies with their experiences and constant hard work in taking care of their bodies and breasts, the celebrities here project themselves as taking *personalized* "responsibility" for their health; shaping their physical appearance to fit dominant beauty norms; emphasizing "choices" around health that ultimately link back to consumption. However, as we will see in the discussion that follows, others, especially patients suffering from breast cancer, are constructed in the magazine in a completely contrary way.

In addition to having celebrities as its spokespersons, the magazine also invites patients to send photos and/or write articles about themselves to be part of the special issue each year. These articles stress a discourse of attributing the responsibility for getting breast cancer to patients themselves. The patients interviewed are mainly urban so called "white-collar" women; for example, Lisa Chang, who is the owner of a famous spa club in China, and Zhang Fu, who has a PhD in literature from Peking University, the top Chinese university. By describing their occupations and educational backgrounds, the campaign tries to indicate that these women should have known the seriousness of breast cancer and taken action to prevent the disease. It is claimed that they failed to do so, simply ignored the signs in their breasts, and delayed seeing a doctor. "It does not matter since it's not painful at all," said Zhang (2006, 137). Due to this perceived unawareness, some of them lost their chance to obtain early treatment and, as a result, their cancer metastasized. Nearly all of the patients interviewed in the magazine alluded to their "irresponsibility," suggesting that they had neglected their physical health by working too hard or being under too much work pressure. They said that "working overtime is almost a daily routine" (ibid., 137). As opposed to the celebrities, who seemingly always manage to balance their workloads and lives and to take care of themselves, the patients tend to be blamed in the magazine's account for neglecting themselves and for leading unhealthy lifestyles. Zhao Chengguang (2008) said: "I was always wanting to have more money before I got the disease and never thought of my own health." Zhao, who is now a housewife, is enjoying a life of cooking and relaxing at home. Lewis (2008, 14) contends that "confessional modes of neoliberal self-surveillance are particularly central to reality-based lifestyle formats, whose narrative development is often strongly reliant on self-disclosure." Similarly, here the process of rationalization (via experts) goes hand in hand with self-surveillance and the confessions of patients themselves. The gaze of the expert has turned inwards upon the self.

Contemporary popular advice culture can be seen to "emerge out of a context in which structural social issues, such as the issue of obesity in the West, are increasingly privatized and psychologized, and where 'the well-being of all' … 'has increasingly come to be seen as a consequence of the responsible self-government of each'" (Lewis 2008, 14). As we saw above, this also pertains in China, following the withdrawal of the state from healthcare provision. In the October editions of *Trends Health*, the term "health management" was mentioned repeatedly, both by the editors and the celebrity interviewees. For example, in 2008, chief editor Sun Yajun wrote in the editor's letter that "among all the risk factors of breast cancer, only 40 percent are genetic and environmental issues, while 60 percent depends on ourselves (*you women shuole suan*). That is called breast health management" (Sun 2008, 18).

Along with time, money, marriage and career, "health" has finally been defined as something manageable and under one's own control. Readers of the articles written by breast cancer patients could easily sense the sharp contrast between the patients' self-confessed lifestyle attitudes and those of the celebrities who have spent considerable money and time on taking care of themselves, especially their breasts, in order to maintain health and beauty.

Why, though, have the female white-collar workers failed to manage their health? Why are they, as is suggested above, under so much pressure and eager to earn more money? Why do they not realize the importance of having their breasts checked annually? While public health and medical research literature based on large-cohort studies shows that certain lifestyle factors do increase the risk of developing breast cancer – for example smoking, high alcohol consumption, the use of oral contraceptives, and obesity – scientific studies also confirm that key risk factors also include gender, aging, genetic factors, and race and ethnicity (American Cancer Society 2013), factors that are almost impossible for women themselves to "manage" and control.

Despite breast cancer being a public health issue, it is constructed in the campaign as something private and "self-manageable." Considering how the shortage of investment in the healthcare sector in China has had a negative influence on breast cancer prevention and cure, the flourishing of the self-responsibility and entrepreneurial subjecthood in the current campaign is perhaps easier to understand. Regular physical examinations can help early detection of breast cancer and bring about a mortality rate decline. In Shanghai, today, the rate of women participating in regular physical examinations is only 47 percent. According to the Shanghai Female Workers Health Care Regulation, every woman in the workplace should have a gynecological check-up every two years and the expense should be covered by their work units (China Shanghai n.d.). However, because this is not a national regulation, compulsory regular physical examinations are still not common in China. For women in the country's other cities, or for those in Shanghai who are out of work, a physical examination is simply an additional financial burden. As indicated by a survey undertaken by Shanghai municipal government in 2002, 14 percent of the total female population is either unemployed or has been laid off in Changning District, Shanghai. The rate of unemployment for women aged 44, who are included in the high-risk age bracket of breast cancer in China, is more than 21 percent (Women of China 2002). The expense of a physical examination is not included in their health insurance policies, and the cost is relatively high for unemployed women. For example, the normal charge for a mammogram in Shanghai is approximately 200 RMB (approximately US$30), which is almost one-third of the monthly basic living allowance provided by the Shanghai municipal government to the unemployed (Chen 2009b). The circumstances are much worse for women in rural areas, where 90 percent of all peasants are uninsured (Hsiao 2007). Few of the 260 million rural migrant workers have health insurance cover in the places in which they stay and work. If the 200 RMB charge for an examination poses problems for some women, both in urban and rural areas, then how could the majority find 10,000 to 100,000 RMB (between $1,500 and $15,000) for medical expenses to treat the disease?

Breast cancer: a chance for class mobility through consumption

While the "breasts" constitute an integral part of the celebrities' beautiful figures, breast cancer has been constructed as having a devastating impact on the beauty and integrity of the female body. For example, many celebrities who have represented the Pink Ribbon Campaign were asked how or through which channels they had learned about breast cancer and/or which incident had made them aware of the disease. Several stars, for example Ke Lan, Mao A'min and Tan Weiwei, to name but a few, mentioned their experiences of casually meeting breast cancer patients who had undergone full mastectomy. They described the uneasy feeling they had when contemplating "incomplete" female bodies. "I was little then and very scared when seeing one of my classmates' mother without breasts and wondered why she has no breasts on her chest," said Mao A'min, one of China's famous female singers (Chen 2009a). Zhang Yuqi, a Chinese movie star, compared the shape of the scars left by a mastectomy to several centipedes creeping towards each other (Song 2010).

The campaign not only depicts breast cancer as a devastating disease for women, but also represents it as providing a chance for individuals to "grow up" and develop as people. In 2006, a patient named Zhang Fu was interviewed and photographed naked for the campaign (Zhang 2006). Unlike the celebrities, who shielded their breasts with their hands or pink ribbons, Zhang's chest was completely revealed to the readers' eyes. In the photo, Zhang smiles happily, one arm cushioning her head and the other resting naturally on her leg. Her smile and the natural position of her arms indicate that Zhang is quite relaxed and comfortable in front of the camera. In contrast to her confident smile, however, the image reveals six vivid, eye-catching pink scars on the left side of her chest. In articles written by Zhang for the campaign, she expresses her happiness regarding her chance to have early surgical treatment. Although her treatment for breast cancer and the risk of losing her breast are temporarily over for Zhang, there is still the possibility that her breast cancer will recur. Her choice of breast conserving treatment, rather than mastectomy, could make that risk higher. However, Zhang said: "I chose to do the conservative therapy because I think I have enough ability now to face and deal with the risks brought by breast cancer." Her article also stresses the self-confidence and ability she developed through her experience of the disease. Compared with the optimism Zhang is evincing now, she was understandably upset and nervous when she first learnt she had cancer. "I could not help but keep crying from afternoon until night and called all my friends and family, telling them what had happened to me … I had never been so freaked out and devastated before." This is how Zhang described her feelings when she was first informed of the diagnosis. Breast cancer, she indicated, forced her to calm down, to learn more about the disease and to fight against it. Finally, she has been able to become a happy, confident woman again. Another patient said that in effect, the disease provided her with the opportunity to start her current career as a volunteer and yoga trainer and to pursue her personal values. The pink and colorful images featured on every page of the magazine, along with photos of the patients, indicate the warm, happy and exhilarating atmosphere they are enjoying now.

Breast cancer is depicted in the magazine not only as providing women with the chance to mature intellectually, but also as an opportunity to achieve class mobility and higher status. The new lifestyles that breast cancer survivors enjoy after their surgery, according to the magazine, are not only healthy, but also "fashionable" and accord with modern, middle-class tastes. Survivors, who were once patients, and have suffered from their own perceived irresponsibility regarding their health, are now experts at keeping healthy, and role models leading popular "health fashion." Lisa Chang said: "As a woman, you should take care of yourself, because it's never too much for you to do to keep yourself healthy." She now goes to hospital for her quarterly check-ups and does a certain amount of exercise every day. In addition, she often enjoys a spa, which is her favorite form of relaxation. She even owns a spa club.

Other survivors are described as engaging in many forms of sport to keep their bodies and spirits in balance. Guo Jian, who saw breast cancer as a "gift from God," now regards yoga as a tool to use to fight the disease. Nowadays, she is recognized as a famous yoga trainer in China. She owns a chain of yoga clubs around the country. "I do yoga every day and it has become part of my life. I like to do yoga at any time, even when waiting for a flight," she commented. The article also emphasized her view that because many women in contemporary China have mental health problems (*xintai wenti hen yanzhong*), yoga is a perfect way to ensure a slow and balanced lifestyle. Today, yoga is a fashionable form of exercise in China. Each year, the third weekend of October is set aside as the "Day of Yoga" (Guo 2008).[2]

Such discourses can be seen as a part of a broader focus by Chinese media to introduce and establish middle-class tastes and values for their audiences (Lewis et al. 2012). Doing yoga everyday, enjoying a spa regularly, and using luxury skincare products are increasingly constructed as essential elements of the perceived superior, Western, healthy, middle-class ways of living by the Chinese media. In the campaign, all of the above practices are seen to have been adopted by breast cancer survivors. By juxtaposing and comparing the patients' lives before and after developing breast cancer, the campaign tries to indicate that breast cancer provides an opportunity for Chinese women to review their lifestyles and commence the projects of self-making, self-management and, perhaps, finally realize a better self and way of living.

When discussing lifestyle TV in China, Lewis, Martin and Sun claim that in China, in contrast to Euro-American programming, such programs are concerned "more with the purpose of teaching viewers what they will need to do in order to achieve status and less about how to construct a social identity" (Lewis et al. 2012, 552). They therefore need to display superior taste and the statues of the lifestyles they promote in the programs are often "beyond ordinary people's wildest dreams" (ibid., 552). By presenting both the celebrities' beautiful bodies, and the dramatic change in patients' lifestyles before and after their diagnosis, the magazine reveals just such an endeavor to "introduce and establish" middle-class values and tastes.

Pink Ribbon Campaign: a global force situated in the Chinese context

Thus far, I have analyzed how celebrities in the Chinese Pink Ribbon Campaign have been constructed as embodiments of self-entrepreneurial subjecthood through idealized representations of their beautiful bodies and femininities, as well as through their constant work on their bodies, health and lifestyles. They spell out their secrets for sustaining their beauty and health. By doing this, their lifestyles are constructed in the campaign as fashionable and healthy for the female readers to learn and to imitate. By contrast, patients in the campaign are described as those who did not follow a healthy or fashionable way of living. They are told that the only way to win the battle against breast cancer and to retain their happiness and beauty is to pursue more healthy and fashionable lifestyles, like relaxing by doing yoga, taking a spa, undergoing breast reconstruction, and/or buying those fashionable, luxury goods "you deserve to have." In this way, breast cancer has been constructed not only as a devastating disease for women, but moreover as a precious chance for readers to scrutinize their own lifestyles, to take action to improve them and to even achieve class mobility, if they work hard enough.

China's recent participation in the global Pink Ribbon Campaign and its popularity in China also need to be placed in the context of the rise in the privatization and marketization of the Chinese media sector, especially of fashion magazines. As an important part of reforms towards commercialization in the Chinese media and cultural sector, the Chinese Party-state has maintained control of these sectors while at the same time allowing the operation of private capital, both domestic and foreign. Non-news content, including recreational and entertainment themes, and advertisements, are considered to be politically less sensitive and are open to the private sector (Lewis et al. 2012). Regarding Chinese fashion and lifestyle magazines, whose viability mainly depends on advertisements (Chen 2010) and foreign investment, the localization and translation of global popular culture into content that caters for Chinese readers and advertisers becomes increasingly essential. Breast cancer prevention campaigns, which have already achieved massive success in the global sphere and proven their great potential to attract advertisements, therefore provide a good opportunity for the magazines to win local markets.

The Pink Ribbon Campaign that appears in the *Trends Health* magazine, which has been sponsored by Estée Lauder in recent times, has attracted many domestic and international companies as sponsors and advertisers. In its 2010 edition, pages 29 to 35 featured all kinds of products in pink, some featuring a pink ribbon. The categories of the goods ranged from perfume, shoes, bags, clothes, watches and home wares to electronic goods, even cars. Most of the brands were world-famous luxury brands, including Chanel, Dior, Miu Miu and Longines, to name but a few. The pink color of both the products and the pages made all of the products look extremely feminine and (supposedly) attractive to female consumers. The whole layout, which put emphasis on "must-have" products, together with the prices listed beside the photos, was designed to arouse women's craving for the products and to urge them to open their purses and buy them.

According to the media kit promoting the Pink Ribbon Campaign in 2010, which was released online, companies that wanted to be advertisers in or sponsors for the campaign had to design a special product featuring pink. It cost at least 300,000 RMB (approximately $50,000) to display the products in the campaign. The most expensive package for sponsoring the campaign cost 800,000 RMB (approximately $130,000). This included displaying the pink product, as well as other media exposure opportunities. It would definitely be worthwhile for companies and brands to invest in the campaign considering the niche market of *Trends Health* magazine. The magazine's official website clearly stated that the average age of its readers was 29. "They are faithful supporters of brand consumption" (Trends Group 2013). This is confirmed by Chen (2010), who concurs that urban middle-class citizens in large Chinese cities are the target readers of fashion magazines. With a total consumption of €40 billion (approximately $52 billions) on luxury goods by Chinese people in 2010, and their potential to become the world's number one luxury products market (163 News 2013), Chinese consumers seem to be the essential target group for major global brands. It thus comes as no surprise that the magazine can attract so many high-end advertisers. The breast cancer awareness cause, which proclaims its care for female readers, provides a major opportunity for imparting a favorable impression to China's middle-class female market.

Building on the above, it becomes easier to answer the questions raised in the previous section about why the magazine has ignored – or at least downplayed – other risk factors for breast cancer, such as environmental and genetic factors, by only stressing lifestyle factors. Li (2012, 122) claims that over the past decade in China, emerging lifestyle magazines have been consistently conscious of a middle-class eagerness for a "Western lifestyle." To this end, they have attempted to provide content "which reflects the readership's social aspirations in a bid to generate profits for their overseas investors." She further argues that to avoid political retribution as well as to generate profit, the magazines have functioned as information vehicles in the service of the rising middle class and have also contributed to the growing consumerism of society. Therefore, the specific aim of these magazines to attract the urban middle class and to nurture their lifestyles has, from the very beginning, decided the orientation of the campaign. Stress is on the risks particular to the individual woman's "lifestyle": a topic that, with its inbuilt potential to offer commodities as health solutions, readily attracts the financial sponsorship of commercial investors.

While the media and the international luxury brands both aim to attract urban, middle-class females as their target audience, members of minority groups who lack consuming capability – jobless women, those on low incomes, inhabitants of rural areas and migrant workers – are clearly forgotten, and omitted from the breast cancer "prevention" campaign's focus. In terms of the efficacy of the campaign, this is a significant shortcoming. According to research done in the rural areas of Shanxi Province, less than 30 percent of 633 rural women could name one or two risk factors for breast cancer. Some 82 percent were eager to learn more about breast cancer and associated check-up procedures, but none of them had ever done or had any kind of breast medical examination, and only 7 percent of all respondents had received any medical guidance vis-à-vis breast check-ups (Zhang et al. 2009, 11–13).

Conclusion

In an interview conducted by Sina.com in 2007, when asked their reason for using naked female bodies to publicize the campaign, Sun Yajun, the chief editor of *Trends Health* magazine said:

> Breast cancer is devastating to women's physical bodies and mental health. We hope to use perfect, integrated female bodies as a signifier to arouse women's awareness of their health and bodies … We are communicating a "notion of health" (*jiankang de linian*) and the idea of preventing breast cancer … Through the special issue every October, we hope to remind women to do annual physical examinations and breast check-ups.
>
> (Sun 2007)

Most of the staff of *Trends Health* magazine, along with volunteers who help promote the campaign, are very passionate about the campaign and proud to be part of it. As Sun said in the same interview, the workers believe that this is a meaningful and worthy cause to which to devote their time and energy. Indeed, the producers' passion and declared intention to advocate for women's health was the point of departure when I started to research this campaign. Therefore, my examination of how the campaign is represented and constructed must also consider whether and how the campaign has fulfilled its purposes as stated above.

As the first national campaign directed toward breast cancer awareness and prevention in China, this campaign has over the past decade succeeded in summoning scores of female celebrities to speak on its behalf, and has become a successful campaign in terms of brand building and attracting commercial sponsorship. However, although the producers and participating celebrities started the campaign with good intentions to advocate for women's health and breast cancer awareness, the heavy involvement of multinational consumer goods companies has diluted its original purpose and theme. In addition, the fashion magazine, as a highly privatized media platform whose main duty is responsibility to its investors, has from the very beginning determined the campaign's focus on women's lifestyles and cultivating their consumption habits. By packaging the female celebrities as role model in the domain of self-care, a certain lifestyle, which signifies middle-class tastes and values, is introduced and promoted by the campaign. Together with this lifestyle, notions of self-enterprising and self-responsibility are also introduced and promoted to young urban women.

Rose (1989, 1996) argues that the rise of neoliberal governments in many nations in the 1980s, along with the emergence of a wider enterprise culture, has seen a shift in the dominant paradigms through which modern citizenship is conceptualized. In particular, the figure of the self-governing citizen, an individual who is constructed as enterprising and self-directed, has become culturally dominant. In the campaign examined in this chapter, while the experts and breast cancer survivors are constructed as self-responsible, wise, ethical consumer-citizens, ordinary readers who may not adopt the recommended lifestyles or devote themselves to care of the self are deemed, by implication, unethical. I propose that in the current case of the Pink Ribbon Campaign, the use of female celebrities, and the heavy involvement of multinational commercial forces, *contribute to rather than ameliorate* the problems arising due to the withdrawal of the Chinese government from women's health-related causes. Through such cooperation between a commoditized media, celebrities as role models and large transnational companies, the young urban woman is left with few other choices but to assume the position of a self-responsible, ethical consumer-citizen.

Notes

1 See Trends Group 2013.

2 Sina Ladies. 2012. "Zhongguo Yujia ri zhi suoyou yujia aihaozhe de yifengxin" (中国瑜伽日致所有瑜伽爱好者的一份信) (A letter to all the yoga lovers in China). *Sina Ladies*. eladies.sina.com.cn/zc/2012/0929/09411188286.shtml (accessed September 10, 2013).

References

163 News. 2013. "外媒称去年中国奢侈品消费达400亿欧元 (Foreign Media Claim that the Total Consumption of Luxury Products in China Last Year Reached 40 billion euros)." news.163.com/11/0209/00/6SDKUE590001124J.html (accessed September 10, 2013).

American Cancer Society. 2013. "What are the Risk Factors for Breast Cancer?" www.cancer.org/cancer/breastcancer/detailedguide/breast-cancer-risk-factors (accessed September 10, 2013).

Chen, Jing (陈静). 2009a. "毛阿敏 就让美丽的力量顺应自然而行." *Trends Health* 《时尚健康》, October, 59.

Chen, Liyu (陈里予). 2009b. "上海市城镇低保升至每人每月425元 (The Basic Living Allowance for Urban Shanghai People has been Increased to 425 RMB per Month)." *Sohu*, May 5. business.sohu.com/20090605/n264358701.shtml (accessed October 10, 2013).

Chen, Nancy N. 2008. "Consuming Medicine and Biotechnology in China." In *Privatizing China: Socialism from Afar*, edited by Li Zhang and Aihwa Ong, 123–132. New York: Cornell University Press.

Chen, Peiqin. 2010. "Magazines: An Industry in Transition." In *New Media for a New China*, edited by James F. Scotton and William A. Hachten, 61–73. Malden, MA: Wiley-Blackwell.

China Shanghai. n.d. "Shanghai Female Workers Health Care Regulation (上海市女职工劳动保护法)." www.shanghai.gov.cn/shanghai/node2314/node3124/node3125/node3133/userobject6ai655.html (accessed October 10, 2013).

Edwards, Louise, and Elaine Jeffreys. 2010. "Celebrity/China." In *Celebrity in China*, edited by Louise Edwards and Elaine Jeffreys, 1–20. Hong Kong: Hong Kong University Press.

Evans, H. 2008, "Sexed Bodies, Sexualized Identities, and the Limits of Gender", *China Information*, XXII: 361–386.

Estée Lauder. 2013. "Pink Ribbon." www.esteelauder.com/pinkribbon/index.tmpl (accessed September 10, 2013).

Guo, Jian (郭健). 2008. "郭建 前所未有的最好状态." *Trends Health* 《时尚健康》, October, 83.

Hood, Johanna. 2010. "Celebrity Philanthropy: The Cultivation of China's HIV/AIDS Heroes." In *Celebrity in China*, edited by Louise Edwards and Elaine Jeffreys, 85–102. Hong Kong: Hong Kong University Press.

Hsiao, William C. 2007. "The Political Economy of Chinese Health Reform." *Health Economics, Policy and Law* 2(3): 241–249.

Huang, Yanzhong. 2009. "An Institutional Analysis of China's Failed Healthcare Reform." In *Socialist China, Capitalist China: Social Tension and Political Adaptation under Economic Globalization*, edited by Guoguang Wu and Helen Lansdowne, 75–86. Routledge: New York.

King, Samantha. 2006. *Pink Ribbons, Inc.: Breast Cancer and the Politics of Philanthropy.* Minneapolis, MN: University of Minnesota Press.

Lewis, Tania. 2008. *Smart Living: Popular Culture and Everyday Life.* New York: Peter Lang Publishing.

Lewis, Tania, Fran Martin, and Wanning Sun. 2012. "Lifestyling Asia? Shaping Modernity and Selfhood on Life-Advice Programming." *International Journal of Cultural Studies* 15(6): 537–566.

Li, Shuang. 2012. "A New Generation of Lifestyle Magazine Journalism in China." *Journalism Practice* 6(1): 122–137.

McCracken, Grant. 1989. "Who is the Celebrity Endorser? Cultural Foundations of the Endorsement Process." *Journal of Consumer Research* 16(3): 310–321.

Rose, Nikolas. 1989. *Governing the Soul: The Shaping of the Private Self.* London: Routledge.

Rose, Nikolas. 1996. *Inventing Our Selves: Psychology, Power, and Personhood.* Cambridge: Cambridge University Press.

Smith, Peter, Christine Wong, and Yuxin Zhao. 2005. *Public Expenditure and the Role of Government in the Chinese Health Sector, Prepared for China Rural Health AAA.* Washington, DC: World Bank. siteresources.worldbank.org/INTEAPREGTOPHEANUT/Resources/502734-1129734318233/BN5-publicexpenditure-final.pdf.

Song, Feifei (宋菲菲). 2010. "张雨绮的粉红丝带故事." *Trends Health* 《时尚健康》, October, 69.

Sun, Yajun (孙雅君). 2007. "明星做客新浪聊2007粉红丝带 (Talking About Pink Ribbon Campaign in Sina in 2007)". *Sina.* eladies.sina.com.cn/zc/2007/0926/2240551406.shtml (accessed November 20, 2013).

Sun, Yajun (孙雅君). 2008. "Editor's letter." *Trends Health*, October, 18.

Trends Groups. 2013. *Trends Health*. www.trendsmag.com/trendsmag/client/about/ads/health1.htm (accessed September 10, 2013).

Women of China. 2002. "关于上海市长宁区女性就业状况的分析及对策研究 (The Analysis about Women's Employment in Changning District, Shanghai)." *Women of China*, 6. www.women.org.cn/allnews/02/58.html (accessed October 10, 2013).

Wu, Peici (吴佩慈). 2007. "吴佩慈 每个自信的女人都是女神. *Trends Health* 《时尚健康》, October, 67.

Zhan, Mei. 2008. "Wild Consumption: Relocating Responsibilities in the Times of SARS." In *Privatizing China: Socialism from Afar*, edited by Li Zhang and Aihwa Ong, 151–167. New York: Cornell University Press.

Zhang, Fu (张芙). 2006. "张芙 保乳是给自己一个可能." *Trends Health* 《时尚健康》, October, 136–137.

Zhang, Li, and Aihwa Ong, eds. 2008. *Privatizing China: Socialism from Afar*, Ithaca, NY: Cornell University Press.

Zhang, Yinling, Baohua Cao, Qun Yang, He Lei, Qiaoling Xu, and Ruijie Shi. 2009. "Rural Area Female's Demands for Knowledge and Health Education of Breast Cancer." *China Journal of Health Psychology* 17(8): 11–13.

Zhao, Chengguang (赵晨光). 2008. "赵晨光 找到过日子的感觉." *Trends Health* 《时尚健康》, October, 82.

6 *Empresses in the Palace* and the "neoliberalization through China" project in Taiwan

Fang-chih Irene Yang

The phenomenon of the Chinese historical television drama *Empresses in the Palace* (*Hougong Zhen Huan Zhuan*) in Taiwan can be best captured through Henry Jenkins's notion of "convergence culture," defined as "the flow of content across multiple media platforms, the cooperation between multiple media industries, and the migratory behavior of media audiences who will go almost anywhere in search of the kinds of entertainment experiences they want" (Jenkins 2008, 2). Not only has the show been repeated more than ten times in three years since 2012 and, at its peak, aired for nine hours a week on TV (XMTV.CN 2012) and been streamed on the Internet for free, but it has also proliferated into different genres, including variety shows, *kuso* (satirical remakes of the show by viewers), and self-help books, in addition to generating numerous commentaries and news coverage on different media platforms.

Convergence culture is predicated on a network society whose operation of power in shaping subjectivity can be illuminated through Foucault's concept of governmentality (Hay 2010). Scholarship in the West has taken up the Foucaultian lens of governmentality to focus on the production of neoliberal subjectivity (Gill 2003; Hay 2010; McRobbie 2013). If Western scholars have the privilege of taking "neoliberalism" as a body of thought originating, revised and practiced in the West, then in a peripheral location such as Taiwan, a "state without nation" with a democratically elected authoritarian government since 2008, we must address how the process of neoliberalization is a process of articulation and translation (Clarke 2008) which involves struggles and negotiations not only with the American and Chinese empires, but also with the resilient authoritarian culture from the old and now revived KMT (Kuomintang or Nationalist) regime, which ruled Taiwan at the time of writing (2008–2016).

This chapter focuses on the production of a particular kind of *authoritarian neoliberal subjectivity* that I argue is produced via the convergence of different media platforms and genres generated through *Empresses in the Palace*, a Chinese TV drama, in the context of Taiwan having taken on a project that I call "neoliberalization through China" since 2008. The chapter first discusses the concept of neoliberal governmentality in producing subjectivity in a network society, followed by a discussion of the project of neoliberalization through China in Taiwan. The third part discusses the political rationalities inscribed in the institution of the everyday networks of government and the TV industry, which have led to a re-privileging of traditional Chinese culture. Finally, I analyze the flow of *Empresses* texts, from television to the Internet and the business self-help genre, in order to address the authoritarian neoliberal subjectivity that is produced. I argue that neoliberal thought (especially the economization of culture) as a form of political rationality informs the making of the creative industries, including television. This neoliberal thought articulates with the KMT's authoritarian philosophy as well as with Communist China's political strategy in using traditional Chinese culture as an economic resource to unify with Taiwan. The economization of traditional Chinese culture, demonstrated through the television culture generated by *Empresses in the Palace*, works to produce authoritarian neoliberal subjects who are selfish, calculating, self-responsible, and obedient to power and hierarchy – a project that undermines the social and leads to pressing political dangers.

Neoliberal governmentality in Taiwan

For the governmentality school of thought, neoliberalism is defined through "rule at a distance" which emphasizes self-discipline and self-cultivation in producing autonomous, calculating, entrepreneurial citizenship. This is achieved through the circulation of discourses and technologies in different levels and contexts. As such, media plays a significant role in disseminating discourses. As Hay points out, the institution of liberal government requires the multiplication and dispersion of mechanisms for disciplining, guiding and shaping individuals' proper exercise of freedoms. The proliferation of mechanisms constitutes the networks of power which, in a digitally structured network society, enable power to operate as the "little everyday operation of social control" (Hay 2010, 154). Television, the Internet and self-help books, in a convergence society, are such mechanisms of the "everyday network of government" (Hay 2010).

Hay emphasizes the notion of govern-"mentalities" – the political rationalities that operate at different levels and contexts, but synchronize with each other to produce autonomous, free, self-enterprising citizens. Since the KMT took over Taiwan (in the late 1940s), a form of Confucian-influenced governmentality ("cultivate oneself, keep one's family in order, run the country well, bring peace to the world" 修身齊家治國平天下) also relied on "rule at a distance" to produce obedient, productive, patriotic, self-reliant and self-responsible citizens for authoritarian control. What this entails is that "rule at a distance" is not *unique* to neoliberalism (Kipnis 2008), and that neoliberal subjectivity and citizenship need to be seen as the articulation of rule at a distance with specific economic policies (which are informed by particular kinds of political rationalities or "mentalities"). Through neoliberal globalization, today, US-style neoliberalism articulates with Taiwan's unique authoritarian development, and since 2008, with Taiwan's neoliberalization through China project. In the next section, I discuss the political rationalities that enable Taiwan's television industry to become an "everyday network of government" – that is, the historical and geographical "arrangement" of the networks and dispositions through which technologies of control and freedom are exercised (Hay 2010), within the context of "neoliberalization through China."

Neoliberalization through China

A brief account of the history of Taiwan is needed in order to delineate the particular type of political-economic formation that led to the revival of the KMT authoritarian regime and its project of neoliberalization through China. Before economic liberalization and democratization (in the late 1980s and 1990s), Taiwan's economy was structured according to two logics. On the one hand, an export-oriented economic development policy designed and supported by the USA drew Taiwan into the international division of labor, spawning small and medium-sized family firms, which formed the backbone of Taiwan's "economic miracle." On the other hand, all major industries, including those left behind by the colonial Japanese state (1895–1945), were either controlled and owned by the KMT party-state, or structured according to patron-client dependency relationships between the party-state and the capitalists who conformed to the demands of the state (this was the case with the television industry). Since 1985, with the signing of the Plaza Accord, East Asian countries have effectively been forced to begin a process of market liberalization according to US demands (Hamilton 1999, 56–57). In Taiwan, this led to the privatization of public assets into the hands of the KMT party and the capitalists who had close connections with them. At the same time, democratic movements began to gain popular support, demanding elections at both central and local government levels. The need for election funding opened up business's influence over the political agenda (Kim and Im 2001; Kong 2004). Not only did this "dual transition" (economic and political) shape a business-friendly Taiwanese state, but the legacy of the KMT party-state's practice of crony capitalism also led to the formation of KMT-friendly large corporations whose performance became the measure of Taiwan's economic success.

What the neoliberals understand is that they need to control the state so that the market can be regulated to the advantage of the few. The KMT's loss of political power from 2000 to 2008 (following the party's losses to the Democratic Progressive Party (DPP) in the 2000 and 2004 presidential elections) led it to cooperate with its historical enemy, the Chinese Communist Party (CCP) across the straits in China. The Lian–Hu Meeting (*Lian Hu Gonghui*) between the chairmen of the KMT and CCP in 2005 marked an official policy change for both the KMT and the CCP. For the CCP, the agenda is now unification through economic integration, which requires the KMT's power for "institution building" (Xin 2010). For the KMT, "uniting with the CCP to fight against Taiwan's independence (and the DPP)" (*lian gong zhi taidu*) became the political strategy.

The election of KMT president Ma Ying-jeou in 2008 marked the success of this cooperation. Following his election there occurred a process of "neoliberalization through China" according to China's demand for institution building. Neoliberalization through China refers to the KMT's attempt to see Taiwan join the world economic order through China, as the Ma administration believes Taiwan can leverage the rise of China, while China disallows Taiwan to join any trade pact with countries other than China (or only with the permission of China). The signing of the Economic Cooperation Framework Agreement (ECFA) in 2010, the expansion of the free trade agreement with China, and the controversial Cross Strait Service Trade Agreement in 2014 are touted as the only and necessary path to Taiwan's full participation in world trade (such as Taiwan's signing on to the Trans-Pacific Partnership). Neoliberalization through China drew Taiwan firmly into China's economic orbit, making Taiwan an integral part of the Chinese economy, resulting in the formation of a class of pro-China, pro-KMT cross-strait elite capitalists (跨海峽權貴資本家), and producing an increasing gap between the rich and the poor, with the top 5 percent of the rich earning 65.97 times more than the lowest 5 percent of the working poor in 2008, and 96.56 times in 2011 (Zheng 2013).

This "neoliberalization through China" economic policy also worked politically for the revival of the KMT's authoritarian rule. Dirlik (2012) points out that the Chinese "model" or, more accurately, paradigm, itself took inspiration from East Asian authoritarian countries such as Singapore and Taiwan, and relied on investments and technology from these countries in developing "socialism with Chinese characteristics" – that is, the beginnings of economic reform – in the late 1970s and 1980s. At the same time, China's state-managed economy has also been nourished by globalization, and the Chinese regime has been a major proponent of the globalization of markets and production since the 1990s. "What characterizes the Chinese economy is a successful combination of authoritarian management internally with effective activity in the neoliberal market" (Dirlik 2012, 285). Cooperating with China, for Taiwan's revived authoritarian administration under Ma Ying-jeou, entailed exercising unchecked political power in following China's demand for institution building. The Chinese model's combination of authoritarianism with neoliberal globalization allowed Ma to violate democratic procedures guaranteed in Taiwan's Constitution in the name of "striving for the economy" while nourishing pro-China and pro-KMT capitalists.

The economization of culture and TV as an everyday network of government

How has culture, in particular television(-generated) culture, figured since 2008, and what role does it play in this political-economic arrangement of "neoliberalization through China" in Taiwan? A brief discussion of the history of television more broadly is necessary to understand the present configuration of TV as an everyday network of government in producing "neoliberal subjects with Chinese characteristics."

In Taiwan, television was installed as an instrument for governing thc population on a daily basis in the context of both the Cold War and China's civil war of the 1940s (between China's Communist forces and the Nationalist/KMT Republic of China). The goal of the three TV networks, established between 1962 and 1971, was to "correct social consciousness, maintain national interests, and national dignity"; "adhere to government policies and promote anti-communism ideologies"; and emphasize "traditional ethics [Chinese culture and tradition] and morality and maintain free democracy"; in addition to "using Mandarin as the primary language" (Su 1991, 125). The mission of governing Chinese national subjects in the Republic of China on Taiwan was supported by a particular kind of industrial arrangement: a "patron-client dependency" between state officials and capitalists who pledged loyalty to the KMT state (Lin 2006). However, this arrangement also led to inherent tensions between the government's need to use TV as a propaganda tool, and the capitalists' need to earn a profit (Lin 2006).

Following the end of the authoritarian rule of the Chiang family (successive presidents Generalissimo Chiang Kai-shek and his son, Chiang Ching-kuo) and the lifting of martial law, the entanglement of democratization with neoliberalization in the late 1980s led to the deregulation of television and the formation of a "post-network" era dominated by commercial cable and satellite systems in the early 1990s, and later, the formation of a network society powered by the digital revolution, characterized by the convergence of TV and other media platforms. This period of industrial and technological reform was facilitated by the myth that a free market equals freedom of speech, which was supported not only by the neoliberals but also by the popular demand for democracy. These changes, however, have not altered television's role as an everyday network of government, but have strengthened it, as TV is now further woven into the texture of everyday life not only through round-the-clock broadcasting but also through click-on-demand online digital services available at any time and place.

Neoliberalization has played a major role in maintaining the hegemony of Chinese culture in Taiwan (a cultural project that had already been central to the KMT's rule, since the 1940s). First, the opening up of China to Taiwan in the realm of television in the late 1980s triggered "China fever" in drama productions: many producers went to China to shoot the authentic China (as opposed to the imagined "motherland" of Taiwan's previous drama productions) and take advantage of cheap Chinese labor and talent. This allowed television producers and managers (who were all high-level KMT party members) to appeal to the value of "Chineseness" to maintain their power and control as they struggled against the tide of democratization and the concurrent rise of Taiwanese nativism and localism, manifested in the popularity of the Hsiangtu (indigenous) drama genre. Drama productions co-produced in China were praised as an act of searching for quality and authenticity, despite uncertain financial returns. Moreover, the concept of "the China market" (*Zhongguo shichang*) emerged during this period not only to underline its size and desirability, but also used interchangeably with "international" as a rhetorical strategy to devalue the "narrow-minded," local nature of concurrent democratic demands for cultural indigenization/Taiwanization (Yang 2015).

Second, the global neoliberal discourse of "creative industries," which sees culture as economy, began to take center stage from the 2000s. Since the election of Ma in 2008, the democratically elected authoritarian regime used this neoliberal discourse in two ways to facilitate the revival of Chinese culture and tradition, paving the way for political unification. First, the neoliberal discourse relies on the separation of the economy from the political and cultural domains and the assertion that the economization of these domains is an apolitical process. This is achieved through constantly invoking the deep-seated ideology of "striving for the economy" (*pin jingji*) as the ultimate goal of politics. As Hao Min-yi, the former policy consultant for President Ma, stated in 2009: "[w]e need to change our ideas and think of culture as a form of capital and as a technology that brings about economic development" (Hao 2009). Second, in this neoliberal discourse of culture as economic resource, pro-China Taiwanese capitalists, the Chinese state, and Chinese capitalists all construct Chinese culture and tradition as Taiwan's niche and strength in the realm of popular culture production. As a result, the main goal of Taiwan's cultural policy, according to the Ministry of Culture, is to develop "Chinese culture with Taiwanese characteristics" (「具有台灣特色的中華文化」的文化施政主軸) (Yang 2015).

The neoliberal discourse of culture as economy has also led to the prominence of the "Chinese-language market" (*huayu shichang*), a concept that has its roots in the global "Greater China" discourse of the 1990s, enabled by Asia Satellite TV's globalization through regionalization strategy. In the domain of television production, two phenomena emerged as a result of the hegemony of the "Chinese-language market" discourse. First, we have seen the hollowing out of the national television industry as many producers, entertainers and investors moved to China to capitalize on its large market. As a result, most television and cable channels rely on importing dramas to fill up airtime. In 2008, domestically produced drama took up 42 percent of airtime whereas in 2011, it had decreased to 29.6 percent (Ministry of Culture 2013). The Chinese cultural nationalism promoted by the KMT state led to the boycott and hence the decline of the import of Korean dramas, to be replaced by Chinese dramas (in particular, historical dramas) as of 2012.[1] The old networks, including CTS, now a public broadcasting channel, played a major role in this process of disseminating Chinese culture and history through Chinese historical dramas in the name of saving and earning money. Second, in reaching the Chinese-language market, Taiwan's drama production invested heavily in the production of a new genre, Chinese dramas (*huaju*), emphasizing "Confucian" ethics, including filial piety, obedience, family and romantic love (Yang 2012).

In this section, I have mapped out the governmental political rationalities in the domain of culture, and television in particular. I have argued that historically, television has functioned as an everyday network of government, but whereas in the early days of television, governmental rationality was inflected by a contradiction between the mission to cultivate Chinese culture as the superior national culture and the search for commercial interests, the contemporary neoliberal discourse of culture as economy resolves this contradiction by viewing culture *as economy*, and under the pro-China, pro-unification regime, makes traditional Chinese culture and tradition a valuable economic resource for cultural production.

Historical TV dramas, *Empresses in the Palace* and "elite networks"

Empresses in the Palace, an historical TV drama made in China, has to be approached through three contexts. First, we must consider China's appropriation of the global discourse of soft power to fit its nationalistic agenda. While Joseph Nye uses soft power to discuss state-to-state international relations, China's propaganda machine appropriates it to emphasize the role of culture in both national cohesion and international competition. Building a harmonious society through traditional Chinese culture is considered to strengthen China's soft power (Edney 2012). Consequently, cultural productions are obliged to promote traditional Chinese culture. Second, we must recall that it is through the rhetoric of the economy that soft power as political control can be exercised, as was stated in former Chinese President Hu Jintao's policy announcement in 2007, and written in the guidelines for China's cultural development passed in 2011: "We insist on developing culture industry through Chinese style … [We will] expand the scale of our culture industry, increase our competitiveness and power in the culture industry, and actively develop domestic and international cultural markets in order to strengthen the influence of Chinese culture in the world" (Xinhuanet 2007). The politicization of the economy and the economization of politics through the revival of traditional Chinese culture have led to the commodification and proliferation of Chinese history in the popular domain (Liu 2004). Third, we should take into account that the political and economic uses of traditional Chinese culture led the state to promote historical TV dramas. The popularity of historical TV dramas, however, needs to be analyzed as both a critique and a legitimation of the present. Zhu Ying, in investigating the early historical TV drama *Yongzheng Dynasty* (1997), points out that, on the one hand, it offers a critique of the present in the guise of historical figures and events so as to avoid censorship; on the other hand, *Yongzheng Dynasty* legitimizes existing authoritarianism through "totalitarian nostalgia" which celebrates the leadership of a kind and capable emperor (仁君) (Zhu 2005). Moreover, this show also led to a proliferation of Qing dynasty dramas, an historical period when China was at its peak in terms of territorial expansion and national strength. *Empresses in the Palace*, also set in the Qing dynasty's Yongzheng period, follows this generic tradition of glorifying China's rise and strength. At the same time, it needs to be read in relation to the present situation.

The predominant mode of interpretation considers *Empresses in the Palace* as a contemporary workplace tale presented in the form of history: "*Empresses in the Palace* itself is a show about contemporary ethics of the workplace, dressed in the guise of history" and "[it is] a reflection of contemporary Chinese social realty, be it in the workplace or the realm of love" (Hou 2013). As the director of *Empresses*, Zheng Xiao-long, indicates: "even though this is an historical palace drama, it is a drama that adheres to official Chinese history, you can learn real history from this show. Moreover, the back palace is the workplace, the show also helps young people to deal with their career" (Zhao 2011).

The reading of an historical drama centered on love struggles as a workplace cautionary tale needs to be analyzed through China's gendered political-economic configuration. A brief plot summary will be provided here to illustrate this point.

Zhen Huan is forced by the emperor to be a royal concubine in the back palace, a place where women compete for power by trying to win the love of the emperor (Figure 6.1). There, she becomes embroiled in power struggles and almost loses her life several times, which transforms her from an innocent girl (Figure 6.2) into a conniving, calculative and mature woman (Figure 6.3). In order to survive, she relies on several close friends as her network in fighting her enemies. When she loses the emperor's love, she flees the palace and stays in a monastery where she has an affair with the emperor's brother, Lord 17, and is impregnated by him, but due to unpredictable circumstances, she comes back to the palace and becomes even more scheming and hard-hearted in eliminating her enemies. To eliminate the queen, she aborts her own baby and claims it was the queen's fault. She even poisons the man she loves, Lord 17, in order to gain the emperor's trust. Finally, when the emperor dies, she is consecrated as queen (the mother of the new emperor) and enjoys a life of power and wealth.

John Osburg (2013) uses the term "elite networks" to refer to the state-business complex at the heart of China's development of capitalism and discusses the gender politics of these elite networks. He argues that "the moral economies of elite *guanxi* networks are at the very heart of 'capitalist' development in urban China." "*Guanxi* relationships are composed of mixtures of interest, affect, and morality, a mixture that distinguishes them from other types of relationship" (ibid., 32). By and large, elite networks are a men's world that relies on Confucian brotherhood, in particular the concept of *yiqi* (義氣) – "honor or a sense of obligation in personal relationships" – to mask the utilitarian nature of what is in fact an elite *guanxi* network. The men who

Figure 6.1 *Empresses in the Palace* – analysis of combat capabilities: the episode on various concubines 後宮甄嬛傳-戰力分析:眾妃篇

Figure 6.2 The young, innocent Zhen Huan, *Empresses in the Palace*, episode 10

Figure 6.3 The mature Zhen Huan, *Empresses in the Palace*, episode 56

dominate this network rely on women (hostess, girlfriends, and *ernai* or mistresses) to boost their masculinity and build up fraternity. As a result, the masculine ideal in China today is the "boss-patron" who gives out material favors to support the lower-status men in his network and the women who depend on him for a living. The moral economies of *guanxi* networks serve to exclude outsiders and consolidate power. Excluded from the major field of power play, women rely on their youthful body and their "quality" (artistic cultivation and education) to exchange for a short- or long-term relationship with these wealthy and powerful men who can offer them material wealth. What is interesting in Osburg's account is its illumination of the way in which the elites understand the significance of *guanxi* in building power, while the women who are excluded from the elite networks use the trope of market competition to legitimize their trading of sexuality for material comfort and frame the sale of sex "as a 'developed' form of entrepreneurialism: as the rational exploitation of marginalized women's only resource in a competitive economic environment" (Osburg 2013, 148–149). Women see the instrumental "capacity" of their body in building their marriage/relationships, and therefore rely on a neoliberal discourse of market competition, individualism, self-reliance and entrepreneurism to prepare themselves as successful mistresses. Within this gendered social arrangement, the domain of love and marriage effectively becomes the *workplace*, for women.

Empresses in the Palace depicts the plight of women within the structure of such gendered elite networks, with the emperor representing the boss-patron. As the show emphasizes, every exchange of sex with the emperor is compensated by material gifts, while no sex means literal death from material deprivation. Love has to be sacrificed in order to maintain life and material wealth, as symbolized by the murdering of Lord 17. Moreover, women's social status, while hierarchically structured, is determined by the emperor's favors. As a result, the realm of love/sex is equated with the workplace and is a matter of survival for women. This structures women's relationship with each other in the form of a friend-foe binary, with competition and elimination being the primary ethos. To compete for the emperor's love, *guanxi* is seen as an essential strategy: an instrumentalized human relationship in the form of cooperation in eliminating the foe within the structure of the friend-foe imaginary. Moreover, the concept of competition requires a calculating, selfish, self-interested subject who will grab power by any possible means without any moral concerns. These constructions of the society as hierarchical and human nature as selfish and rational are essential to the working of authoritarian neoliberal Chinese capitalism.

Workplace literature and the production of authoritarian neoliberal working subjects in Taiwan

Through media convergence, *Empresses in the Palace* has extended into the genre of self-help books, which interpret the show as a cautionary workplace tale, with the historical back palace likened to the modern workplace. The self-help genre of "workplace literature" is produced by fans who become experts because of their training in economics and management, or their personal experiences in the workplace. Written by both male and female Chinese and Taiwanese fan-authors, and circulated through books, business magazines and the Internet in Taiwan, along with the show's daily, repeated appearance on television, these cultural texts constitute the "ethical substance," "the primary material of [...] moral conduct," in Foucault's words, which individuals use to cultivate subjectivity (Foucault 1990, 28). The material this section analyzes includes texts like *The 80 Things that Empresses in the Palace Teaches Me* (Xiyan 2013), *Survival Tactics in the Workplace*

(The 36 Rules that Zhen Huan Teaches Me) (Luo 2013), *The Workplace is the Back Palace: The Base Tactics that Zhen Huan Teaches Me in the Office* (Jinfei and Gao 2013), *The Knowledge that Huafei (Royal Concubines) Should Know: The Mines that you Should Not Step On in the Workplace* (Luoshi 2013), and *From Apprentice to the Ultimate CEO* (Wang 2013). It also includes an excerpt from "The Six Management Philosophies in *Empresses in the Palace*," circulated in the *Business Weekly* Forum (one of the most prestigious business magazines in Taiwan), and written by a "leadership training expert" in China.

As texts generated through *Empresses* belong to a genre of self-help workplace advice literature with a specific Chinese history, I will discuss the political rationalities that govern this genre's production. This genre began to gain visibility in the 1990s when big corporations consolidated to become the dominant form of the economy as a result of neoliberal globalization.[2] There has been a boom in this genre with the recent neoliberalization through China and the concurrent commodification and popularization of Chinese history in the Taiwanese cultural scene. Ziyang (a Chinese writer) published the popular text *The Economics Behind History* (2013) at a time when copious workplace literature was being generated through *Empresses.* The book captures the rationalities at the heart of this genre, and is therefore worthwhile considering in some detail. Assuming the character of an economist, the author declares in the introduction that "all problems can be seen as economic problems and can be solved through economic means" (Ziyang 2013, 2). Similarly, "all histories can be analyzed through economics, and you can solve all of the problems of history if you can think like an economist." The goal of analyzing history is to analyze the present and "offer guidance for the present," and this present is a market economy characterized by the ascendancy of the economic. Present reality, no matter whether it concerns "power, life, love, [or] learning and living," can be made "simple and clear" "if we think like an economist" whose principle is a question of making choices after cost-benefit analysis (ibid., 4). Moreover, "we have to see through all the appearances in order to understand the essence of economics: the maximization of profit as human nature. It is individuals' drive for the maximization of profit that turns endless human desires into the driving forces of living, determines all human behavior, and motivates the movement of history" (ibid., 5). The obvious point here concerns the reduction of history and all domains of human life to economics, defined through cost-benefit analysis, with individuals seeking the greatest profit framed as human nature.

The analogy of the back palace as the workplace allows for a fairly homogenous imagination about the workplace in the numerous advice books generated. The predominant metaphors used to describe the workplace are those of "jungle" and "war," which articulate the ethos of competition and power struggle as the rule of the game, hollowing out fairness and justice. As Luo (2013) highlights in the blurb of *Survival Tactics in the Workplace*, "[w]here there is a power struggle, there is the back palace. The workplace is a jungle where the weak becomes the meat of the strong. There are no judges, no clear-cut rules, and only survivors can define what success is. Zhen Huan says, in the back palace, even if you do not want to compete, you will inevitably get involved … better to help yourself rather than help others." Built into such discourse of competition is an acknowledgement of the society/workplace as hierarchical. Most of the literature is directed to the "ordinary us" at the bottom of the office hierarchy: "Everybody thinks we are Zhen Huan, but most of us are An Lingrong … Most people do not have well-established families or rich fathers to lean on … once you enter the workplace, you have been selected as a royal concubine in the back palace, and you can only fight alone" (ibid., 16).

Within this hierarchical workplace, human relationships are structured vertically in terms of boss–employee, and horizontally in terms of the friend–foe binary. However, I want to point out that this "jungle" experienced by ordinary workers is in fact an intentional creation of management in order to maintain a workplace hierarchy that favors the "boss." In "The Six Management Philosophies in *Empresses in the Palace*," the author, Tan Xiao-fang, a leadership training expert, makes it clear that "cooperation is just a slogan, the most important thing is to maintain power balance in the workplace." "If everybody works hard and cooperates, the power and status of the boss might be threatened. This is why many managers [create an environment] for their subordinates to fight with each other rather than cooperate as brothers" (Tan 2012).

What needs to be highlighted is the notion of hierarchy, since it is the illiberal element rather than the liberal notion of equality (Kipnis 2008) that is characteristic of Chinese capitalist development (including the East Asian authoritarian capitalist development that provided inspiration to China). The Chinese model combines this hierarchical thinking with the neoliberal notion of competition and pan-economization as its moral foundation for authoritarian neoliberal capitalist development. In addition to the neoliberal construction of the workplace as a jungle where competition is the norm, this body of literature helps to produce a neoliberal subject defined by individualism (self-responsibility), materialism (self-interest), and instrumentalism (of human relationships and the self).

The most famous phrase by Zhen Huan that has caught popular sentiment is "A bitch always fakes her feelings" (賤人就是矯情). What this phrase articulates is the acknowledgement of social inequality that puts us "in hell" (Luo 2013). As such, "a virtuous heart can only lead to destruction, the key is to protect yourself … Being a bitch who fakes her feelings (賤人就是矯情) is a necessary evil … When there are conflicts over interests, everybody sacrifices everything in order to be a bitch" (ibid., 82). The key strategy for faking one's feelings is to stay "low key" (*didiao*). All of the workplace literature, be it for top-level managers (Tan 2012) or office workers, recommends to stay low key and "play stupid as a form of wisdom" (Wang 2013, 93). "No matter whether it's in the back palace or in the workplace, you should stay low key so that you do not make other people jealous of you. Pretend to be weak and show this to other people, so that other people do not see you as a target and you can protect yourself" (Xiyan 2013, 71).

The "bitch mentality" that seeks self-interest above all things leads to the oxymoronic common sense of responsibilization and instrumentalization of the self, and the instrumentalization of human relationships. The former presumes that the self can be instrumentalized and objectified as "capital" which can be used, as in "the basic survival rule in the back palace is be a person who is of good use" (Luo 2013, 23), and the injunction to "feel satisfied in being used, and make yourself usable all the time" (Xiyan 2013, 117). However, the objectified human is then endowed with self-responsibility, to improve competitiveness as value: "a real iron rice bowl is not about finding life-long employment (which is impossible). It means wherever you go, you can always find rice … you need to improve yourself to raise your own value" (Luo 2013, 25–27). Attitude is essential to this self-responsibilization: "Zhen Huan teaches us that our fate is in our own hands. As long as we can cultivate a positive attitude and seize every opportunity we encounter, we can be successful … There is no desperate situation in the workplace, there are only desperate attitudes" (Wang 2013, 200–202). What is promoted here is a neoliberal discourse of psychologized competition which leads to an emphasis on individual responses and responsibility in times of economic insecurity.

Gender politics also operate through this psychologized competition, not only in the form of working on the "self" as consciousness but also vis-à-vis the gendered body. Specific advice is given to women to cultivate a positive attitude in order that they can "behave like blossoms": "Be strong willed and manage your body. People will not treat you as a human being if your body is out of shape …" (Jinfei and Gao 2013, 178–179). Emphasis is placed on the active cultivation of the beautiful body through proper dress code to appear "youthful and feminine": "The first lesson Zhen Huan teaches you is that people need proper clothing … Use this as an investment and an invisible weapon … The second lesson is, make good use of your clothes to achieve your goal … [and] increase your own value" (Luoshi 2013, 77–79). Moreover, women need to "develop your obedient, tender, virtuous, and considerate personality" (Jinfei and Gao 2013, 178). Here, the work of self-care adheres to gender norms that are seen as a form of capital. Gendered subjectivity constituted through performances of gender is instrumentalized to increase competitiveness in the job marketplace.

The "bitch mentality" also leads to the instrumentalization of human relationships, discussed in terms of loyalty and collectivity. Gender plays a role in how loyalty is interpreted. For example, "the Yongzheng emperor is like a CEO in a big corporation, he has to pursue profits for the corporation, but also takes care of all kinds of personal relationships in the corporation … Women should learn from Zhen Huan and step into his shoes and think from his perspective in order to be a good employee" (Wang 2013, 56). This discourse emphasizes the power and benevolence of the male boss and the virtue of femininity as obedience and amiability – a discourse that encourages women to stay where they are as the subordinate/symbolic concubine of male superiors. Relatedly, for women, there is an emphasis on collectivity and harmony: "It is important to have a collective goal, this is how all parts can be harmonized and collective spirit be maximized" (Wang 2013, 137). However, loyalty as willing self-subordination and harmony to "stay on your boss's side of the battle" is to "make him feel that you take his side: this will benefit your career" (Wang 2013, 162–164). For men, however, obedience is not emphasized, but rather the ambition to get ahead and into a powerful position: "Loyalty is like a professional skill … In the back palace where power struggles are common, you should not let your loyalty hold you back from your promotion … Behind all your loyal performances, you should really keep your own interests in mind" (Luo 2013, 184–190).[3]

Conclusion: neoliberalism with Chinese characteristics in Taiwan

This chapter has analyzed present-day political rationalities in Taiwan by means of analyzing the governmental discourses circulating through the TV industry and the textual material generated through this "everyday network of government," emphasizing their articulations with the project of Taiwan's neoliberalization through China. As the Taiwanese uptake of *Empresses in the Palace* makes clear, govern-"mentality" in building and developing the culture industry operates through the neoliberal discourse of economization of culture; in particular, the economization of traditional Chinese history and culture which works to the benefit of the pro-KMT, pro-China cross-strait capitalists in Taiwan. At the level of popular culture, we find the economization and commodification of Chinese history in the Zhen Huan-inspired workplace guides which, through a discourse of instrumentalism and materialism, work toward producing selfish, self-responsible and calculating subjects who conform to corporate hierarchy and the spirit of market competition. This subject is gendered to the extent that a woman's body is instrumentalized to be properly feminine while her mind is trained to stay loyal and obedient to the male boss in order to protect her self-interest. The male worker, in contrast, is encouraged to be ambitious.

The production of this worker subjectivity via *Empresses* and its para-texts needs to be analyzed within the context of neoliberalization through China in Taiwan, which as I have discussed, helped to consolidate and legitimize the KMT regime (2008–2016), supported by the elite class of the pro-China, cross-strait capitalists. The maintenance of this political and class power was legitimized by the economization of politics, in the sense that political decisions were taken in order to create an environment where the cross-strait capitalists can be structurally supported to achieve and maintain a dominant position. At the same time, history and culture were also economized according to the logic of political power centered in Chineseness. The notion of Chineseness or traditional Chinese culture in *Empresses* demonstrates a combination of the illiberal, authoritarian hierarchy with the neoliberal market-driven logic of competition. This subjectivity is conducive to a political-economic order of authoritarian neoliberalism on which Taiwan's KMT and China's CCP regimes *both* relied to maintain their power. This "traditional Chinese culture" emphasizes the "naturalness" of social inequality, with competition being the only means of survival, and encourages human greed and selfishness at the expense of the social collectivity. Competition and individualism promulgate self-responsibility. The worsening of economic inequality is acknowledged but tolerated as a "natural" state of being, with individuals to blame for not being able to make it. Young people are particularly singled out for their lack of competitive power and their lack of strength and perseverance to put up with low wages and endure, or "eat bitterness" (吃苦). The blaming of individuals at the same time generates more workplace self-help books that teach people to be obedient to the boss, to compete with their co-workers (and see co-workers in the friend–foe structure) in order to advance in the workplace hierarchy. The pursuit of power and profits leads to the instrumentalization of human relationships, which discourages workers from forming unions or collectivities to challenge power inequality. Further, as noted above, this is also a gendered discourse: while male workers are encouraged to pursue their interests and become powerful, women are encouraged to use their beautiful bodies as capital while staying obedient to the boss.

However, the success of governing at a distance through self-regulation cannot be guaranteed. Convergence culture, while following the logic of commercial interests, also allows for the generation of counter-hegemonic material by users who challenge the government's neoliberal project. The economic inequality brought about by the Chinese model of neoliberal accumulation by dispossession also helped to seed the conditions for the challenge of such unchecked class power. However, the economization of the political sphere, constituted through the neoliberal logic of competition and the friend–foe imaginary, led Taiwan's former government to see dissenters as threats to be eliminated. As a result, young people who protest against trade with China that cements the cross-strait capitalists' power were seen as "terrorists" deserving to be treated with violence (as evidenced by the government's response to the 2014 Sunflower protest movement). Such appeals to police violence to maintain class power undermine the democratic principle that glues Taiwan society into a collectivity. As should be clear by now, the project of neoliberalization through China that I have been critiquing throughout this chapter has consequences that far exceed the media realm to have a very direct impact on contemporary politics and society. Indeed, adherence to such a project has led Taiwan into an uncertain present – and future – where its young democracy may stand at stake.

Notes

1 In 2011, the National Communications Commission threatened to revoke the license for ET Drama Channel (*Dong Sen Xi Jyu Tai*) for its violation of the quota

for imported dramas by featuring mostly Korean dramas. As a result, many TV channels, including ET Drama Channel, switched to importing Chinese dramas because China is officially considered a "special district," not a foreign nation.

2 One popular book in this genre is *Workplace Winner* (1996), written by Chiu Yi, the former legislator and now perpetual political talk show guest both in Taiwan and China.

3 The gendering processes take place in different forms. The cover of Luo Yi's book, composed of cold office chairs, directs his readership to men mostly. Many of the books, however, have feminine markers such as flowers and an infantilized cartoon character from the show. There are also sections specifically directed at women in these books, such as love and dress codes.

References

Clarke, John. 2008. "Living with/in and without Neo-Liberalism." *Focaal* 51: 135–147.

Dirlik, Arif. 2012. "The Idea of a 'Chinese Model': A Critical Discussion." *China Information* 26(3): 277–302.

Edney, Kingsley. 2012. "Soft Power and the Chinese Propaganda System." *Journal of Contemporary China* 21(78): 899–914.

Foucault, Michel. 1990. *The History of Sexuality Volume 2: The Use of Pleasure*. New York: Vintage Books.

Gill, Rosalind. 2003. "From Sexual Objectification to Sexual Subjectification: The Resexualisation of Women's Bodies in the Media." *Feminist Media Studies* 3(1): 100–106.

Hamilton, Gary. 1999. "Asian Business Networks in Transition: or, What Alan Greenspan Does Not Know About the Asian Business Crisis." In *The Politics of the Asian Economic Crisis*, edited by T.J. Pempel, 45–61. Ithaca, NY: Cornell University Press.

Hao, Min-yi. 2009. "'Culture' Activates the 'Fourth Wave of the Economy'" (郝明義「文化」帶動「第四波經濟」). *Commonwealth Magazine* (天下雜誌). www.cw.com.tw/article/article.action?id=5005826 (accessed July 10, 2013).

Hay, James. 2010. "Television as Everyday Network of Government." In *Post-global Network and Everyday Life*, edited by Marina Levina and Grant Kien, 149–176. New York: Peter Lang.

Hou, J.Y. 2013. "The Highest Rating in China's History: A Discovery of the Popularity of *Empresses in the Palace*" (中國大陸史上最高收視紀錄 《甄嬛傳》為何大熱大揭底 圖 – – 《甄嬛傳》能輸出什麼價值觀?). Ent.Aboluowang.com (阿波羅娛樂). tw.aboluowang.com/2013/0228/287480.html (accessed March 3, 2014).

Jenkins, Henry. 2008. *Convergence Culture: Where Old and New Media Collide*. New York: NYU Press.

Jin, Fei, and Gao, Yan (勁飛與高焱). 2013. *The Workplace is the Back Palace: The Base Tactics that Zhen Huan Teaches Me in the Office* (職場即後宮 甄嬛傳教會我的辦公室賤招。) Taipei: Yage Publications (雅各文創).

Kim, Byung-Kook, and Hyug-Baeg Im. 2001. "'Crony Capitalism' in South Korea, Thailand and Taiwan: Myth and Reality." *Journal of East Asian Studies* 1(1): 5–52.

Kipnis, Andrew B. 2008. "Audit Cultures: Neoliberal Governmentality, Socialist Legacy, or Technology of Governing?" *American Ethnologist* 35(2): 275–289.

Kong, Tat Yan. 2004. "Corruption and the Effect of Regime Types: The Case of Taiwan." *New Political Economy* 91(3): 341–364.

Liberty Times. 2012. "*Empresses in the Palace*: Super Popularity, the Three Networks Bombard the Audiences for Another 9 Hours" (《甄嬛傳》超夯 3台再轟炸民眾9小時). Last modified November 30, 2012. news.ltn.com.tw/news/entertainment/breakingnews/730894 (accessed December 1, 2013).

Lin, Lihyun (林麗雲). 2006. "Capital Formation in Taiwan's Television under the Authoritarian Rule" (威權主義下台灣電視資本的形成). *Chinese Journal of Communication Research* 9: 71–111.

Liu, Kan. 2004. *Globalization and Cultural Trends in China*. Honolulu, HI: University of Hawaii Press.

Luo, Y. (羅毅). 2013. *Survival Tactics in the Workplace (The 36 Rules that Zhen Huan Teaches Me)* (甄嬛教會我的36則 職場生存術). Taipei: Zhiyanguan Publication (智言館出版).

Luoshi, B.N. (螺獅拜恩). 2013. *The Knowledge that Huafei Should Know: The Mines that you Should Not Step On in the Workplace* (華妃早知道該多好的道理⊠這些職場地雷千萬不要踩). Taipei: Gobooks Publications (高寶出版社).

McRobbie, Angela. 2013. "Feminism, the Family and the New 'Mediated' Maternalism." *New Formations: A Journal of Culture/Theory/Politics*80–81: 119–137.

Ministry of Culture. 2013. "Special Research Report on the Trend in Audio Visual Industry in 2011" (2011影視產業趨勢研究專題研究報告 – – 電視及電影產業). ntso.gov.tw/BAMID/Code/NewListContent36.aspx?id=583f46f2-9169-44d1-9397-1dd0da4b14e2 (accessed January 5, 2014).

Osburg, John. 2013. *Anxious Wealth: Money and Morality Among China's New Rich*. Stanford, CA: Stanford University Press.

Su, Heng (蘇蘅). 1991. "The Study on the Cultural Implications of TV Programs in Taiwan: A Case Studies on Dialect Programs" (我國電視節目文化意涵的研究:以方言節目為例). PhD diss., National Cheng Chih University.

Tan, Xiao-fang. 2012. "The Six Management Philosophies in *Empresses in the Palace*", (看《甄嬛傳》學到的職場生存六堂課). *Business Weekly*. forum.businessweekly.com.tw/topic.aspx?fid=62&tid=2285 (accessed May 21, 2014).

Wang, X.S. (王小娴). 2013. *From Apprentice to the Ultimate CEO* (從菜鳥到終極*CEO*). Taipei: Da-guan Publication (達觀出版社).

Xiao, H.F. (2010) "Love is a Capacity: The Narrative of Gendered Self-development in Chinese Style Divorce." *Journal of Contemporary China* 19(66): 735–753.

Xin, Qiang. 2010. "Beyond Power Politics: Institution-building and Mainland China's Taiwan Policy Transition." *Journal of Contemporary China* 19(65): 525–539.

Xinhuanet. (新華網). 2007. "Hu Jintao's Report in the 17th Party Meeting" (胡锦涛在党的十七大上的报告). *Xinhuanet* (新華網). news.xinhuanet.com/newscenter/2007-10/24/content_6938568_6.htm (accessed January 5, 2014).

Xiyan (夕顏). 2013. *The 80 Things that Empresses in the Palace Teaches Me* (后宮甄嬛傳教我的八十件事). Taipei: Gobooks Publications (高寶出版社).

XMTV.CN. 2012. "Chinese Dramas Earn Tens of Billions for Taiwanese Television Industry: *Empresses in the Palace* was Broadcast Ten Times in Three Years." (陸劇為台灣電視臺盈利過億《甄嬛傳》3年播10次). Last modified January 25, 2010. big5.cntv.cn/gate/big5/taiwan.xmtv.cn/2014/01/25/VIDE1390619186456299.shtml (accessed December 1, 2013).

Yang, Fang-chih. 2012. "Gender and Popular Culture." In *Gender Dimensions in Taiwanese Society*, edited Shu-ling Huang and Mei-hui You, 107–127. Taipei: Jyu-liu publications (in Chinese).

Yang, Fang-chih Irene. 2015. "Taiyu Serial Dramas in Taiwan: A History of Problem-Making." In *Television Histories in Asia: Issues and Contexts*, edited by Jinna Tay and Graeme Turner, 164–181. New York: Routledge.

Zhao, Y. 2011. "Four Tips that *Empresses in the Palace* Teaches You: The Rules of the Workplace in the Back Palace Dramas" (《后宫甄嬛传》教你四招 从后宫剧看职场上位法则). CRI Online (國際在線). gb.cri.cn/27564/2011/12/31/111s3504824.htm (accessed March 3, 2014).

Zheng, Qifan. 2013. "The Richest 5% vs. the Poorest 5%" (最富5 VS.最窮5 所得差距逾96倍 2011年最富家庭年均所得達463.5萬 最窮僅4.8萬). *Liberty Times* (自由時報). news.ltn.com.tw/news/focus/paper/686924 (accessed February 2, 2014).

Zhu, Ying. 2005. "Yongzheng Dynasty and Chinese Primetime Television Drama". *Cinema Journal* 44(4): 3–17.

Ziyang (子陽). 2013. *The Economics Behind History* (歷史背後的經濟學). Taipei: Jiu-yun Publications (九韵出版社).

7 Media and cultural cosmopolitanism

Asian women in transnational flows

Youna Kim

Cultural cosmopolitanism is part of the structure of feeling associated with modernity at a global level. As this chapter will demonstrate, young women in modern Asia – especially those in subordinate and marginalized positions, discontent with the gendered socioeconomic and cultural conditions of society – are likely to imagine alternative lifestyles and desire to move out of the national and local forms of life and to seek a more open, more inclusive, alternative life experience elsewhere. Globalization, as a mediated cultural force, routinely presents an imaginary of consumer cosmopolitanism that can be commonly shared in the images of something better, seemingly progressive and emancipatory lifestyles. Women's mediated experience as global consumers in everyday life is locally situated but globally connected by imagined, cultural cosmopolitanism. Media consumers, especially of the middle and upper classes in modern urban centers, come to embrace the new and imagine themselves as cosmopolitan participants in global commodity culture.

This chapter will argue that imagined, cultural cosmopolitanism is intrinsically bound up with the intensification of media globalization in Asia and its effects on young women, as it provides a condition for everyday reflexivity and possible self-transformation. Cultural cosmopolitanism expands the framework of the meaning of identity and engages with a self-development project, while encouraging individualization and the liberation of desire from established structures. The social imaginary of global modernity is increasingly present in neoliberal capitalist media culture and everyday cultural practices. Educated, middle-class and upper-class urban young women are held up as exemplars of global modernity. Trying to be mobile transnationals is intimately linked to the experiential tensions rooted in the home, tradition and patriarchal meanings of life that are negotiated through media and cultural consumption. Imagined, cultural cosmopolitanism is now creating greater motivations to travel beyond the nation and enter a broader sphere of modern experience.

However, does the abstract and decontextualized form of global consumer cosmopolitanism move beyond its own abstraction? Whose cosmopolitanism is it? Based on ethnographic data on Korean, Japanese and Chinese women caught up in transnational flows, this chapter will consider how East Asian women make sense of their own transnational lives and globalized media consumption, and examine the paradoxical consequences for their identities. The consequence of actually embracing the world is not necessarily an increased significance and better potentiality of cosmopolitanism. This chapter will argue that, as a lived experience, the possibility of becoming cosmopolitan subjects is contingent upon discursive dialogic encounters with global Others, context-sensitive relational experience, and exclusionary practices. The possibility of cosmopolitan identity requires taking account of uneven social relations of power, cultural difference and situated human contexts in which one defines the self and Others not necessarily in terms of pleasures but in terms of tensions to cope with. Actual border-crossing movements may not produce better conditions for the development of cosmopolitan identity, but may involve rejection or resistance. Overall, this chapter will recognize these resulting paradoxes by discussing in detail four interrelated themes: first, everyday reflexivity; second, female individualization; third, transnational mobility; and fourth, cosmopolitanism as global consumer culture.

Media and reflexivity in everyday life[1]

The media involve complex processes of social change and transition – from the conduct of everyday life, to the reflexive understanding of a global world, to the construction of a new identity and a constant tension in its expression within the everyday (Kim 2005, 2008, 2011, 2012). Media globalization in Asia needs to be recognized as a proliferating, indispensable, yet highly complex and contradictory resource for the construction of identity within the experience of everyday life. The media are central to everyday reflexivity; that is, the capacity to monitor action and its contexts to keep in touch with the grounds of everyday life, confront uncertainties, and understand the relationships between cause and effect, yet never quite control the complex dynamics of everyday life. Reflexivity is an everyday practice. It is intrinsic to human activity, since human beings routinely keep in touch with the grounds of what they do, what they think and what they feel, in a circular feedback mechanism. However, there is a different and significant process in contemporary everyday life, which has changed the very nature of reflexivity by providing conditions for increased capacities for reflexivity in the light of new information and knowledge (Giddens 1991). The difference consists in the scale of information and knowledge made available in a global modern condition under which reflexivity takes place. This heightened reflexivity involves the routine incorporation of new information and knowledge into environments of action that are thereby reconstituted or reorganized. It can operate more intensively not in a situation of greater and greater certainty, but in one of methodological doubt in the ambivalence of modernity, as a way of dealing with social change and defining how to act. Everyday people have the ability to reflect on the social conditions of their existence and to change them accordingly, going beyond traditional markers and the givens of social order (Beck et al. 1994). Reflexivity is increasingly understood, in contemporary Western/European social theory, to be central to the constitution of subjects under conditions of global modernity.

The question, however, is to what extent and in what ways? Whose reflexivity? It should be recognized that reflexivity is experienced differently by different social subjects in different social locations, defining those societies as distinctive (Kim 2005, 2008). Reflexivity should not be understood as a universal capacity of subjects or a generalized experience that cuts across social divides (Beck 1998), but should be understood in specific life world contexts where reflexivity arises unevenly and often ambiguously with competing reflexivities. There is a need to recognize situated reflexivity, specifying the different experiences of reflexivity situated within different social spaces. The degrees of reflexivity and its particular character and content may differ in Asia – stronger and weaker, emotional and rational, positive and negative in its implications – which can be recognized within specific, everyday life contexts.

It is in the everyday that the reflexive and cultural dimensions of the media are worked through, through the various ways in which women engage with and incorporate the media into the familiar, ordinary and more or less secure routines of their everyday life, while constructing relationships and meanings within it (Kim 2005, 2008). It is also in everyday life that genuine "creations" are achieved, those creations that women produce as part of the process of becoming human; the human life world that is not defined simply by historical, ideological and political super-structures, by totality or society as a whole, but defined by this intermediate and mediating level of everyday life or the "power of everyday life" (Lefebvre 1971).

The media are among sources of the creation, the working out of significance in everyday practices. They give shape to the social and cultural environments of everyday life and provide a framework for making sense of the world; herein lies the possibility of a multitude of meanings to emerge and circulate. The circulation and movement of meaning, or mediation (Martin-Barbero 1993), involves a constant yet dialectical transformation of meaning with consequences, whether intended or unintended, significant or insignificant. The media are central to everyday experience – as a mediating, not determining, process through which women constitute and reconstitute identities in their distinctiveness within a shared, yet contested and highly differentiated social space governed by different power, resources and constraints. Although media consumption may not lead to dramatic social or political change in the short run, and although the importance of the transformations generated by the media in the long run are problematically obscured by the attention to short-run immediate effects (ibid.), women's mundane changes, imagination and critical reflection triggered by the media and expressed in the practices of everyday life can be the basis of social constitution (Kim 2008).

Case study

The following data from my ethnographic research in Korea demonstrate that reflexivity is an integral process of media talk and that women's reflections on themselves and their worlds are major elements of their experiences of the media in everyday life (for details, see Kim 2005, 2006). In order to understand how popular media culture, television in particular, intersects with the everyday lives of Korean women of different generations and classes, I conducted fieldwork which included a varied sample of women in their twenties, thirties and fifties from both working-class and middle-class backgrounds: six different socioeconomic categories, with seven women in each category. This case study draws on the accounts of the middle-class women in their twenties, as this younger age group demonstrated an active use of global television, now available on the Internet at any time.

> English is a must for employment [in Korea]. I withdrew from the university for one year and went to Australia for an English course. To brush up English now, I keep the TV on and listen to CNN, drama, movies. Who would find CNN interesting? But it's good for a listening practice. I don't find American drama interesting, but it's best for learning spoken English.

Transnational culture today tends to be tied to the job market. English, as a language of global modernity and a means of making a living, has become a crucial precondition for women's attainment of well-paid work and economic independence. As a consequence, these young women learn English, whether they like it or not. Learning English and involving themselves in wider Western culture through travel and global television are distinctive characteristics of the lives of middle-class women. Their openness towards new cultural experiences is increasingly self-reflexive, characterized more by a search for "differences" rather than universalities. What is common to this experience is a "learning of the self" that is reflexively interpreted and understood by a contrast between imagined (Western) freedom and practical (Korean) restrictions. The following extract illustrates what some young women mean by Western free lifestyles, and its details reveal some of the constraints on being free in Korean society:

> In *Friends* [an American comedy drama], they often get together in the coffee shop and chat sitting comfortably on the sofa. None of them seem to worry about life or work. Everyday life is just ha-ha-ho-ho happy and simple. They don't seem to have a nice job, yet life is jolly. The long blond works in the coffee shop as a waitress. The tall stupid woman sings stupid songs. Did they go to university? Probably they did, they don't look smart though. In Korean society, if we are a university graduate and work in a coffee shop, people will think of us as a total loser. Not to

> mention parents' fury, "Have I sent you to university to see you work in a coffee shop?" None of their parents seem to compel, "Quit fooling around, get married and settle down!" In their culture it seems OK to fool around and enjoy life. Because nobody interferes in their life. I like such free social atmosphere.

This remark illuminates the media's great capacity for evoking reflexivity in an endless chain of referentiality, intersected with the microcosms of everyday life. In the context of new cultural experiences, Korean ways of life and traditional norms are interrogated and criticized. Young middle-class women commonly criticize Korean gender models and appropriate forms of behavior predicated on rigidly defined matrimonial roles, family expectations and direct parental control. On the other hand, they derive new interpretations of life through Western images of free lifestyles. Significantly, their yearning for Western freedom crystallizes around the meaning of "individualization," which is fundamentally incompatible with traditional family values. The intensified self-reflexivity signals a deliberately hopeful movement, a transformative quest for individualization.

Female individualization

The troubling signs of female individualization as intersected with everyday media culture have become a new arena of anxiety for women in contemporary Asia (Kim 2010, 2012). Signs of female individualization have been proliferating as a defining feature of contemporary modes of identity, albeit untenable and ambivalent, within the discursive regime of self – embodied in regulatory practices in society where individualism is not placed at the heart of its culture. Arguably, the media are central to the signs of emergent cultures of female individualization producing the alternative social, cultural and symbolic relations women wish to live within and define the kind of self they wish to become.

From the 1980s onward, women in Asia have gained higher levels of education and the commensurate expectations have become a driving motor in women's aspirations for work, economic power, independence, freedom and self-fulfillment. However, women often experience gendered labor market inequity, setting limits on patterns of participation, reinforcing women's socioeconomic position on the margins of work systems, and thus revealing the illusion of the language of choice that the new capacities of education appear to promise. The enlargement of choice can be particularly illusory for women in contemporary Asia, where gendered socioeconomic and cultural conditions persist and continue to structure labor market outcomes and lifestyles (Kim 2005, 2011, 2012).

In contemporary Korea, 95.3 percent of women go to high school and 63.0 percent of women go on to higher education. Similarly, high school education in Japan has also reached equal levels for men (96.0 percent) and women

(96.7 percent), and 45.3 percent of the women advance to higher education (Kim 2012). Young women in urban China, who were born in the era of the single-child policy with the emphasis on individual success, have become the focus of parental expectations and the product of a fiercely competitive education system, in which gender difference is not recognized (Thornham and Feng 2012). Despite the impressive level of higher education in Korea, only 46.7 percent of female university graduates are employed, mostly on traditional female career tracks such as non-managerial and secretarial positions. A wage differential of 76 percent compared with male wages gives Korean women little economic security. Japanese women in full-time employment earn only 65 percent of male wages, far from being economically rewarding or emotionally fulfilling (Kim 2012). Middle-class women in urban China have to compete for jobs in a post-socialist context in which gender difference, officially denied in their school years, seems "suddenly very pronounced" (Thornham and Feng 2012). Increasingly, educated Asian women are choosing to invest their resources into their career, rather than into marriage and family. The average age of marriage for Japanese women increased from 24.5 in 1975 to 28.5 in 2008, making Japan one of the latest-marrying populations in the world. Non-marriage for women has become common in many urban areas of East Asia (Jones 2005).

The social transformations in urban Asia appear to engender similar, but not quite the same, trends and consequences of individualization which are notably linked to contemporary Western/European social theory (Giddens 1991; Beck and Beck-Gernsheim 2002). Western individualization is characterized by a growing emphasis on individual autonomy and independence from traditions and social institutions. Women are now released from traditional gender roles, and find themselves forced to build up a "life of their own" by way of the labor market, training and mobility (Beck and Beck-Gernsheim 2002). Confronted with a plurality of choices, individuals' life politics are organized around an increasingly reflexive and calculable mode of thinking to colonize the future with some degree of success (Giddens 1991). At the heart of life politics lie enterprising agents, who strategically plan, avidly self-monitor and manage a life of their own.

However, what it means to be a free and independent individual in Asian societies is a more complex and paradoxical issue. What does individualization mean in the context of the family? Traditional external constraints on marriage and family, and the hetero-normative expectation of marriage by the age of 30 in East Asia, have not progressively disappeared. The family, not the individual, is still the basic unit of social reproduction. Oftentimes, an imagined future of individualization is simultaneously organized around the modalities of marriage and family. Amidst the proliferation of the media, the seeming pluralization of choices in life and the deepening of the self, ongoing identity work is struggled over by women, who create the expressive possibilities for identity transformation but may also face considerable difficulties, or may still not know which way they are going (Kim 2012).

Transnational mobility

The limitations and contradictions of female individualization in Asia are continually salient yet unresolved, giving rise to transnational mobility as a temporary solution and a form of departure from a socially expected, normative biography. From the mid-1980s onward, there has been a rising trend of women leaving their country to experience life overseas either as tourists or students, eventually surpassing the number of men engaging in foreign travel. Women are travelling out of Korea, Japan and China for very different reasons from those that sent them into the diaspora only 20 years ago. Women's desire to move is constituted by contradictory contemporary socioeconomic relations, as well as by the cultural-symbolic forms by which everyday life is lived out, rethought and rearticulated in its intersection with the emergence of precarious individualized identities.

Case study

This phenomenon frequently figures in women's imagination of the West through the everyday media, as demonstrated in the following data from my ethnographic research on Korean, Japanese and Chinese women in their twenties and early thirties (for details, see Kim 2010, 2011). This case study offers insights into the implications of women's migration, with data drawn from personal in-depth interviews and diaries. I conducted interviews with 60 women (20 Koreans, 20 Japanese, 20 Chinese) who had been living and studying in the UK/London for three to seven years. The women's ages were between 26 and 33 years: single women of middle-class and upper-class status. Also, a panel of 30 diarists (ten Koreans, ten Japanese, ten Chinese) were recruited from the women interviewed and asked to write/email diaries about their experiences and to express in detail key issues raised from the interviews. This method was designed to generate biographical material accounts from the women and incorporate a reflexive biographical analysis.

> My job might be OK, my life might be OK compared to my mother's [in Korea]. But I didn't feel happy, couldn't be satisfied with just that! I have bigger desires … The more I got to know bigger things through the media, the more I thought about them.
>
> This [Korean drama] showed beautiful scenery of Cambridge and London where they met while studying. It's a typical romance, an illusion made by TV. But I wanted to believe that could happen. Life would feel different there … I imagined myself and anticipated to go.

Young Korean women appear to have more choices and capacities in life, higher education and better material provisions compared with past generations, yet this does not necessarily translate into greater happiness. Expectations of satisfaction have risen, affected by what other people have or insatiably, endlessly desire to have, which occurs by the intrusion of cultural Others through the media and has the consequence of causing both rising expectations and rising frustration. The construction of an autonomous illusion ("I wanted to believe that could happen"), the ability to create an illusion which is known to be false but felt to be true, suggests that the knowing individual creates the existence for herself in her imagination. Considerable meaning is gained, not merely from the illusion but from "imagining that illusion as actuality," mobilizing the self towards a hoped-for future.

> So sick and tired of office work [in Japan], one day I decided to do nothing and watched this film *Notting Hill*. Romance, freedom, laughter, London parks are so green! I felt, go there! It makes you feel something good can happen there ... You know that is an illusion but you want to believe that illusion and go.

The aestheticization and romanticization of Western cities is known to be false but felt to be suggestive of possibility: "something good can happen there." A general awareness of the link between media consumption and physical displacement exists in the Japanese women's emotional investment in the media at a level of utopian sensibility. It is intertwined with the good feelings the media embody and evoke. The media certainly construct an illusion or an image of something better that women's day-to-day lives do not provide, but it is the intelligently detectable illusion that is put to work by the knowing individuals with intentionality of knowledge: "You know that is an illusion but you want to believe that illusion and go."

> Life in China is so competitive, crowded and stressful. People work so hard, try to survive and win in competitive society ... Bus is so crowded that you have to squeeze in. There is no space for your self. I started the everyday with this crowded bus ... A bus ride in the West seemed fun, pleasant [on TV], people easily got on and got off. Wouldn't it be nice to live in that environment? I saw this empty bus on TV a long time ago but still remember ... Here, London bus is not crowded, most of time I can sit down and think. There is a space for thinking about my self.

This mediated experience can powerfully create and allow a space for the self to emerge in the fluidities of transnational imagination, while engaging with a newly found curiosity and a search for a new self that can be played out and actualized. Different ways to conceive the self are emerging in more individualist terms marked by an outward-looking reflexivity. Contemporary Chinese female identities are being shaped by cultural consumption within mediated transnational networks. Chinese women have been subject to different imaginary social spaces which enable them to reflect upon their lived experiences within multiple and competing regimes of identification, expanding potentialities for self-invention that the divergent cultural experiences give rise to and mobilize.

Cosmopolitanism: beyond global consumer culture?

East Asian women's mediated experience, as discussed above, can have the effect of transforming their sense of self, of the world beyond and their imagined place in it, while mobilizing the sedimented orientation toward displacement. New kinds of transnational networks, connections and various capacities for mobility are now changing not only the scale and patterns of migration but also the nature of migrant experience and thinking. Importantly, a provisional nomadic sensibility ("willing to go anywhere for a while") has been facilitated by the mediation of rapidly evolving media technologies (Kim 2011). Transnational Asian women on the move may appear to be new signifiers of change or self-expressive icons of hybridity with possibilities for self-creation that liberate thinking from localism and make a break to a transgressive, rootless identity. Are they becoming cosmopolitan subjects? Can they afford a cosmopolitan identity?

In the current debate on transnational mobility, cosmopolitanism has become the privileged term of analysis for characterizing qualities in people and their identities. Transnational groups are figured as the bearers of deterritorialized cosmopolitanism, as "always already cosmopolitan," moving beyond the grasp of any individual state. Their cultures are characterized as worldly, productive sites of crossing and as exemplary instances of active resistance to national cultures and localism (Clifford 1992; Bhabha 1994). The recent revitalization of cosmopolitanism has been in fashion since the 1990s, amid the intensifying globalization of late liberalism, capital, mobility and the media. Greater frequency of travel and transnational media and cultural flows create a zone in which emergent global forms of cosmopolitanism are brought into a conflictual relationship with nationalist forms of culture (Appadurai 1996). Such a condition called cosmopolitanism, mixed with the vision of a global, hybrid and rootless culture, has been celebrated as an alternative to ethnocentric nationalism. Cosmopolitanism suggests a more outward-looking disposition, a mode of engaging with the world and such an experiential openness and willingness towards divergent cultural experiences (Hannerz 1990). In its cultural and political dimensions, cosmopolitanism lives a double life: a pop cultural evocation of openness to a larger world, and a political claim about the moral significance of transcending the local, even achieving the universal (Calhoun 2008). Invoked as a moral and ethical ideal, cosmopolitanism means learning from each other's differences through conversation and taking an interest in the practices and beliefs that lend them significance (Appiah 2006). It represents a normative philosophy transcending all identities – a universal identification that does not place love/loyalty of country ahead of love of mankind and universal humanity (Nussbaum 1997), assuming that extensive learning of human diversity will lead to a finding of common human qualities and purposes. The cosmopolitan position of the so-called "citizen of the world" indicates the impending obsolescence of national cultural identity or national self that is understood as a naturalized ideological constraint to be overcome (Beck 2006). This emergent form of cosmopolitanism has come to be cast as a potentially liberatory space, a locus of progressive politics and rejection of parochial nationalist positions. In short, much of the theory on cosmopolitanism suggests that existing transnational movements give rise to the emergence of new world communities with emancipatory forms of global consciousness and lifestyles.

Case study

Who is it that experiences cosmopolitanism? As this case study will demonstrate, frequent border crossings in the wake of globalization do not necessarily generate greater levels of cosmopolitan attitudes and motivations. Cosmopolitanism is readily identifiable by globalized media cultures and media talk as imagined cultural space, but not necessarily as lived experience. The social reality of cosmopolitanism is much more ambiguous, marked by global structures of power and inequality, exclusion and inclusion governing one's relationship to Others and the world. The following data from my ethnographic research in the UK/London will foreground the tensions and struggles at the heart of the cosmopolitan subject in a hierarchically defined world of the West (for details, see Kim 2011).

Korean women: "We never invented cosmopolitanism"

> They have no interest in us. Whether inside school life or outside, depending on whom we meet, depending on the luck! Generally they don't bother to know about us.
>
> Some people ask, "Are you from North Korea or South Korea? When are you going back home?" I do not say it aloud but continually feel racism, everyday little things that I try to ignore. I say "not aloud" because what we have to say will not matter to them anyway.
>
> I don't feel connection in human interactions. I come to realize, why try to know them when they don't try to know us?

"They have no interest in us." Much of the motivation and possibility of becoming cosmopolitan subjects depends on the contexts, discursive and communicative encounters and common existential experiences. Britain, London in particular, has been a center of the renewed talk of cosmopolitanism since the 1990s, with developments towards globalization, European integration and rebranding of cities to attract financial and cultural investment and tourism, envisaging a space for the transformation of national identity to cosmopolitan Britain (Calhoun 2008). Cultural difference and human pluralism have been revalued as resources and opportunities and appropriated into the re-visioning of the cosmopolitan space, yet this can present an exclusionary rhetoric, rather than an open-minded interest or an awareness of the existence and equal validity of other cultures. In celebrating the supposedly inclusive cosmopolitan consciousness, which forms of cultural difference are seen as desirable and valued, and which are excluded? A world of increasing flows of people and cultural melange with its allure of diversity and cosmopolitan gloss may appear to be a comfort zone for strangers, but they are routinely confronted with an implicit racism ("everyday little things"), subtly signaled hostility that can coexist without manifesting conflicts and come to be internalized. Any possible viability of cosmopolitan identity formation is seen to be a relative one ("depending on whom we meet"), hence, a matter of luck and contingency, more than a matter of choice; one cannot freely choose and operate its potentiality through one's own agency alone. Cosmopolitanism should be understood as a situated and relational experience. It is a dialogic formation in the specific contexts encountered, wherein the meaning of identity operates from its interaction with a system of differences and the inequitable exercise of power shapes the extent of one's belonging, or non-belonging, to the world as a whole. A resulting response by the excluded ethnic minorities is often feelings of rejection and self-doubt, characterized by a reflexive distantiation and potentially subversive resistance, or a self-determined withdrawal from cosmopolitan openness ("why try to know them when they don't try to know us?"), through a hidden contestation of asymmetrical knowledge and asymmetrical ignorance.

> I will always be a foreigner. I feel so alone. There is a boundary like a wide river between us and them, which cannot be crossed … We hear people in the classroom talk about cosmopolitanism. We just listen. Whatever that means, it is their idea. We never invented cosmopolitanism. If that means following them, losing our own identity, it is meaningless to desire that.

"We never invented cosmopolitanism." A strong disassociation or repudiation from the concept of cosmopolitanism as a Western invention, as well as its situated reason, can be underpinned by the marginalizing experiences of unequal, West-centric contexts and sometimes antagonistic human interactions. This affective and lived dimension of displacement can reinforce non-cosmopolitanism and, even more, anti-cosmopolitanism. An increasing awareness of global connectivity through the media and imagined cosmopolitanism back home may project an inclusive world of strangers that openly receives them, yet the actual experience of inhabiting the world is often devoid of social affiliation and can be unbearably lonely. The consequence of increasing transnational movement is not necessarily the emergence of robust cosmopolitan subjects and a loss of distinctive identity, of difference that undermines its own cultural particularity. Transnational mobility does not easily generate a cosmopolitanizing experience of the world, a fluid and extended sense of belonging beyond national boundaries, but rather presents concrete manifestations of the limits of imagined, cultural cosmopolitanism.

Japanese women: "Just imagine through the media but cannot act"

> People ask, "Are you from Japan?," so I say, "Yes, I am from Tokyo." Then they really like it! They ask lots of questions … They want to know about the Japanese hair style and kimono, temples, how to use traditional wrapping cloth that we don't even use now … They worship us. In their fantasy, they want to believe we wear kimono usually and serve tea nicely.
>
> They seem to know Japanese culture through the media … geisha in kimono, Pokémon, advanced technologies … I came here to become modern and independent, not a traditional Japanese woman. But Western men like traditional images of Japanese women, and they expect traditional Japanese women when meeting us.

The overall interest in, or fascination with, the appeal of a uniquely Japanese culture in touch with tradition signifies the modern West's desire to be cosmopolitan by intermixing with Japanese otherness in its capacity and willingness to take pleasure from the transnational cultural exchange. The representation of Japan in the Western popular imagination is paradoxical and complex: on one hand, the Western fear of Japanese corporations, economic power and powerful masculine nationalism by which Japan is seen as a site of potential threat, but on the other hand, the Western attraction to an orientalist fantasy and subservient object of desire ("geisha in kimono"), which is constructed through the West's sexualization and feminization of Japanese culture. Gendering Japan as female (Yamamoto 1999) is the primary mechanism through which Western discourse controls and shapes the ideological image of Japan. Japanese media culture has increasingly invented an identity of "cool Japan" as a form of cultural nationalism through technologically advanced, utopian and futuristic entertainment including animated movies, comics and video games, while establishing distinctively Japanese styles and particularism that are differentiated not only by Japan but also by the West. If multicultural diversity is celebrated in a cosmopolitan vision of the world, Japan could stand in a distinctive, albeit ambiguous, positioning within the reciprocal recognition. Cosmopolitanism, as a relational and dialogic term, operates within the contexts of encounters, favorable or unfavorable, inclusive or exclusive, thereby a cosmopolitan possibility may emerge or not. Such interplay may generate a situated, but characteristically thin cosmopolitanism: even while women denounce and repudiate Japan's traditional masculine culture, they become more attached to the place called home with its cultural particularities, yet simultaneously embracing pleasure from the interactions with the modern West; however, in contradictory and implicitly forced ways ("they want to believe we wear kimono usually") with struggles in the language of paradox ("they expect traditional Japanese women").

> They are interested in traditional Japanese culture I don't even know about. This is a surprising discovery. I have to learn to explain to them.
>
> In Japan, I was not Japanese. I was liberal, against old traditions. I preferred the Western world and imagined changing my self through the media … I just imagine through the media but cannot act. I am becoming more Japanese while living abroad … There is no reason to change or become like them. Being distinctively Japanese is an advantage.

The Western worship of traditional Japanese otherness, often seen as accidental knowledge ("surprising discovery") to many women on the move, can impact upon and interplay with how women come to redefine a new subject position: "just imagine through the media but cannot act." The fluidity of conceptions of identity and change were once powerfully imagined through the Western media and occidental longings in their homeland, but the actual interactions – discursive and communicative encounters with the West – recontextualize such imagined cosmopolitan identification and precariously expose, or impose to some extent, a fixed categorical distinction of Japaneseness. Why be a woman of the world? The motivational reasons, which would allow for the possibility of cosmopolitan subjectivity and the determination to act on it, depend on what distinction and gain stand to be made, to what end. Far from a robust cosmopolitan projection, a self-determined reaction to how best to act from the learning of cosmopolitan knowledge rather foregrounds a national self through the distinctiveness of cultural difference, representing Japaneseness even more strongly than before ("becoming more Japanese") in the relational experience of the transnational field. Ironically, the so-called cosmopolitan city may be confronted with the dynamics of nationalisms of mobile transnationals, who conceive themselves primarily as national, orient themselves toward a sense of distinct identity and differentiation, and sustain its potency and relevance, while dealing with the ambivalent tensions of the working of identity in response to the hegemonic worship of otherness as well as to what are perceived as common problems.

Chinese women: "We are seen as a problem"

> I see how Western people think about Chinese through the media … we are uncivilized, even dangerous immigrants, pollute the world … we are seen as a problem.
>
> They have negative images about us. I explain history but give up! They are the top of the mountain. The superior vs. inferior judgment is fixed. Even if I so wish to be cosmopolitan, I alone cannot be cosmopolitan.

> Despite weak English I tried to talk to Western students at school parties … They leave us alone. They think they know about everything. There is no common subject to talk about. We become mixed with people like us … I know Chinese women married to British men. What do they talk about?

Crucially, much of the cosmopolitan possibility, willingness and motivation, is predicated upon the context of encountering otherness and the way in which cultural identity is projected: "we are seen as a problem." China's constitutive cultural difference appears to be perceived as bearers of potential problems, or lacks, hardly desirable sources of cosmopolitan unity. Social distance and tensions are expressed by the excluded women who find seemingly inescapable orientalist projections ("uncivilized, even dangerous") in Eurocentric discourses that tend to create a threatening Other in order to construct a universalized self (Pan 2004), a Western normality that may secure the West's self-imagination and self-affirmation ("top of the mountain," "know about everything"). World cities like London deploy and celebrate cosmopolitan signifiers, cultural diversity and multiculturalism, yet these values are celebrated highly selectively. The media frequently evoke warnings that China has destroyed as much as it has created (Macfarlane and Yan 2004). Cosmopolitanism is not a free-floating, but a situated and relational term operating from a degree of dialogic experience and a mode of interaction in a global system of differences. Cosmopolitan identity, if any, is not in itself a matter of choice. Although one may choose to be a cosmopolitan ("I so wish to be"), one cannot automatically be cosmopolitan by oneself. One's willing agency is not a sufficient condition, since the cosmopolitan possibility or what seems like free individual choice is highly contingent upon, and regulated by, mutual understanding and validation, recognition of otherness as equally worthy of respect, if not always necessarily desirable. In the internationalized academy, the mere mixture and co-presence may not give rise to new forms of global subjectivity and cross-cultural dialogue. The lived reality is quite segregated ("mixed with people like us"), without a depth of encounters across national cultural boundaries.

> I am becoming more Chinese … Shopping here [in London] is easier, more choices. Through the Internet we easily connect to users who know where to buy brands at affordable prices … I have a collection of Western perfumes. A Western roommate said, "You are not a Chinese any more."
>
> If people ask, "Where are you from?" I say, "I am Chinese" instead of saying "I am from China." Being Chinese is the unchangeable truth.

The resulting consequence can be described as a more rigidly inscribed national body ("becoming more Chinese"), yet wrapped in a more conspicuous cosmopolitan consumer culture to the extent of its misunderstanding and negation to the eyes of encounters ("not a Chinese anymore"). The key to an understanding of cosmopolitanism lies in the realm of media cultural consumption and the realistic possibility of the transformation of excluded ethnic groups into interchangeable global consumers, if not citizens, enabled by global capital and the media transcending time and space in different world cultures. For many women, cosmopolitanism may be limited to a world that is an object of consumption: a wider range of options available to be consumed for pleasure and gratification in constrained lives. Beneath that apparent cosmopolitan consumption practice, a profound process of nationalism is at work, deemed one of the central forces for identification and belonging in displacement, which involves a painful struggle for a dialogue, understanding and reciprocal respect for each other's constitutive cultures constructed differently in historical embeddedness. Women's struggle implicitly carries a denial and repudiation of an exclusionary form of cosmopolitanism that is not as acceptable or accessible to them.

Conclusion

Cosmopolitanism as a lived experience may not actually exist, but imagined, cultural cosmopolitanism prevails within the realm of global consumer culture. Apparently, in localized settings back home, more widespread and mundane experience of the cosmopolitan existed as new forms of consumer subjectivity, cultural disposition and cultural transformations invoked by the global forces of the media. Often, young East Asian women talk about their sense of identity in relation to popular culture consumption practices while resisting systems of inequality and simultaneously generating imaginations of alternative lifestyles and work; therefore, transnational subjectivities are possibly constituted in and through their "imagination" and reflexive "talk" about popular media culture (Kim 2005, 2011).

However, the consequence that follows from the actual border-crossing movements may not produce better conditions for the development of a cosmopolitan identity. The actual experience of transnational mobility is inevitably caught up within the uneven transnational field and its relational context with the hierarchical emphasis on difference and diversity. The unconditional inclusiveness of the cosmopolitan theoretical formulation, its theoretically claimed openness and recognition of difference, can consign particular nations or ethnic groups to peripheral status, non-acceptance and subordination. While such a celebratory manifestation of cosmopolitan inclusiveness may occur for, and motivate, some people, others may find this way of life not as progressive or emancipatory. Moving beyond national boundaries and moving freely into other cultures and societies can reveal a sense of intensified contradictions (Kim 2011).

Acknowledgements

This chapter is based on a part of my empirical research and book, *Transnational Migration, Media and Identity of Asian Women: Diasporic Daughters* (Routledge, 2011).

Note

1 This section appears in both Kim 2008 and 2013.

References

Appadurai, Arjun. 1996. *Modernity at Large*. Minneapolis, MN: University of Minnesota Press.

Appiah, Kwame Anthony. 2006. *Cosmopolitanism: Ethics in a World of Strangers*. New York: Norton.

Beck, Ulrich. 1998. *World Risk Society*. Cambridge: Polity.

Beck, Ulrich. 2006. *Cosmopolitan Vision*. Cambridge: Polity.

Beck, Ulrich, and Elisabeth Beck-Gernsheim. 2002. *Individualization*. London: Sage.

Beck, Ulrich, Anthony Giddens, and Scott Lash. 1994. *Reflexive Modernization: Politics, Tradition and Aesthetics in the Modern Social Order*. Cambridge: Polity.

Bhabha, Homi. 1994. *The Location of Culture*. New York: Routledge.

Calhoun, Craig. 2008. "Cosmopolitanism in the Modern Social Imaginary." *Daedalus* 127(3): 105–114.

Clifford, James. 1992. "Travelling Cultures." In *Cultural Studies*, edited by Lawrence Grossberg, Cary Nelson, and Paula Treichler, 96–116. New York: Routledge.

Giddens, Anthony. 1991. *Modernity and Self-identity: Self and Society in the Late Modern Age*. Cambridge: Polity.

Hannerz, Ulf. 1990. "Cosmopolitans and Locals in World Culture." In *Global Culture: Nationalism, Globalization and Modernity*, edited by Mike Featherstone, 237–254. London: Sage.

Jones, Gavin W. 2005. "The Flight from Marriage in South-East and East Asia." *Journal of Comparative Family Studies* 36(1): 93–119.

Kim, Youna. 2005. *Women, Television and Everyday Life in Korea: Journeys of Hope*. London: Routledge.

Kim, Youna. 2006. "The Body, TV Talk and Emotion: Methodological Reflections." *Cultural Studies/Critical Methodologies* 6(2): 226–244.

Kim, Youna. 2008. *Media Consumption and Everyday Life in Asia*. London: Routledge.

Kim, Youna. 2010. "Female Individualization?: Transnational Mobility and Media Consumption of Asian Women." *Media, Culture & Society* 32(1): 25–43.

Kim, Youna. 2011. *Transnational Migration, Media and Identity of Asian Women: Diasporic Daughters*. London: Routledge.

Kim, Youna. 2012. *Women and the Media in Asia: The Precarious Self*. London: Palgrave Macmillan.

Kim, Youna. 2013. *The Korean Wave: Korean Media Go Global*. London and New York: Routledge.

Lefebvre, Henri. 1971. *Everyday Life in the Modern World*. London: Penguin.

Macfarlane, Alan, and Xiaoxiao Yan. 2004. "China Diaries." *Cambridge Anthropology* 24(2): 75–90.

Martin-Barbero, Jesus. 1993. *Communication, Culture and Hegemony.* London: Sage.

Martin-Barbero, Jesus. 2003. "Cultural Change: The Perception of the Media and the Mediation of its Images." *Television & New Media* 4(1): 85–106.

Nussbaum, Martha. 1997. *Cultivating Humanity.* Cambridge, MA: Harvard University Press.

Pan, Chengxin. 2004. "The 'China Threat' in American Self-imagination: The Discursive Construction of Other as Power Politics." *Alternatives: Global, Local, Political* 29(3): 305–331.

Thornham, Sue, and FengPengpeng. 2012. "Just a Slogan: Individualism, Post-feminism and Female Subjectivity in Consumerist China." In *Women and the Media in Asia: The Precarious Self*, edited by Youna Kim, 96–114. London: Palgrave Macmillan.

Yamamoto, Traise. 1999. *Masking Selves, Masking Subjects.* Berkeley, CA: University of California Press.

8 Differential (im)mobilities

Imaginative transnationalism in Taiwanese women's travel TV

Fran Martin

This chapter focuses on how television travel shows in Taiwan that are targeted at and/or popular with female audiences mediate the wider cultural imagination of available gendered identities.[1] By considering how these programs represent the relationship between women and transnational mobility, I explore how they connect with the ongoing transformation of gender as a result of economic, cultural, social and demographic change in Taiwan today. This is interesting, in the first instance, because as feminist geographers have long insisted, questions of mobility and immobility are always gendered questions; and historically, in Taiwan as elsewhere, women have tended to be associated with home, family and stasis, while the outside world, work and movement have been culturally gendered as masculine (Massey 1991; Hanson 2010). In light of that, the tendency in Taiwanese popular media over the past ten-odd years to represent women in association with mobilities at various scales comes as an interesting development (Shaw and Lin 2012). My focus is on the televisual imagination of women's international mobility in travel and lifestyle programs directed at and/or largely watched by female audiences. The popularity of such programs raises a series of questions. What has materially changed to make such representations possible? How are such shows "implicated in the imaginative pull toward mobility" (Kim 2010, 36)? What kinds of women are imagined in such representations – and imagine themselves – to be the subjects of these types of mobility? What forms of *im*mobility underwrite the new televisual imagination of (certain) women on the move (Massey 1991; Skeggs 2004, 45–61; Sheller and Urry 2006, 210–11)? How does the media imagination of mobile women square with women's actual opportunities for transnational movement?

In exploring these questions, I will present two main examples. These are: first, young, urban Taiwanese women's reception of the Discovery Channel's daughter channel, TLC Taiwan (旅遊生活頻道); second, a locally produced travel show directed at young women considering non-package tourist travel in the Asia-Pacific region, *Miss Traveler* (WOMAN愛旅行/小姐愛旅行, originally produced for free-to-air CTS). Each of these targets female viewers and/or is mainly popular with women; each focuses on a twenty- or thirty-something, unmarried, middle-class female subject; and each associates that subject with potential for transnational mobility. My analyses reveal that both in the minds of female viewers and at a textual level, such programming mediates tensions between the *imagination of women's mobility*, on the one hand, and the *gendered limitations on actual mobility* that women experience, on the other.

Unmarried middle-class women: demographic trends and media imaginaries

Unmarried, urban, middle-class working women in their twenties and thirties represent a growing population in Taiwan today, as they also do in several other East Asian countries (Jones 2007; Dales 2012). Taiwanese women's education rates are high – indeed, their participation rate in higher education, now nearing 90 percent, has for the past two decades exceeded men's – while the gender-wage gap continues to narrow, standing at 16.1 percent in 2013 (comparable to the European Union average) (DGBAS 2014; Ministry of Education Taiwan 2014; Yu and Liu 2014, 239–240). Unmarried women's workforce participation rate has for some years been virtually identical to unmarried men's (60.57 percent of women versus 61.29 percent of men in 2012). However, for women, paid employment drops off markedly after marriage (down to 49.05 percent in 2012), while men's rises (up to 72.14 percent); and by far the most significant reason that unemployed women cite for not taking on paid employment is housework (DGBAS 2013b).[2] Over recent years, a strong trend toward "late" marriage and childbirth has drawn much attention: by 2012, the average age for women's first marriage had risen to 29.5, while 82.8 percent of women between 20–29 remained unmarried, along with 31.4 percent of 30–39 year olds (DGBAS 2012, 2014; *The China Post* 2013).

The above indicators show a trend whereby upon marriage, women tend to transition out of the workforce and into unpaid care work in the domestic sphere. In this situation, it seems, Taiwanese women are collectively deciding to delay the onset of marriage. Interpreting this trend, social analysts point out that with the twin impacts of feminism and women's increased education, a chasm has opened up between dominant understandings of women's social and familial roles, and the way that young women themselves tend to view them (Chen 2009). An older-style ideology that places the major burden of familial care work onto wives' shoulders remains functionally dominant, but now comes into direct conflict with young women's own increasingly post-traditional view of gender roles (Yu and Liu 2014). Along with the availability of paid employment that enables women to support themselves independently, this makes the opportunity cost of marriage significantly higher for women (especially educated women) than for men (Jones 2007, 463).

Taiwanese news media are regularly awash with stories about twenty- and thirty-something women's growing unwillingness to get married, with commentators expressing varying combinations of pop-feminist triumph and conservative anxiety over the growing numbers of highly educated women getting "married to the job" rather than to a husband (Dong 2012). A group of common neologisms describing such women – several of which originated in Japan, where comparable patterns are evident – includes 熟女 (*shounü*: "mature (yet sexy/glamorous) woman"), 輕熟女 (*qingshounü*: "young-mature woman"), 敗犬 (*baiquan*: "loser dog"; i.e. unmarried woman over 25), 剩女 (*shengnü*: "leftover woman"), and 勝女/盛女 (*shengnü*: "triumphant woman": pop-feminist re-scriptings of the derogatory homophone "leftover woman"). The wide currency of such terms indicates the extent of social anxiety and popular debate over women's "late" and non-marriage in Taiwan today (Yang 2002; Martin 2016).

The analysis that I present below shows how some unmarried, middle-class women cultivate a *mobile imaginary* as a key aspect of their identity, and how travel television responds to this emergent conceptual linkage between unmarried middle-class women and the potential for international mobility. Such a linkage is to some extent material as well as imagined. Accompanying the demographic changes outlined above that have seen greater material resources flow to young(ish) middle-class women in Taiwan, there has been an increase in Taiwanese women's overseas tourism, both in absolute numbers and as a percentage of all travelers. In 2003, 2.4 million women traveled abroad, representing 40 percent of all departures by nationals that year; by 2013 the total figure had more than doubled to over 5 million, representing 47 percent of departures (Taiwan Tourism Bureau 2014). Responding and probably also contributing to Taiwanese women's growing enthusiasm for travel, there has emerged over recent years a niche in Taiwanese travel television that is explicitly directed at female viewers. To contextualize my analysis of two examples of such television and its viewers, I will first briefly sketch out the broader context of travel TV in Taiwan.

Travel television in Taiwan

Travel shows on Taiwanese television can be seen to constitute a spectrum in terms of style, mode of address and geographic focus. At one end sits TLC Taiwan: a niche travel and lifestyle cable channel provided by Discovery Networks Asia-Pacific in Singapore, the regional headquarters of the American global media company Discovery Communications Inc. TLC offers mainly imported content in English (usually with Chinese subtitles), though with some Asia-specific content made to order for Discovery by production houses within the region. In the context of the Taiwanese television landscape as a whole, the style of TLC shows sits far toward the documentary-naturalistic end of the spectrum, while the mode of address centers a global, cosmopolitan subject, and the geographic focus is on the USA and Western Europe. Essentially, TLC Taiwan narrowcasts to a very specific target audience: young, highly educated, English-competent, professional city dwellers. Conceived by Discovery as a women's channel, targeting female viewers through a focus on "relatable life moments," TLC is indeed popular with middle-class Taiwanese women (Discovery Communications 2014). In the final quarter of 2012, female viewers outnumbered males 3:2, and most viewers were full-time workers over 25 years of age with higher than average income (AGB Nielsen Taiwan, private data purchase).

If TLC represents the "global" end of the spectrum, then at the "local" end we find a quite different type of programming: locally produced travelogues introducing holiday spots within Taiwan, often sponsored by town tourist boards. The style of these shows differs greatly from TLC programming. Focusing on travel as "having fun" (玩), these shows frequently incorporate elements of the all-popular Taiwanese variety genre, including comic byplay between multiple hosts, upbeat extra-diegetic music, post-production audio effects and animations, and in-studio segments. Popular shows on commercial cable channels like TVBS-G's *Super Taste* (時尚玩家) and Star Chinese's *Travel Relief Team* (旅行應援團) use a convivial-collective mode of address, centering a highly localized formation of Taiwanese identity through a focus on familiar everyday street scenes and modes of sociality as well as some linguistic code switching between Mandarin and Minnan ("Taiwanese") languages.

Between these two poles of the global (TLC) and the local (Taiwanese travelogues) stretches a broad middle ground incorporating, for example, locally made variety-style travelogues taking in overseas destinations (commercial cable channel GTV's *World's Number One*, 世界第一等); a locally produced TLC show introducing travel destinations within Taiwan, in English (*Fun Taiwan* 瘋台灣); and a range of more sober, documentary-style travelogues focusing on Taiwan and mainland China (such as the long-running *Taiwan Walker*, 台灣腳逛大陸, from commercial cable channel CtiTV). An interesting development in this "middle ground" of Taiwanese travel television is the establishment of Asia Travel TV, a satellite channel that commenced business in 2003, targeting regional Sinophone audiences across Asia and the Pacific (Asia Travel TV 2014). The channel's strategy appears to be to develop a Chinese-language, Asia-regional version of the Discovery model, targeting middle-class, ethnically Chinese viewers across the region to whom the idea of non-package leisure travel – and the urbane, cosmopolitan identity it entails – is likely to appeal. Sometimes aired on the Asia Travel channel, and also falling into this wide "middle ground" of Taiwanese travel TV, is an emergent subgenre of locally produced international travel shows targeting young(ish) female solo travelers. These are the focus of this chapter's second case study.

TLC Taiwan: women imagining lifestyle mobility

In 2011, together with research assistant Claire Tsai, I interviewed 16 TLC viewers in Taipei. Interviewees were aged between 20 and 27, and represented a mix of students and white-collar workers. Ten were women, and it is on their responses that I focus in this section.

Interestingly, while TLC Taiwan offers a mix of Euro-American lifestyle and travel shows, our interviewees tended to view even the non-travel themed lifestyle programming – such as cooking and makeover shows – *as travel shows.* For example, Ms. Cai,[3] a 26-year-old worker in a trading company, observed:

> Of course I think that [TLC cooking shows] feel foreign, because they have all those sorts of things that we rarely see, dishes that we rarely see. [Watching] is like absorbing new knowledge; like: oh, it turns out foreigners eat pretty different things from what we eat.

Similarly, sisters Ms. A. Zhang (a 28-year-old editor) and Ms. B. Zhang (a 24-year-old logistics assistant) noted about the shows of Jamie Oliver, Curtis Stone and Anthony Bourdain, all of which they enjoyed:

A: Their shows are pretty much travel shows, with fine dining added: take a look at fine dining in different countries; take a look at culture in different countries [...] It looks like foreign food, foreign chefs [...] Other countries, other cultures.

B: Yes, yes, [you see] how they live in that kind of world.

Consistent with their enjoyment of TLC Taiwan as "travel television," the urban-dwelling, tertiary-educated middle-class women (like the men) who we interviewed tended to present themselves as consciously "internationalist" subjects (to borrow Karen Kelsky's term for a certain group of young, single Japanese women in the 1990s; Kelsky 2001, 5–6). That is, they represented their interests, aspirations, values and life plans as closely entwined with their hopes for traveling, studying and/or working overseas. They explicitly connected this outward orientation with their enjoyment of TLC, and in the case of some of our female interviewees, they also linked their internationalist imaginary in interesting ways with their gendered identity.

The 26-year-old Ms. Zhu is an interesting example to consider here. Ms. Zhu was a talkative, bubbly young woman who we interviewed in Taipei during her break from studying Korean in Seoul. She was a keen viewer of TLC, including shows like *Take Home Chef, Jamie At Home, Passport to Europe* and *Man Versus Food.* At the very start of our discussion, after chatting about the fact her younger sister married young (at 21) while Ms. Zhu herself remained unmarried, Ms. Zhu spontaneously – and somewhat tongue-in-cheek – classified herself as a member of the *baiquan* ("loser dog": unmarried over 25) category. She presents her understanding of the genesis and experience of the category below:

> Nowadays at 25, from 25 onward [...] girls will start to feel – there's that word that appeared, "*baiquan.*" As soon as it came out everyone was like: oh no! I'm a *baiquan*! [...] These last few years in Asia, women have got

> more and more opportunities to pursue their rights. Maybe while they're concentrating on their career, they're unable to spend a lot of energy on relationships and dating. Women now have many opportunities and rights, maybe even opportunities to [...] compete with men in the workplace [...] And once they've received these high levels of education, their hopes and standards for choosing a marriage partner rise too. You get this situation where when the girl likes someone, he doesn't like her. And the ones that do like her, she won't accept [...] Actually this has happened in Japan, and in Korea too I think. I was chatting with some Korean girls; it seems that the deal in Korea is basically, once you're 25 you hope to get married. People will ask you, have you got a boyfriend. It happens in Taiwan too [...] Most mums and dads will be like, "Hey, where's the boyfriend? Bring him home so we can look him over!" and stuff like that.

Ms. Zhu emphasized that her own situation was unusual insofar as her mother had said to her directly that it would not matter if she never got married, so long as she is happy. However, her discussion above shows that she nevertheless sees herself as part of that demographic that is currently the subject of so much popular debate in Taiwan (and elsewhere in East Asia, including Japan and Korea): unmarried young women who are seen to value personal development over marriage, and are widely judged as too slow to marry and "too picky" in their choice of men.

Interestingly, speaking – albeit with some irony – as a self-confessed "loser dog," Ms. Zhu also represented her identity as structured almost entirely around an international orientation. She said she had always been interested in the world beyond Taiwan, and during her undergraduate years had acted as a volunteer guide for international students at her university, which enabled her to make foreign friends whom she now visited during her frequent international travels across Asia and Russia for recreation, study and sporting competitions (she was also an elite athlete). She had previously gone out with two European boyfriends, and all of her good friends were either non-Taiwanese people or fellow Taiwanese students whose main point of connection was their shared interest in overseas languages and cultures. Ms. Zhu said that TLC "widens your field of vision," "opens Taiwan's eyes to the world" and provides a "bridge" between Taiwan and the rest of the world. She framed her own viewing of TLC as a logical extension of this cosmopolitan outlook.

Somewhat similarly, 27-year-old medical imaging technician Ms. Li connected her TLC viewing with her own internationalist desires, as follows:

> [When watching Curtis Stone] I really like it, because [...] I really want to go overseas to live, or work. So every time I watch that show I think that maybe one day I'll come across that kind of ... food, or come across that kind of person [...] [I hope to go to] North America, I guess. Because I've been to Canada before, and I really liked it [...] I stayed with friends in Canada, yeah, and their kitchen was SUPER-BIG! I happily started

> making all sorts of things in that kitchen of theirs. It was just like the feeling in the show when [Stone] goes to someone's kitchen and starts cooking: just fantastic [...]
>
> I really like traveling, I like to go and look at different countries, different people, different cultures [...] Through TLC we can find out about the customs of different countries, it's like it opens a window for us [...] You feel like it's a small-scale global village.

In these comments Ms. Li, like Ms. Zhu, uses TLC to construct herself as a certain type of internationalized person: a citizen of the "global village" projected by the channel.

Ms. Li, like most of our interviewees, felt that the mobile imaginary presented by TLC would be especially attractive to young female viewers (and as we saw above, the data on audience demographics support this). Speculating on why this may be so, Ms. Li offered the following discussion:

> I think maybe [girls like TLC] because girls tend to fantasize; they tend to hope more to go [overseas] for fun, and plan for that [...] Girls – romantic types – sort of think, if I go away for fun, I might meet someone great, I might have an adventure, some handsome guy might pick me up, or something. Maybe she [hopes to] make a heap of new friends. But boys aren't like that [...] Of the boys I know at the moment, if they were going overseas it'd be either for study or for work. Some of them go for fun, but not many [...] Maybe it's because the traditional Taiwanese society thinks that once a boy grows up he should earn money, raise a family, find a job – added to that is the rising unemployment rate over the last ten years [...] They also have to do the military service. So they tend to think, just get that over with, and hurry to find work. They won't tend to plan or fantasize about where they're going to travel for fun, or what life might be like overseas.

Following this discussion, I asked Ms. Li whether she thought that TLC's popularity with young women might connect with women's normative life stages, too, insofar as they could be seen to have a "window of opportunity" for self-directed consumption between university graduation and marriage, which the channel encourages them to explore through overseas travel. Ms. Li responded enthusiastically:

> Yes, yes, and I think I'm in that group myself! [...] Because ever since university I've been thinking that way [...] Starting at university and right through 'til grad school, this way of thinking has become clearer and clearer for me.

Like Ms. Zhu (above), then, Ms. Li discerns a connection between her own current life stage and the allure of overseas travel. Her remarks strongly underscore the perceived gender specificity of her experience: while still-dominant social norms underline the importance for young men of establishing one's business or other career as soon as possible, career development may be considered of less defining importance for young women. This plus the lack of compulsion to complete military service, reasons Ms. Li, means that women have greater time and inclination for travel at this particular time of life. Such a view resonates somewhat with Karen Kelsky's study of the gendered situation of "internationalist" women in Japan:

> [I]f women are blocked from the safe and secure paths of male professional achievement within Japan, women also, as a result of these very exclusions, enjoy a special freedom to explore alternative life choices, such as devoting several years to studying a foreign language, experimenting with foreign firms, working or studying abroad, or engaging with foreigners in Japan or the world outside.
>
> (Kelsky 2001, 3)

As in Kelsky's analysis, for Ms. Li it is the relative de-emphasis on young women's professional development in Taiwan that paradoxically opens up greater possibilities for them to consider international mobility.

Ms. Li also speculates on whether some women (among whom she seems, perhaps, to include herself) may harbor a fantasy of meeting new friends and even a romantic partner overseas – implicitly, given the geographic focus of our conversation, in a Western country. As Kelsky's in-depth study of a related phenomenon in Japan shows, the issue of such transcultural romantic fantasy is a complex one, and our interview data do not support further extrapolation.[4] Ms. Li's comment, though, does suggest at least the possibility of another explicitly gendered element in young heterosexual women's dreams of transnational mobility. A feminine fantasy of moving overseas for love would connect with the entrenched structures of patrilocal marriage in Chinese societies, in which the bride traditionally moves to the groom's family home, not vice-versa, making women more likely than men to become geographically mobile as a result of marriage or long-term heterosexual relationships.

However, for the most part our interviewees' international mobility was much more a (perceived) potential than a current reality. Consider the following response from 24-year-old product manager Ms. Peng, who was hoping to undertake graduate study in the USA:

> I feel like what we're watching is a kind of "Oh … someday." You often say, "Someday I want to go there too." For example if [the show] is about Spain, then, [I feel] I must go there someday. Or if it shows you somewhere really fun you'll be like, oh it looks gorgeous, I'll go there someday. It makes you look forward to it; a kind of … hope, that someday you'll be able to do whatever […] What I mean is, these shows create a lot of expectancy […] I think [they create] a *wish*[5] […] A dream.

Combined with the transnational orientation that TLC represents, this temporality of "oh, someday …" suggests that the channel is used by these young viewers for the imaginative elaboration of their own abstract *potential* for (future) movement (Kaufmann et al. 2004). The sorts of lives these interviewees hazily projected for themselves through their imaginative engagements with TLC resonate with Cohen, Duncan and Thulemark's conceptualization of "lifestyle mobility": voluntary geographic movement as an ongoing lifestyle choice that blurs the boundaries between travel and migration, work and leisure, and home and away (Cohen et al. 2013). The kind of mobility these interviewees imagine – blending leisure travel with working abroad and tourism with migration – is always unfinished and ongoing; a long, still unfolding, segmented line linking a series of places across a lifetime of movement.

Bearing in mind this abstract, future-oriented focus in our interviewees – TLC programming as more about imagining one's potential for movement than a reflection of concrete opportunities for becoming mobile – Ms. Li's speculation, above, that female viewers in Taiwan may see TLC's Euro-American lifestyle shows *as a fantasy genre* is an intriguing possibility. Lending strength to this idea, Ms. B. Zhang (introduced above) commented frankly:

> Those Euro-American shows [on TLC], I think they just look very "wow!" They feel great, but they're just for looking at and going "wow!" Because what they show is – well, from the point of view of normal people, it's things we couldn't possibly hope to ever experience.

Responses like this suggest that while on one hand TLC may represent a collective imagination of "lifestyle mobility," on the other hand, interviewees were also aware of the material constraints on their access to such a dream. The following conversation between two viewers of *Project Runway*, Anthony Bourdain, Kylie Kwong, and several TLC travel and home makeover shows, Ms. Cai (26, a trading company employee) and Ms. Qiu (25, a government bureaucrat), acknowledge the gap between the TLC dream of limitless mobility and the realities of their own material constraint:

CAI: I do really hope [to go overseas], but I've never … I can't find a reason, a concrete reason, an opportunity, yeah. Of course if I got the chance I'd love to go overseas and try it, yeah, I'd go and try living in some little village, or somewhere […] really different from Taiwan, yeah. I've thought about if I had the chance, going to see how it would feel to live overseas.

QIU: When I was in high school, I really wanted to go overseas someday to work, but … as I've grown older, and that's turned out to be impossible, I've thought: OK, so I'll earn lots of money and not go overseas to work, but when I'm exhausted from working [here], just go there for travel. Stay overseas for two or three months, half a year, yeah.

Like many of our other interviewees, these women's responses to TLC are characterized by a gap between the "oh, someday …" fantasy of the mobile self, and consciousness of the material factors weighing on the side of their fixity in Taiwan: lack of opportunities to find work overseas, the prohibitive costs of travel, and (in other interviewees' accounts) limited language skills. Interestingly, our most self-consciously "internationalist" respondent, Ms. Zhu (introduced above), cited gender-bound family obligations as a factor mitigating against the possibility of her remaining overseas long term:

> Actually I very much wish I could work and live overseas, I really do, but … to a certain extent, because of my family, since after all I'm a girl … even though my little sister has set a precedent! […] To a certain extent I've let my family know, I mean if I had a [work] opportunity overseas I actually might not immediately want to turn it down.

Ms. Zhu draws back from spelling it out, but the implication of her elliptical discussion is that, "since she's a girl," she feels she has a duty to return to Taiwan to take care of her aging parents. Although she has discussed "to some extent" with her parents the possibility that she could take a job overseas, it is clear that Ms. Zhu feels torn between her internationalist desires and her gendered sense of familial obligation.

Overall, then, these Taiwanese TLC viewers are positioned slightly differently in relation to the dream of internationalism from the young, internationally active Japanese women studied by Kelsky. While Kelsky argues that her respondents' internationalism enabled their full-scale "defection" from the expected female life course (Kelsky 2001, 2), our interviewees were engaged, rather, in negotiating the contradiction between the *imagination* of lifestyle mobility – playing with the dream of living, working and maybe meeting a romantic partner overseas – and material constraints on their *actualization* of such mobility, including constraints arising from gendered social and familial expectations.

With the dream of full-scale lifestyle mobility that TLC represents often pragmatically seen as out of their reach, an alternative – as Ms. Qiu suggests, above – may present itself in the temporary mobility of tourism. As we saw above, this is an option increasingly being taken up by Taiwanese women, and TV producers recognize this in their development of a new subgenre: "pink" travel TV.

Traveling solo: pink travel TV and the single girl

As noted above, unmarried middle-class women have become both a growing demographic and a focal point for public anxieties in Taiwan today. These developments have spurred the emergence of a new interest in such women in locally produced popular media, where they feature both as characters and as a target audience (Martin 2016, forthcoming). From idol dramas about the trials and tribulations of late-twenties career women negotiating the twin perils of getting married versus being left on the shelf (sometimes called "pink dramas"), to fashion and beauty advice formats that school unmarried women in looking and feeling fabulous at work and at play, there has emerged a cross-genre cluster that, based on its centering of unmarried, middle-class female identity, we might dub "pink TV."

Addressing the increasing accessibility of leisure travel for young women and expanding "pink TV" into a new genre, in 2010 free-to-air network CTS launched a new show specifically aimed at young women planning non-package overseas tourist travel. The program, sponsored by the tourism boards of the destinations featured, was originally titled *Miss Loves to Travel* (小姐愛旅行) before being retitled in 2011 (WOMAN愛旅行: literally, *Woman Loves to Travel*, official English title: *Miss Traveler*). In May 2012, the show returned to its original Chinese title and a new home on cable channel Azio TV (Dongfeng), and in 2013 it spawned a spin-off entitled *Miss Traveler: Air Hostess* (空姐愛旅行) on the cable channel CtiTV (in which each episode is hosted by an air hostess and a young female celebrity). Indicating the wider marketability of the young women's travel show concept beyond Taiwan, *Miss Traveler* is now syndicated to China's iQiyi web TV portal (iqiyi.com).

Miss Traveler is hosted by a rotating group of glamorous, unmarried, thirty-something female models, actresses, singers and other media celebrities (Sonia Sui, Tien Hsin, Tammy Chen, Novia Lin, Miranda Lu and Yuli Lin, among others). Originally aired at 10pm on Friday nights, at the time of writing, different versions of the show are airing across a wide range of time slots – including the primetime slot of 8–9pm on Saturday, Sunday and Wednesday – on both Azio TV and the Asia Travel Channel. While the program's logo in CTS's 2011–12 version centers the Eiffel Tower and the Arc de Triomphe against a pink background (Figure 8.1) and its promos state that it "takes you to see the world," in fact the vast majority of the locations visited are in Taiwan's local Asia-Pacific region (including Macau, Hong Kong, Beijing, Hokkaido, Palau, Guam, North Vietnam, Manila, Seoul, Angkor Wat, Hawaii, and Taiwan's own Matsu islands, among others).

CTS's promotional blurb for the 2011–12 version of the show introduces it as follows:

> Is travel nourishment for the soul, a search for the self? Is it the search for an answer? Ever since the popularity of the film *Eat, Pray, Love* [Chinese title: *One Person's Travels*], travel has taken on a new meaning. In the midst of the craze for group tourism, women have begun to reflect on whether the value of solo travel may be even greater. Let us recall the words of English philosopher Alain de Botton: "If our lives are dominated by a search for happiness, then perhaps few activities reveal as much about the dynamics of this quest – in all its ardor and paradoxes – than our travels." The search for meaning makes the journey more

> valuable than *dailylife* [sic]. You needn't consider your companions' time and whether your schedules align, meaning that your trip begins in freedom and becomes a whole journey of *relief.* From 2011, CTS presents a new production: *Miss Traveler,* which will explore the meaning of life and of travel through profound images. Let us *Eat, Play and Enjoy your life!*
>
> There are precious few opportunities in a woman's life for her to treat herself; there are precious few holidays she can enjoy alone. When life no longer offers just a single option … let yourself be thoroughly liberated!
>
> (CTS 2011)

With its references to a Hollywood chick-flick (whose Chinese title emphasizes the value of traveling alone), a Swiss-British popular philosopher, and several words and phrases in English, the blurb clearly addresses its reader as a member of an individualized, pop-intellectual, female cosmopolitan elite. It also plays up the imperative for women to make the most of their "precious few" chances to travel "freely" and enjoy a holiday alone, "liberated" to "eat, play and enjoy," unencumbered by the demands of travel companions. It is interesting to note that similar rhetoric is common in Taiwan across advertisements for feminine-coded luxury items like desserts, jewelry and designer accessories: such appeals to the allure of female freedom encourage women to consciously visualize their own gender-limited resources and opportunities, and offer consumption as a salve for the worn-down female self that emerges from such visualization.[6] The blurb's framing of young women's independent overseas leisure travel as a time of hard-won freedom is reinforced in the show itself, where celebrity hosts reflect on travel as providing a unique time "when I can truly relax and be myself," away from the pressures of a hectic work life (January 20, 2012).

Figure 8.1 Opening credits for *Miss Traveler* (CTS, 2011–12)

Most episodes are hosted by a single presenter (occasionally a pair of "friends"), and the central scenario visualized is that of the young female traveler enjoying the destination's highlights by herself (shopping and dining alone; striking up conversations with locals, etc.), while chatting breezily to the camera about her experiences. The style of leisure consumption is middlebrow – some high-end luxuries are sampled (a two-star Michelin yum cha restaurant in Hong Kong; April 20, 2012; a luxury yacht cruise in Guam February 3, 2012) – but the majority of the activities are more affordable. For example, in addition to the luxury dinner-for-one, a Hong Kong episode hosted by Sonia Sui (April 20, 2012) sees Sui browsing in boutique curio shops featuring the work of French and local designers; riding on the long moving sidewalk in Central; queuing up for local street food delicacies; wandering through a fishing village and markets; having coffee and a snack at a classic 1950s-style teahouse; and being talked through a local folk-religious ritual on the street at night. The show's presentation of this mid-budget range of shopping, eating, sightseeing and "cultural" activities is clearly designed to appeal to female, solo middle-class travelers – perhaps like the interviewees cited above, for whom leisure travel represents a more affordable alternative to the lifestyle mobility project that TLC Taiwan encourages them to imagine.

What is most notable for my purposes is *Miss Traveler*'s framing of women's independent travel as the site of a new kind of value: the value of finding "the real you," actualized through traveling alone. Mobility through *Miss Traveler*'s cultural capital-rich style of solo tourism becomes linked with the existing media imaginary of the self-focused, unmarried career woman in a way that underlines the "freedoms" available to such women while also acknowledging the constraints on those freedoms. Regional tourist travel is presented as a means of mediating the tensions that being a single, over-25 working woman entails: hard work, the pressure continually to manage other people's needs, and, implicitly, the need to justify to others that "it's OK to be alone."[7]

The limits of mobility?

On Taiwanese television the strongest potential for international travel thus tends to be associated with unmarried women: we have seen this both in the mode of address of *Miss Traveler*, and in the gendered engagements by unmarried female viewers with the idea of "lifestyle mobility" made imaginable through TLC. There exist no comparable examples enabling viewers to envisage the same kinds of international mobility on the part of married women. Indeed, if we focus on TV genres targeting married women, the association between femininity and mobility all but disappears. In the popular variety-talk show genre, we find multiple examples that address the adult female viewer as by definition married, a mother, and concerned principally – if not solely – with the management of affective labor in the domestic sphere (Martin 2013). Religious programming such as that found on the Da Ai Buddhist channel similarly addresses its (largely married, retired) female audience as concerned mainly with local community and family matters (Lewis et al., 2016, Chapter 6). The replacement of a mobile imaginary with a strong local and domestic focus in many programs targeted at married women points to familial care-work duties, which as we saw above typically intensify significantly after marriage, as a key factor mitigating against the imaginability of women's mobility. Thus, while on the one hand this chapter has underlined a class limitation on the popular imaginability of mobile women – insofar as transnational mobility has emerged as a central component of middle-class identity formations, specifically – on the other hand, these comparative examples support my parallel argument that women's age and marital status also ramify for the perceived plausibility of their mobility.

However, although the correlation between the televisual figuration of women's capacity for movement and these extant forms of cultural power holds true at a broad level, nevertheless, as we have seen, in each of the examples above mobility and immobility have not actually appeared as diametrically opposed states but rather in a more analogue relation, illustrating what Chris McMorran has recently called "the daily reality of living between mobility and stasis" (McMorran 2013, 2). While young, urban, middle-class women watching TLC find that the channel enables a dream of future lifestyle mobility, such viewers are simultaneously aware that the material limitations on their potential for travel may reveal that dream as a fantasy. While a show like *Miss Traveler* encourages single, middle-class women to see regional solo tourist travel as a way to experience freedom for "the real me," the show's promotional framing simultaneously hints at the social constraints that make the pleasures of traveling (and simply being) alone a luxury rather than a normal state of affairs. Such complexities lead us away both from simplistic characterizations of women as *either* mobile *or* immobile; and from any overgeneralized view that women in advanced East Asian capitalist societies like Taiwan are moving from a state of general immobility into one of general mobility, with travel television "reflecting" such a trend. Instead, women's television in and from Taiwan speaks to complexly imbricated and highly context-dependent forms of gendered (im)mobility.

Acknowledgements

Many thanks to Claire Tsai and Phyllis Yu-ting Huang for their invaluable research assistance. This research was funded by the Australian Research Council (ARC DP1094355).

Notes

1 This chapter draws on, and redevelops, some material that is also discussed in Lewis et al. (2016). In chapter 4 of that book, we discuss Taiwanese viewers of TLC as "internationalist" subjects; here, I develop the gendered implications of that identification for female viewers specifically.

2 A 2011 study shows that 64 percent of housework domestic responsibilities are undertaken by wives, and just 3 percent by their spouses; the remaining percentage is undertaken largely by the wives' parents (DGBAS 2013a, 9).

3 All names are pseudonyms. All translations from the original Chinese are by the author.

4 Although Curtis Stone's supermarket pick-up scenario in *Take Home Chef* was extraordinarily popular with the women we spoke to.

5 With the exception of media titles, words in italics appear in English in the original.

6 Thanks to Ta-wei Chi for this observation.

7 I refer here to the social pressures toward marriage to which unmarried women are subjected: as noted above, this has been a constant theme of "pink" idol dramas in recent years, and I think forms one subtext for *Miss Traveler*'s defense of the value of women's solo travel as offering much-needed "me time."

References

Asia Travel TV. 2014. "About Asia Travel TV." www.hitravel.tv/about.aspx (accessed October 15, 2014).

Chen, Yu-hua. 2009. "A Cohort Analysis of the Transition to First Marriage Among Taiwanese." *Population and Society* 5(1): 25–44.

The China Post. 2013. "Average Marriage Age for Men, Women Rises to 31.9, 29.5." May 27. www.chinapost.com.tw/taiwan/national/national-news/2013/05/27/379657/Average-marriage.htm (accessed August 20, 2013).

Cohen, Scott A., Tara Duncan, and Maria Thulemark. 2013. "Lifestyle Mobilities: The Crossroads of Travel, Leisure and Migration." *Mobilities* 10(1). doi: 10.1080/17450101.2013.826481.

CTS. 2011. *Miss Traveler Introduction*. event.cts.com.tw/misstraveler/index.html (accessed June 10, 2011).

Dales, Laura. 2012. "Singlehood and Agency in Japan." Paper presented at the 19th Biennial Conference of the Asian Studies Association of Australia, University of Western Sydney, July 11–13.

Directorate General of Budget, Accounting and Statistics (DGBAS). 2012. *Women and Men in R.O.C. (Facts and Figures) 2012*. eng.stat.gov.tw/public/data/dgbas03/bs2/gender/eb/2012/EGI/index.html.

Directorate General of Budget, Accounting and Statistics (DGBAS). 2013a. *Women and Men in R.O.C. (Taiwan): Facts and Figures*. ebook.dgbas.gov.tw/public/Data/331910471453.pdf.

Directorate General of Budget, Accounting and Statistics (DGBAS). 2013b. *Employment and Economics*. eng.stat.gov.tw/ct.asp?xItem=4561&ctNode=6032&mp=5.

Directorate General of Budget, Accounting and Statistics (DGBAS). 2014. *Women and Men in R.O.C. (Taiwan): Facts and Figures*. eng.stat.gov.tw/ct.asp?xItem=33469&ctNode=6032&mp=5.

Discovery Communications. 2014. "TLC." corporate.discovery.com/brands/us/tlc/ (accessed October 15, 2014).

Dong, Yujia (董俞佳). 2012. "女性晚婚 「勝女潮」來襲 不嫁男人嫁工作", 聯合報 May 20. www.pcdvd.com.tw/showthread.php?t=969599 (accessed December 15, 2012).

Hanson, Susan. 2010. "Gender and Mobility: New Approaches for Informing Sustainability." *Gender, Place and Culture: A Journal of Feminist Geography* 17(1): 5–23.

Jones, Gavin W. 2007. "Delayed Marriage and Very Low Fertility in Pacific Asia." *Population and Development Review* 33(3): 453–478.

Kaufmann, Vincent, Manfred Max Bergman, and Dominique Joye. 2004. "Motility: Mobility as Capital." *International Journal of Urban and Regional Research* 28(4): 745–756.

Kelsky, Karen. 2001. *Women on the Verge: Japanese Women, Western Dreams.* Durham and London: Duke University Press.

Kim, Youna. 2010. "Female Individualization? Transnational Mobility and Media Consumption of Asian Women." *Media, Culture and Society* 32(1): 25–43.

Lewis, Tania, Fran Martin, and Wanning Sun. 2016. *Telemodernities: Television and Transforming Lives in Asia.* Durham and London: Duke University Press.

Martin, Fran. 2013. "'A Tangle of People Messing Around Together': Taiwanese Variety Television and the Mediation of Women's Affective Labour." *Cultural Studies* 27(2): 207–224.

Martin, Fran. 2016. "'From Sparrow to Phoenix': Imagining Gender Transformation Through Taiwanese Women's Variety TV." *Positions: Asia Critique* 24(2).

Massey, Doreen. 1991. "A Global Sense of Place." *Marxism Today* 38: 24–29.

McMorran, Chris. 2013. "Mobilities Amid the Production of Fixities: Labour in a Japanese Inn." *Mobilities.* doi: 10.1080/17450101.2013.825439.

Ministry of Education Taiwan. 2014. *Gender Proportion, All Levels – By Year.* english.moe.gov.tw/ct.asp?xItem=14508&CtNode=11431&mp=11.

Shaw, Ping, and Chin-yi Lin. 2012. "Moving Freely: Single Women and Mobility in Taiwanese TV Advertising." In *Women and the Media in Asia: The Precarious Self,* edited by Youna Kim, 130–142. New York and Houndsmills: Palgrave Macmillan.

Sheller, Mimi and John Urry. 2006. "The New Mobilities Paradigm." *Environment and Planning A* 38: 207–226.

Skeggs, Beverley. 2004. *Class, Self, Culture.* London and New York: Routledge.

Taiwan Tourism Bureau. 2014. *Outbound Departures of Nationals of the Republic of China by Gender by Year (1984~).* admin.taiwan.net.tw/statistics/year_en.aspx?no=15.

Yang, Irene Fang-chih. 2002. "Constructing Shounyus' Identity and Desire: The Politics of Translation in Taiwanese Sex and the City." *International Journal of Cultural Studies* 14(3): 235–249.

Yu, Ruoh-Yong, and Yu-sheng Liu. 2014. "Change and Continuity in the Experience of Marriage in Taiwan." In *Wives, Husbands and Lovers: Marriage and Sexuality in Hong Kong, Taiwan and Urban China,* edited by Deborah S. Davis and Sara L. Friedman, 239–261. Stanford, CA: Stanford University Press.

9 Locating the mobile

Intergenerational locative media in Tokyo, Shanghai and Melbourne

Larissa Hjorth, Heather Horst, Sarah Pink, Baohua Zhou, Fumitoshi Kato, Genevieve Bell, Kana Ohashi, Chris Malmo and Miao Xiao

Location-based services like Google Maps and practices like geotagging have become an integral part of everyday life, entangling movements across relationships, lifestyles, places and spaces. Existing research has shown that the growth of locative media is impacting upon cultural practice and policy, and on how people experience place, time and mobility, in ways that are uneven across cultural, generational and temporal scales (Farman 2011; Gazzard 2011; de Souza e Silva and Frith 2012). Yet we still know very little about how privacy and surveillance are actually being practiced in the age of "Big Data," or how these now everyday lifestyle practices are changing over time and in different cultural contexts. Few studies have tried to understand how different generations are using locative media for everyday "friendly" surveillance – to stay in touch, to keep children "safe," and to monitor the activities of children, partners and parents (Sengupta 2012; Clark 2012). Understanding the cultural and intergenerational dimensions of people's locative media use can provide new insights into contemporary and culturally nuanced practices of lifestyle. In particular, mapping the digital practices through and around the family can help us to comprehend the tension between the tenacity of kinship ties and their transformation through digital entanglements.

This chapter presents new research into how locative media are shaping, and being shaped by, practices of intimacy and privacy in intergenerational families. While debates around lifestyle and consumer culture in Asia have focused upon individualization and the idea of a "break" with traditional values, especially as a result of new media (Robison and Goodman 1996; McVeigh 2003b; Chua 2010), we argue for a middle-ground approach that focuses on the reproduction of kinship through media rituals. These quotidian media practices both re-enact older familial rituals and give birth to new ones.

Drawing on three vignettes developed as short-term ethnographies (Pink and Morgan 2013) with families in Tokyo, Shanghai and Melbourne in November 2013, this chapter outlines a framework for conceptualizing the mundane ways in which locative media are used. In all three locations, we conducted in-depth interviews involving scenarios of use and solicited a-day-in-your-life narratives from family members. As we illustrate, the comparison of three different cultural contexts enables an exploration of multiple configurations in the adoption of locative media – including the uneven development of locative media, their uses and their intergenerational uptake.

Tokyo, Shanghai and Melbourne provide three contrasting sites through which to understand locative media practices. Residents of Tokyo have been using locative media for over a decade. Shanghai is an example of rapid and large-scale uptake of locative media by the youth – generations born post-1980 including the *ba ling hou* and *jiu ling hou* (literally, the post-1980 and post-1990 generations) (CNNIC 2013; Pink and Hjorth 2013; Hjorth et al. 2014). In comparison with Tokyo and Shanghai, Melbourne has a more recent uptake locative media through high rates of smartphone penetration over the past two years (ABS 2013; Our Mobile Planet 2012). By contrasting these three divergent technocultures and the genealogies of their emergence, this chapter seeks to understand the emerging and existing practices, motivations and perceptions around intergeneration uses of locative media in mundane settings in everyday life. We then consider these practices in terms of four underlying themes – *digital kinship, intimate co-presence, affective ambience* and *the intimate mundane.*

These four concepts underscore the ways in which intimacy, family and place are being transformed in an age of locative media. *Digital kinship* is a central tenet of the project, which embeds the study into broader debates about the changing (or residual) nature of what it means to be a "family" in an age of networked media (Horst 2010, 2011; Clark 2012). Kinship has always been important to ethnographic understandings of culture. With the added dimension of the digital, we see how kinship moves in and out of online and offline spaces and, in turn, how these spaces have come to develop their own histories, connections and memories. Our attention to digital kinship also accounts for the changing family structure associated with contemporary Asian cities such as Shanghai and Tokyo, including the increasing trend towards nuclear families. It also acknowledges changing definitions of family in multicultural urban areas like Melbourne, such as the growth in LGBT families, single parents and families without children. These new forms of families are, in turn, shaping emergent meanings and forms of kinship and relatedness.

Throughout this chapter we focus upon the ways that families, in all their specificity, use social media to create and maintain connection as well as disconnection. While the concept of digital kinship enables us to understand the new formations of families, we have been particularly interested in understanding the mechanisms through which kinship and relatedness are made and maintained. One concept that emerged during the initial phases of the study is *intimate co-presence.* Intimate co-presence is both a practice and a quality, even a sensibility, through which family members maintain their relationships. Co-presence has been viewed as a productive way for rethinking traditional binaries such as online versus offline that are no longer adequate to everyday life (Licoppe 2004). The rubric of co-presence provides a broader conceptual framework for understanding intimacy and mediation as something that has always been an integral part of being human. As we have noted elsewhere, intimacy has always been mediated, if not by technologies then by memories, language and gestures (Hjorth 2009; Horst and Miller 2012). The concept of intimate co-presence allows us to connect the contemporary with the historical by considering the evolution of mediated intimacies. Intimacy can be understood on various levels from individual and personal to social and cultural (Hertzeld 1997). Our usage of intimacy engages with personal, cultural and social notions of intimacy as always mediated.

Just as mobile media amplify debates around intimacy and degrees of co-presence, they are also embedded in the everyday through their relationship with the creation of ambience. *Affective ambience* plays to the idea that media often drop into the background of everyday life. Its particular affects and textures become embedded in the everyday. Mimi Ito's notion of the "full-time intimate community" captures this definition of ambience. As Okabe (2004) argues, "[t]he visual information shared between intimates also represents a similar social practice, of sharing ambient awareness with close friends, family and loved ones who are not physically co-present." Ambience is often used to describe sound, music and lighting but has also been used in computing and science (especially human-computer interaction) to evoke information and music to provide feeling. In short, ambience is about the *texture* of *context, emotion* and *affect*. In this study we noted a type of ambience we define as affective ambience, whereby one's use or non-use of locative media shapes and affects the production of ambience around people, media and contexts.

Lastly, the concept of the *intimate mundane* provides a lens through which to understand how locative media practices are embedded in the ordinary and mundane detail of everyday life – the often not explicitly thought about or spoken about tasks that we perform, sometimes with family members, as we go about our everyday routines. Attention to the mundane means attention to the essential activities that underpin the more enchanting manifestations of the everyday (Pink et al. 2013). Attention to the digital in this context is no less important (for example, see Coleman 2010), particularly since uses of digital media are very often dispersed throughout other everyday practical activities such as laundry, showering, getting up in the morning and going to bed (see Pink and Leder Mackley 2012). Through the vignettes below, we explore how these four concepts play out across and through locative media in relation to digital kinship. As we argue, digital kinship involves entanglements between older-style kinship relations and rituals, and new modes of understanding within digital spaces.

Genealogies of locative media in Shanghai

Not everyone in the world owns a computer, but the ubiquity of mobile phones has allowed many people access to online media, and globally, the mobile phone is becoming a dominant platform for accessing online content.

In China, the total number of mobile phones in 2012 was 1.04 billion (CNNIC 2013). The significant role played by mobile phones as the dominant portal for social and online media is highlighted by the China Internet Network Information Center (CNNIC) 2013 report, which noted that mobile web users now total just over 463 million. In China, mobile phones have made online content accessible across the urban–rural divide. With over 200 million smartphone subscribers,[1] increasingly mobile social media like QQ and Weibo are an important part of China's media space (Hjorth et al. 2014, 291). A Chinese family with only one child per couple in the youngest generation(s) exemplifies the impact of three and a half decades of government policy. Many in the *ba ling hou* and *jiu ling hou* single-child generations are experiencing a type of economic and geographic mobility their parents could never have imagined. In the midst of this mobility, mobile media feature as a way to maintain familial rituals and belonging.

A key part of this mobile media space involves the convergence of locative, social and mobile media. While mobile media provide a bridge for cross-generational intimacy, it is location-based services (LBS) that is a distinctive practice of China's younger generations. Through smartphones equipped with cameras and GPS (Global Positioning System), young people are able to document, illustrate and narrate a sense of identity, sociality and place in new ways. Through LBS, they are providing new visualities of their journey as they experience emergent forms of geographic and socioeconomic mobility (Hjorth and Gu 2012).

Locative media have burgeoned with the expansion of the mobile Internet in China. There are not only LBS-focused apps like Jiepang (similar to Foursquare), but also social networking service (SNS) apps that integrate LBS functions like Weibo (microblog) and WeChat (a media-rich messenger-like app). In fact, apps like Jiepang with its relatively simple LBS function are losing popularity to SNS apps that not only include an LBS function but also build in more ways to show location besides "check-in," like photo sharing.

In 2013, we interviewed six families in which at least two of the younger generations (grandparents sometimes, plus always parents and children) used locative media. All families were trans-local, meaning that the young people were studying and living in Shanghai, while their parents and grandparents lived far away, in the family's hometown. The main interview questions covered how they use LBS and how such usage influenced intergenerational communication. In all six families, WeChat was the main online communication tool connecting parents and children. As a result, they received each other's locative information mainly through posts that marked the location, or clues to the location in photos. In five families out of six, the parents' WeChat apps had been installed by their children. Both parents and children described WeChat as a convenient, money-saving and fashionable way to communicate.

This led us to ask how parents and their children think about the influence of WeChat on intergenerational communication. We found that while children noted both the advantages and the disadvantages of adding parents as "friends" on locative media, all parents emphasized the benefits of knowing about their children's immediate status and detailed daily lives from WeChat (especially since they were not living with their children). Here we see friendly surveillance (what Matsuda calls "mom in the pocket"; see Matsuda 2009, 67–70) at work whereby the locative media capabilities of geotagging afford parents with ways in which to monitor their child's mundane movements in a manner that is intimate and yet not invasive. Parents all felt relieved to know more about their children's daily lives in such an efficient way without appearing like they were interfering.

Through indirect snooping on WeChat, parents could gain an ambient sense of their children's movements. To add their children as friends on WeChat provided parents with a sense of intimate co-presence with their children and engagement in their children's lives. For example, one mother noted that by checking her daughter's "moments" (social network uploads), "I can know what she is doing at the moment. I feel we're closer. I see where she is and see her photos, so it's just like I'm staying with her." This is an example of how locative media can afford an overlay between intimate co-presence and affective ambience to create digital kinships. That is, the (online) co-presence is both intimate and ambient, reflecting and expanding upon existing kinship ties through digital analogies.

Another advantage is that family members have more topics to talk about as they weave the online with offline. This weaving between different forms of intimate co-presence across physical, electronic and psychological realms is further enhanced by the nature of WeChat. For example, incidental details about the everyday might not warrant direct discussion. When parents asked about mundane matters, children would often answer "nothing much [happened]." However, with locative media interweaving the social with the geographic, stories on the move were made present to both parties. Shared camera phone pictures could offer a site for discussion. One schoolboy interviewed noted that he was aware of his mother stealthily following all his social and locative media accounts, yet he accepted this friendly surveillance because it allows his mother an ambient sense of his life that makes her content. The boy stated, "I'm not the kind of child who likes to share my daily life with my parents, but mom cares a lot about it … Sometimes she pretends to casually mention something she saw on my posts, for example, 'you went to Suzhou last week?' and we'll talk about that."

Locative media usage was most significant when the geographic distance was greatest. When the children were still in middle school, they lived with their parents and the parents knew a great deal about their daily lives. In this situation, the impact of location sharing is not obvious. When the children enroll in university, however, their lives become more varied and parents know less about that, so parents have a stronger desire to follow their children's lives. It is at this stage in the cross-generational relationship that the affective ambience extended across distance by social and locative media becomes more important.

The disadvantages perceived by children are mostly about monitoring from their parents. Children are aware that certain movements and moments might worry their parents, and hence choose to negotiate this in various ways, such as "self-censorship" before posting messages, selective exposure to their parents, and strategic blocking of their parents for a while and then adding them back. Generally speaking, many felt there was little worth hiding from their parents. Moreover, parents deployed emotional means to dissuade their children from blocking them, as was illustrated in two interviews. When mothers found they could not see their daughters' uploads, they questioned their daughters as to why they had blocked them and requested them to "add them back." Both mothers phoned their daughters to express how they cared about them and their disappointment and unhappiness about being blocked. The daughters then unblocked them and have since had to self-edit more systematically.

Patterns of family interaction manifest in particular ways through locative media. For those "democratic" families in which parents and children enjoy relatively independent spaces, parents will not ask much about children's daily activities because they know that their children would not like it. They just watch *quietly*. Other parents have more power and want to know almost everything about their children. The media literacies of parents can also influence how they use locative media to interact with their children. In families where both parents are adept at new technology, mothers seem to be more active than fathers in social media use, and communicate more with their children. In a counter-example, however, in Tintin's family, her mother is not proficient with mobile apps, so she has to live vicariously through her husband's media connections with Tintin. Tintin used to be closer to her mother, but she admits that now that she interacts with her father more frequently on social media, their relationship has become more intimate. Tintin's media usage such as geotagged photos with her parents shows how digital kinship can be recast through intimate, ambient and mundane gestures of media co-presence.

Genealogies of locative media in Tokyo

In Japan from the mid-1970s, a nuclear family consisting only of "a couple and child(ren)" came to be regarded as an exemplary model of the family (Nonoyama 2009). However, in recent years, the composition of the typical family has diversified due to the decrease in the number of people getting married, the tendency to marry later and the decline in the number of children. The number of couples married in 2012 was 670,000, which was 60 percent less than the level in 1972, when the number was 1.1 million (Ministry of Health, Labor and Welfare 2013).

In light of these familial and lifestyle shifts, Hisaya Nonoyama, an advocate of the "family lifestyle approach," argues that today, the notion of "family" indicates various forms of family selected by individuals' lifestyles, and family has become an important object of choice for individuals. Thus, within a context of "family" – which is selected and formed *as* a lifestyle – individuals have to exert active effort to build and maintain "familiar relationships," otherwise they cannot enter or they fall out of the family circle. Nonoyama's research leads us to ask: how do family members communicate with each other to form or maintain lifestyle-based "families of choice" in Japan today?

In Japan, mobile phones, which started to become common in the mid-1990s, are used as a tool to connect family members in these families of choice (Ito et al. 2005). From the late 2000s, smartphones started to become an integral communication tool among family members, not only through their provision of email, SMS (text messages) and telephone services, but also as a portal to social media. According to a survey conducted by the Institute for Information and Communications Policy (IICP) in 2013, the utilization rate of smartphones was 52.8 percent, which was 20 points up from the previous poll (IICP 2014). The age group that uses smartphones most frequently was people in their twenties (87.9 percent), followed by those in their thirties (78.7 percent), teens (63.3 percent), forties (58.8 percent), fifties (32.4 percent), and sixties (8.7 percent). These statistics are echoed in our fieldwork with families. In the next section we discuss some of our key findings in terms of media practices, lifestyles and digital kinship.

Rika is a 32-year-old female flight attendant who lives in a bedsit about an hour by train from Tokyo. Just a stone's throw away from her apartment, Rika's only family, her 72-year-old mother, lives alone. Rika often leaves home for work early in the morning and returns home late. Reflecting the "family-as-chosen-lifestyle" trend noted above, she and her mother respect each other's daily rhythms by living separately. Rika's first mobile phone was the one that her mother bought her when she was in junior high school, for personal security purposes on her way home from after-school cram school. Since then, she has been using her mobile phone for communicating with her mother on a daily basis. After graduating from university, the mobile phone became even more important in maintaining Rika's relationship with her mother as Rika started to fly all around the world as a flight attendant. Overseas flights occasionally cause unexpected delays. "I couldn't come back to Japan when there was a flood in Thailand and a volcanic explosion in Iceland. In these situations, if it wasn't for mobile phones, my mother would not have been able to find out if I was OK," she says. In her airline, the family of employees are not allowed to make calls directly to the airline if a hijacking occurs. This makes the mobile phone indispensable in allowing Rika to communicate with her mother especially when she is abroad.

Until two years ago, Rika used to use SMS when she was abroad, which costs \$1 (per message) anywhere in the world, to communicate with her mother. After she bought a Samsung Galaxy smartphone and tablet PC two years ago, and a tablet PC for her mother, they started to use Facebook and LINE instead of SMS. When she was in junior high, her mother bought a mobile phone for her. Now the roles are reversed, with Rika buying her mother the communication devices. Rather than buying a smartphone, Rika bought an easy-to-use tablet PC with a large screen, given her mother's age. Rika always gives a fully charged tablet PC to her mother before she leaves Japan.

Rika often does a "check-in" on Facebook when she visits abroad on business. One reason is to let her mother know where she is. Her mother does not have her own Facebook account, so Rika keeps her own Facebook account logged-in on the tablet PC, and gives it to her mother so that she can check Rika's timeline without it being bothersome. In the past, she used to give a paper-based hotel list to her mother, but now Facebook "check-ins" suffice. LINE also has a key role in connecting the pair when they are away from each other. They can talk or chat for free by using LINE – now the most used social media app in Japan – when they have Wi-Fi connection, regardless of their location (80.3 percent of those in their twenties, 70.5 percent of teens and 65.4 percent of thirties use LINE; IICP 2014).

For example, Rika communicated with her mother using LINE video calling while she was traveling in Sedona, Arizona. "We can talk face-to-face using LINE video call. And it's free. When I was in Sedona, I wanted to tell my mother that 'I am in *this* kind of place!' by showing the scenery and my face." On being able to communicate easily with her daughter using Facebook and LINE, Rika's mother says: "It's nice. I can feel safe." There are few people who use social media in her generation. In the sixties age group, only 5 percent use Facebook and 4.3 percent use LINE (IICP 2014). Rika's mother does not know much about how to use Facebook and LINE yet, but she is thinking of taking a tablet course to master these technologies in the near future.

Through this interview, we recognize that the relationship between mother and daughter was gradually changing as they begin to adopt new mobile media technologies. During the age of the *keitai* (mobile phone), children were the ones monitored by their parents. In contrast, children now became the ones who monitor the use of technologies by their parents. Growing up with *keitai*, the interviewee's generation (thirties) can be understood as one that tends to be an early adopter of new technologies and services. Thus children are now in the position to introduce, teach and facilitate the use of social media services for their parents, rather than being introduced and taught by them. These participants suggest how social and locative media can contribute to our understandings of the notion of "family." Interestingly enough, we found that a definition of "family" may derive from the function of the media themselves. Like the phenomenon of "friends" in social network sites (Boyd 2008), users understand and define their "family" by applying the classifier of "friends/family members" provided by the app. By doing so, users are beginning to generate new forms of digital kinship.

Our interviewees also illustrated situations in which they felt togetherness or connectedness with their family members, while they are physically apart.

Smartphones and tablet PCs are utilized to create and maintain their intimacy. The "stamp" function (cartoon emoticons) of LINE and other messenger services is becoming an integral part of social and locative media, giving users access to emotional, non-verbal aspects of communication. Another key concept, the intimate mundane, also resonated with our Japan interviews. Given the historical entrenchment of *keitai* culture in Japan, smartphones and tablet PCs are inextricably embedded in day-to-day activities. Daily "check-ins" to Facebook timelines and exchanges of stamps via LINE are no longer "new" events for the users. Rather, they seem to play a key role in organizing their mundane practices, providing a template for tempo-spatial micro-coordinations around differing schedules.

Genealogies of locative media in Melbourne

Melbourne provides a compelling site for studying a relatively recent locative media uptake. Here, as in Shanghai and Tokyo, smartphones play a key role in mediating and representing lifestyle. Smartphones with locative technologies are relatively pervasive in Australia, and this rate of pervasiveness is increasing rapidly. Smartphone penetration is Australia was 37 percent at the beginning of 2011; two years later that figure had risen to 65 percent (Our Mobile Planet 2012; ACMA 2012). However, unlike Tokyo, which has already experienced a decade of mobile Internet, Melbourne is relatively new to the phenomenon. Other recent research has indicated that the number of people who own either a smartphone or a tablet has risen to over 70 percent in this Australian city (Deepend 2014). Device penetration is relatively high across most age demographics. Within certain age brackets, such as the 25–29 demographic, ownership of smart devices is over 90 percent; however, even older demographics, such as the over-sixties, report smartphone ownership of 55 percent (Deepend 2014).

In June 2012, there were an estimated 6.4 million families living in Australia consisting of a total of 19.4 million family members. The vast majority of families were couples (83 percent), with about half of the couples having dependants living with them (43 percent). The next largest group was one-parent families (15 percent), and two out of every three one-parent families had dependants living with them (67 percent). Of the 961,000 one-parent families, 81 percent were single mothers (ABS 2013).

Unlike Shanghai and Tokyo, which are characterized by a relatively monocultural permanent population with a steady tide of international visitors, in Melbourne multiculturalism is a key feature of the permanent population, with 42 percent of its residents born overseas and the most commonly spoken language after English being Mandarin (10 percent) (City of Melbourne 2013). In a City of Melbourne report, a total of 207 ancestries were identified for residents, along with 138 overseas countries of birth and 121 languages other than English spoken at home (ibid.). It is clearly important to engage with this multicultural aspect of Melbourne's social tapestry.

In a preliminary study in October and November of 2013, we conducted some initial probing into relationships with, and through, locative media within families. We sought to recruit participants whose backgrounds reflected cultural diversity and diaspora. We initially conducted a survey via Survey Monkey, recruited via Twitter, Facebook ads and AirTasker. The majority of respondents fell between the ages of 20–39 (60 percent). Some 70 percent used locative media and the Internet to keep in touch with family "very often" or "extremely often"; 90 percent had a smartphone; and attitudes to locative media were mostly positive, although 40 percent stated privacy as a concern. From these 40 surveys we then recruited two families to conduct preliminary home visits, diary studies and interviews.

The first family were Japanese migrants. This was a self-described "nuclear" family of four: mother (Nina, 63), father (Tony, 68), son (Phil, 34), and daughter (Kate, 31). The family was originally from Yokohama, and had lived in Australia for 25 years, with the kids being eight and ten years old when they moved. Both parents are now retired, both children are married, and Phil's wife (Yin, 31) was present for the interviews. Kate uses her work iPad to check her Facebook feed at home. She is not "friends" with her parents on Facebook, although her husband is "friends" with her dad, and he sees most of her pictures through his profile. Kate checks her social media profiles in and around her work day as a Japanese teacher. After work is when she will often call her brother, and comment on his Facebook posts. Her checking reflects Kate's daily rhythms through a type of affective ambience that is located in the intimate mundane. Mundane thoughts and images are posted to give her friends and family an intimate co-present sense of her everyday life. In this way, locative media move in and out of the background of everyday life to help Kate navigate social and spatial assemblages, and entanglements between her Japanese and Australian self.

This family's media use showed how locative media are important in navigating transnational relationships by giving users the ability to gain a sense of place through online maps. In maintaining relationships with friends and family overseas, social and locative media become pivotal for both parents and children to maintain digital kinship through intimate co-presence. Tony, the father, used Facebook to keep in touch with people in Japan, posting comments about weather and traffic, and sometimes photos. Nina, the mother, said early on that she was "not good at technical things," but later on Tony showed us her desk, with her own computer housing social media pages.

The second family was a Chinese Australian family consisting of husband (Jack, 32), wife (Laura, 30) and wife's mother (CiCi, 60). Jack and Laura were recently married, and CiCi had recently moved in with them, beginning a year-long stay. Jack and Laura had been in Australia for seven and three years, respectively; both are from Shandong province and work as professionals in the IT sector. Jack's mother still lives in Shandong, and does not visit Australia often. He is more likely to go back to China, as he likes visiting his friends there as well as seeing his mother (and cousin). He emails her once a week, and they talk about how life is going. His mother wants to know if he works too much. They do not use anything other than email to communicate.

Jack uses Weibo and WeChat to keep in touch with his Chinese friends, both in China and in Australia. He and his wife are connected on a number of social networks, including both "Aussie" and "Chinese" ones. They do not communicate on them very often, however. Jack thinks that Laura posts more than him. Laura complains that he only posts sports and car news, although he will sometimes post pictures of Laura in Melbourne parks and other beautiful locations so that her friends can see. Laura uses Weibo, WeChat, QQ, Facebook and Twitter. Much like Jack, she uses these for different purposes and different sets of friends and family. She accesses these on her iPhone (when out) and her iPad (when home; Figure 9.1). She mainly uses the "Chinese" services to update her friends in China on her life in Melbourne. She also likes to check what her friends in China are doing, and how they are. She leaves messages for them on Weibo and WeChat so that they can see them at their convenience: the time difference is important, especially during the working week when they would struggle to have free time that overlaps.

CiCi primarily uses QQ on her mobile phone (an iPhone). When she is in Australia, CiCi enjoys going on walks in the neighborhood, and taking photos on her phone. Social and locative media provide CiCi with the ability to map her experiences in Australia in an ambient manner that is both intimate and co-present with contacts in China. She can share images and experiences with friends and family in China and have discussions with them in real time. This affordance for digital kinship that transcends geographic distance is important for CiCi as a visitor. In contrast, for both Laura and Jack, as they try to settle in Melbourne, the social and locative media they use have been compartmentalized according to geographic location and social relation. Media like QQ are overtly for digital kinship (that is, communication with family members). Weibo and WeChat are for intimate co-presence with friends back in China. Facebook is for Melbourne friends.

Figure 9.1 Laura's iPad and the affective ambience of a traditional lotus flower image as screensaver

Conclusion

In this chapter, through paralleling three very different cultural, linguistic and technological contexts, we have explored how similarities and differences in cross-generational media literacy and intimacy are emerging. By examining familial media practices, we have tried to show how we can gain insight into both emergent and residual-traditional cultural practices. We have deployed the notion of digital kinship to understand digital media practices within familial lives as both re-enacting older rituals and providing new ways of imagining the contemporary family. Our initial research with families' use of locative media technologies suggests that the concepts of *intimate co-presence, affective ambience* and the *intimate mundane* enable the understanding of the relationships and atmospheres that are being generated across our three focus cities.

We have seen how locative media are being interwoven into the development of new norms of what we are terming digital kinship. From Rika and her mother in Japan, to Kate and her Japanese family in Melbourne, locative media are being used to mediate the intimate mundane. From blocking familial friend requests, to developing a stronger relationship with one's father due to frequent social media connection, contemporary families are using these media to negotiate the knowing and unknowing, tacit and spoken. Providing affective ambience to "fill in" the gaps of cross-generational contact and affording new ways to provide constant comfort for family members separated by geographic distance, locative media entangle with everyday lives to provide a lens onto contemporary negotiations of family, place and intimacy.

As mobile apps are domesticated into the everyday routines of our participants, we can see how people shape the media, just as the media shape them. Mobile apps like LINE in Japan and DayMap in Australia are allowing parents and children to monitor and surveil each other's practices while also affording new modes of negotiating co-presence in an increasingly mobile world. Parents have always watched children and children have always edited their behavior in the presence of their parents, but as the locative media apps become a more integral part of everyday life, we have a new opportunity to understand emergent and enduring forms of kinship and intimate co-presence (Matsuda 2009).

When kinship becomes a digitally inflected phenomenon, the three concepts of *intimate co-presence, affective ambience* and the *intimate mundane* offer us ways of theorizing digital kinship. As we have demonstrated, living with digital media in families is differently experienced in different places. However, these three concepts effectively pull together the common threads of residual and emergent meanings and practices of family in the three research localities we have considered.

Acknowledgements

This research is funded by an Australian Research Council Linkage grant with Intel (LP130100848).

Note

1 This is the official rate. However, unofficial rates are believed to be higher, with countless millions of *shanzhai* (or pirate) hardware versions linked to prepaid subscriptions.

References

Australian Bureau of Statistics (ABS). 2013. *Labour Force, Australia: Labour Force Status and Other Characteristics of Families, June 2012*. www.abs.gov.au/AUSSTATS/abs@.nsf/Latestproducts/6224.0.55.001Media%20Release1Jun%202012?opendocument&tabname=Summary&prodno=6224.0.55.001&issue=Jun%202012&num=&view= (accessed May 28, 2015).

Australian Communications and Media Authority (ACMA). 2012. *Communications Report 2011–2012 Series: Report 3–Smartphones and Tables Take-Up and Use in Australia, Summary Report*. www.acma.gov.au/webwr/_assets/main/lib310665/report-3-smartphones_tablets-summary.pdf (accessed May 28, 2015).

Boyd, Danah. 2008. *It's Complicated: The Social Lives of Networked Teens*. New Haven, CT: Yale University Press.

China Internet Network Information Center (CNNIC). 2013. *Statistical Report on Internet in China*. www1.cnnic.cn/IDR/ReportDownloads/201302/P020130221391269963814.pdf (accessed May 28, 2015).

Chua, Beng Huat. 2010. "Disrupting Hegemonic Liberalism in East Asia." *boundary 2: An International Journal of Literature and Culture* 37(2): 199–216.

City of Melbourne. 2013. *Multicultural Community Demographic Profile*. www.melbourne.vic.gov.au/AboutMelbourne/Statistics/Documents/Demographic_profile_Multicultural_2013.pdf (accessed May 28, 2015).

Clark, Lynn Schofield. 2012. *The Parent App: Understanding Families in a Digital Age*. Oxford: Oxford University Press.

Coleman, E. Gabriella. 2010. "Ethnographic Approaches to Digital Media." *Annual Review of Anthropology* 39: 487–505.

Deepend. 2014. *Making Digital Work Harder: Australian Mobile Device Ownership and Home Usage Report 2014*. www.deepend.com.au/download-white-paper-device-usage-in-the-home (accessed May 28, 2015).

de Souza e Silva, Adriana, and Jordan Frith. 2012. *Mobile Interfaces in Public Spaces: Locational Privacy, Control, and Urban Sociability*. New York: Routledge.

Farman, Jason. 2011. *Mobile Interface Theory: Embodied Space and Locative Media*. London: Routledge.

Gazzard, Alison. 2011. "Location, Location, Location: Collecting Space and Place in Mobile Media." *Convergence* 17(4): 405–417.

Hertzeld, Michael. 1997. *Cultural Intimacy: Social Poetics in the Nation-State*. New York: Routledge.

Hjorth, Larissa. 2009. *Mobile Media in the Asia-Pacific*. London: Routledge.

Hjorth, Larissa, and Kay Gu. 2012. "The Place of Emplaced Visualities: A Case Study of Smartphone Visuality and Location-Based Social Media in Shanghai, China." *Continuum: Journal of Media & Cultural Studies* 26(5): 699–713.

Hjorth, Larissa, Jack Linchuan Qiu, Baohua Zhou, and Wei Ding. 2014. "The Social in the Mobile: QQ as Cross-Generational Media in China." In *The Routledge Companion to Mobile Media*, edited by Gerard Goggin and Larissa Hjorth, 291–299. New York: Routledge.

Horst, Heather A. 2010. "Families". In *Hanging Out, Messing Around, and Geeking Out: Kids Living and Learning with New Media*, edited by Mizuko Ito et al., 149–194. Cambridge, MA: MIT Press.

Horst, Heather A. 2011. "Grandmothers, Girlfriends and Big Men: The Gendered Geographies of Jamaican Transnational Communication." In *Migration, Diaspora and Information Technology in Global Societies*, edited by Leopoldina Fortunati, Raul Pertierra and Jane Vincent, 65–77. London: Routledge.

Horst, Heather A., and Daniel Miller, eds. 2012. *Digital Anthropology*. London: Sage.

Institute for Information and Communications Policy (IICP). 2014. "Heisei 25 nen jouhou tsushin media no riyou jikan to jouhou koudou ni kansuru chousa sokuhou" (The results of a survey of the utilization time of telecommunication media and information behavior). www.soumu.go.jp/iicp/chousakenkyu/data/research/survey/telecom/2014/h25mediariyou_1sokuhou.pdf (accessed June 30, 2014).

Ito, Mizuko, Daisuke Okabe, and Misa Matsuda, eds. 2005. *Pedestrian, Portable and Personal: Mobile Phones in Japanese Life*. Cambridge, MA: MIT Press.

Licoppe, Christian. 2004. "'Connected' Presence: The Emergence of a New Repertoire for Managing Social Relationships in a Changing Communication Technoscape." *Environment and Planning Design: Society and Space* 22(1): 135–156.

Matsuda, Misa. 2009. "Mobile Media and the Transformation of the Family." In *Mobile Technologies: From Telecommunications to Media*, edited by Gerard Goggin and Larissa Hjorth, 62–72. New York: Routledge.

McVeigh, Brian J. 2003a. "Individualization, Individuality, Interiority, and the Internet: Japanese University Students and E-mail." In *Japanese Cybercultures*, edited by Nanette Gottlieb and Mark McLelland, 19–33. London: Routledge.

McVeigh, B. 2003b. *Nationalisms of Japan: Managing and Mystifying Identity*. Oxford and New York: Rowman and Littlefield.

Ministry of Health, Labor and Welfare. 2013. "Heisei 25 nendoban kouseiroudou hakusho" (White Paper on Health, Labour and Welfare 2013). www.mhlw.go.jp/wp/hakusyo/kousei/13/dl/1-02-2.pdf (accessed August 26, 2014).

Nonoyama, H. 2009. *Ronten Handbook Kazoku shakaigaku (Handbook of Family Sociology)*. Kyoto: Sekaishisosha.

Okabe, Daisuke. 2004. "Emergent Social Practices, Situations and Relations through Everyday Camera Phone Use." Paper presented at the International Conference on Mobile Communication in Seoul, Korea, October 18–19. www.itofisher.com/mito/archives/okabe_seoul.pdf.

Our Mobile Planet. 2012. "Our Mobile Planet: Global Smartphone Users." www.slideshare.net/tessierv/google-our-mobile-planet-feb-2012 (accessed June 2, 2015).

Pink, Sarah, and Larissa Hjorth. 2013. "Emplaced Cartographies: Reconceptualising Camera Phone Practices in an Age of Locative Media." *Media International Australia* 145: 145–156.

Pink, Sarah, and Kerstin Leder Mackley. 2012. "Video and a Sense of the Invisible: Approaching Domestic Energy Consumption Through the Sensory Home." *Sociological Research Online* 17(1). www.socresonline.org.uk/17/1/3.html.

Pink, Sarah, Kerstin Leder Mackley, Val Mitchell, Carolina Escobar-Tello, Marcus Hanratty, Tracy Bhamra, and Roxana Morosanu. 2013. "Applying the Lens of Sensory Ethnography to Sustainable HCI." *Transactions on Computer-Human Interaction* 20(4).

Pink, Sarah, and Jennie Morgan. 2013. "Short-Term Ethnography: Intense Routes to Knowing." *Symbolic Interaction* 36(3): 351–361.

Robison, Richard, and David S.G. Goodman, eds. 1996. *The New Rich in Asia: Mobile Phones, McDonald's and Middle Class Revolution*. London: Routledge.

Sengupta, Somini. 2012. "'Big Brother'? No, It's Parents" *The New York Times*, June 25. www.nytimes.com/2012/06/26/technology/software-helps-parents-monitor-their-children-online.html?_r=0 (accessed May 28, 2015).

10 Dishing up diversity?

Class, aspirationalism and Indian food television

Tania Lewis

Watching television in Delhi at 10pm (primetime in urban India) on a Saturday night in 2011, I flicked through the meager offering of 50-odd channels available on my hotel room TV (there are now 600 plus channels in India, and rising). There was the usual mix of *saas bahu* (mother-in-law/daughter) soaps, Bollywood movies ("vintage" and new), endless news and sports channels, quiz shows, a couple of English-language shows (including an endlessly recycled episode of *Friends*), singing competitions and the odd reality offering: *Bigg Boss*, the long-running Indian version of *Big Brother*, was airing that night (the extra g on Big coming courtesy of advice from celebrity numerologists). However, what caught my eye was the small but significant proportion of programming that might best be designated as lifestyle or life advice television. While these shows varied considerably in terms of style and mode of address – ranging from a glossy Indian-made English-language cookery show on TLC and a Hindi-language women's magazine show on the well-being channel Pragya (*Just for Women*), to a no-frills studio-based health show on the major Tamil channel, Jaya TV – they were all underpinned by a concern with advising viewers on various lifestyle issues, and invariably featured an array of "everyday experts" of some kind, whether celebrity chefs, health gurus or more traditional, credentialed experts such as the doctors interviewed, chat-show style, on the Jaya TV health show.

This chapter examines emergent trends in lifestyle culture in contemporary India by focusing on a popular sub-genre of lifestyle television, namely food shows. It comes out of a larger Australian Research Council-funded project I have been working on with Asian cultural studies specialists Fran Martin and Wanning Sun, on lifestyle television in Asia, especially the styles and practices of life conduct, "ethicalised" selfhood and consumer-citizenship performed and promoted on some of these shows (Lewis et al. 2012). In focusing on food television in India, the chapter is centrally concerned with the way in which this particular form of television and its respective modes of "ordinary expertise" (Lewis 2008) foreground key dynamics and tensions around contemporary discourses and practices of selfhood, lifestyle and modernity in India today. Acknowledging the limits of applying Euro-American-inflected theories of class, lifestyle and cultural citizenship in the context of South and

East Asia, and India in particular (Robison and Goodman 1995; Chua 2000), I use food television as a lens through which to examine how the middle classes have been positioned in Indian public life as "the sociocultural embodiment of India's transition to a committed liberalizing nation" (Fernandes 2006, 30).

Drawing on extensive empirical research with self-identified "middle-class" households (in which colleague Kiran Mulenhalli and I conducted interviews in Mumbai), and interviews I undertook in Delhi and Mumbai with numerous media professionals involved in making lifestyle and reality TV, I focus in particular on issues of class, taste and aspirationalism: key concerns for TV programmers, executives and producers alike, but concerns, as the following discussion indicates, that are negotiated in diverse and complex ways in and through people's everyday viewing and lifestyle practices.

A serving of cheese and broccoli: taste, consumption and cookery shows

Lifestyle programming has emerged in India in the context of broader shifts over the past couple of decades in social identity, and family and gender relations, accompanied by highly uneven processes of individualization, and pressures for labor mobility and flexibility (Derné 2008; Kotwal et al. 2011). A shift since the early 1990s from a developmental, socialist state-supported economy to a *laissez-faire* economy and job market has occurred hand in hand with the nation's opening up to a global commodity market, a transition that has seen an emergent and growing consumer culture and a "new" middle class (against the backdrop of colonial, gendered and caste-inflected forms of social stratification) (Fernandes 2006). Meanwhile, the liberalization and privatization of the TV industry have dramatically changed the look and feel of Indian television. While, from the 1960s to the early 1990s, television was state-supported with minimal program diversity (the state broadcaster Doordarshan was the sole content provider), the deregulation of the industry and the rise of satellite have seen as explosion in the number and variety of channels available, with focus shifting away from morally uplifting TV aimed at educating citizens, to light entertainment formats oriented increasingly to consumers (Roy 2008). Indian television has transformed from a rather narrow and exclusionary model of "nationalized" state television to become, today, one of the largest and most diverse television industries in the world. Programming has become highly commercialized with entertainment channels, featuring a mix of soap operas, movies, talent shows and reality TV, taking out the lion's share of viewership.

It is in this setting that cookery programming has become highly popular in India, with culinary shows accompanied by a more general growth in "foodie" culture in recent years and an interest in "luxury" food items like broccoli, mushrooms and kiwi fruit (Fernandes 2006, 74). Meanwhile, lifestyle supplements in major newspapers like *The Times of India* feature regular articles listing the top ten "masterchefs" of the moment, and food "entrepreneurs" like Sanjeev Kapoor (who appears as a regular judge on *MasterChef India* and launched his own food channel in 2011) are considered major cultural icons. This is not to suggest that food TV is a new phenomenon in India; magazine-style cookery shows have long been a feature of Indian daytime TV. The past decade, however, has seen a proliferation and mainstreaming of food programming, from low-budget regional TV shows aimed at rural housewives to glossy food-travel shows targeted at socially mobile urbanites. Such trends are commonly read in India as suggesting a democratization of taste. Nilendu Sen, an executive at the major news channel Aaj Tak (TV Today), sums up this commonly held view when he contends that "[s]uddenly, middle-class homes are talking about pasta, salsa sauces and different kinds of cheeses […] The emergent lifestyle patterns are such that people are experimenting with their lives and they are doing that with food as well".[1]

Niret Alva, TV presenter and cofounder of the production company Miditech, goes further than this, suggesting that food TV is one of the few lifestyle genres that speaks across social divisions in India:

> Food is something Indians are passionate about. In fact, a few months ago there was this *Outlook* magazine lead article about the most popular foods, apparently the most popular food was Masala Dosa (a South Indian dish) followed by Chhola Bhatura (a North Indian dish) so these are local dishes that go across all regions […] Food can be a huge unifier more than language and other things. Even with *MasterChef* the lady who cooks at our place, she was watching it with her eyes open, she said she wants the recipe and she was telling us to write down the details.[2]

Certainly in our fieldwork and interviews with Mumbai households, from poorer families living in informal housing to solidly middle-class and well-to-do upper middle-class households, cookery shows were a universal favorite across gender, age and caste. Indeed, we were surprised by the number of families who had watched or at least were familiar with *MasterChef Australia*, a show that received considerable favorable press when it was first aired in India in 2011 (partly due to the poor reception of *MasterChef India*, which was widely seen as inferior to the Australian version of the British format, both in terms of content and production values).

However, while there is increasing access to and familiarity with glossy international food formats in India, such shifts in program availability do not necessarily equate with a widespread shift in taste or an increasing uptake of cosmopolitan-style consumer practices. The complexity of the TV audience in India, where both programming and television viewing practices are strongly shaped by linguistic, class, caste, gender and regional differences, means that any sweeping generalizations about the "uses of television" need to be closely scrutinized. I would suggest that in the Indian context, cookery programming and the figure of the celebrity chef can be equally understood as speaking to questions of difference as they can be read as social unifiers. I would argue that, through often very distinctive modes of address, performance and forms of "embodied expertise," Indian cookery shows *do* speak to questions of contemporary selfhood, taste, consumption practices and lifestyle – but they do so in ways that suggest a complex negotiation of and articulation between classed, caste inflected and gendered identities.

Food to go: culinary tourism and critical cosmopolitanism

One of the main spaces where lifestyle programming and associated forms of expertise have proliferated on Indian TV is on dedicated lifestyle cable channels aimed at aspirational middle- and upper middle-class audiences, such as Discovery Travel and Living, which came to India in 2004 (and became TLC India in 2010). High-end niche channels like TLC primarily import English-language programming, with the odd locally made program featuring local hosts and personalities. For the purposes of this chapter, however, New Delhi TV (NDTV) Good Times, which was launched in 2007 and featured in the top two lifestyle channels in 2011 according to the TAM Media Research (TAM 2011), until recently the key ratings agency in India, offers a more critically engaging example of Indian lifestyle programming than does TLC, as it largely airs locally made and culturally hybridized shows featuring home-grown hosts and experts.

Targeting young urban viewers and focusing on fitness, beauty, parenthood and marriage, cars and technology, travel, cookery and pets, NDTV Good Times offers a range of locally produced, primarily English-language lifestyle and advice programming (though it is increasingly shifting to Hindi and Hinglish, the playful blended "language" favored by savvy young urbanites). Its extensive programming list ranges from highbrow "conversation" and advice shows (*One Life To Love*), through to magazine-style travel (*Miss Traveler* – see Chapter 8 in this collection), cars (*All About My Car, Honey*) and pet shows (*Heavy Petting*). Recognizing the broader appeal of reality-style shows within a general entertainment market, the channel has more recently moved into reality-lifestyle programs; these include *Daddy's Day In*, a fly-on-the-wall show about men attempting to run a household (an almost revolutionary theme in a country where men very rarely cook or do household chores); *Band Baajaa Bride*, a makeover-style wedding format; and playful new hybrid genres such as NDTV's new Bollywood-ized cookery show for 2013, *The Kitchen Musical*.

While the channel offers a wide range of cooking shows including various home-grown *MasterChef*-like competitive formats, given that upper middle-class Indian households usually employ someone to cook for them, it is perhaps not surprising that NDTV's dominant mode of programming is culinary tourism rather than cookery shows *per se*. As Arati Singh from NDTV Good Times' Mumbai headquarters sums up, "we don't do cookery, we do food." One of the most popular offerings in this genre and across the channel more broadly is the long-running series *Highway on my Plate*. The show is presented by Rocky and Mayur, two rather generously built men who travel round India on motorbikes tasting and critically evaluating local foods – for instance at a roadside *dhabba* in the Punjab – while discussing the specificity of local customs and cuisines. Despite the Indian setting and the frequent use of extra-diegetic elements such as traditional music, the show has the feel of an international format in the tradition of *Two Fat Ladies* or *The Hairy Bikers*, what Niki Strange categorizes as the "tour-educative" genre of cookery show (Strange 1998). As Rocky and Mayur visit various traditional food establishments, they inform the audience – in a comic, conversational style – about the particulars of the cuisine of the area they are visiting, while critically assessing the food outlet on the authenticity of its décor and the quality of the food.

Despite presenting themselves as authoritative food critics, Rocky and Mayur have no particular expertise in this area. In this sense, they reflect the broader rise of "ordinary experts" and the democratization of expertise on lifestyle TV globally. However, in this case they have little in common with the majority of ordinary Indian viewers, embodying instead NDTV Good Times' imagined audience of highly educated, English-speaking, globe-trotting professionals: Rocky is an HR consultant based in Dubai while Mayur is an "outdoor experiential educator." On the show they perform and promote a reflexive and playful kind of cosmopolitan Indian identity, asking audiences to see India and its culinary riches through the eyes of a tourist while adopting a self-consciously hybrid, transnational yet Indian identity (both Rocky and Mayur often refer to their own specific cultural roots). Cosmopolitan in taste but immersed in and knowledgeable about the local and the customary, Rocky and Mayur also embody a kind of critical evaluative habitus where spaces and practices of leisure and lifestyle become sites of constant assessment and evaluation.

Shows such as *Highway on my Plate* address their audience as expert-tourists, as "socially upbeat, well-travelled, cosmopolitan viewers who live in style […] are adventurous about food and travel and want more out of every moment in life" (NDTV Good Times 2011). Such a vision of enterprising global subjecthood is of course well beyond the reach of many Indian viewers. As Arati Singh, head of fashion at NDTV Good Times in Mumbai, emphasized in an interview in 2011, "our programming is very very very aspirational."[3] Indeed, a recurrent theme in our interviews with TV producers and executives in Mumbai and Delhi was the acknowledged gap between this kind of high-end programming and the lives of more "ordinary" Indians, whether the lower-middle or middle classes or "the masses," with one TV executive arguing that "we are focusing on the classes and forgetting about the masses."[4]

In the next section, then, I want to discuss cookery programming in relation to the more solidly *middle*-middle-class (rather than upper- and upper middle-class) viewers we spoke to and watched television with in Mumbai.

While some of these households occasionally watch NDTV Good Times, their viewing and lifestyle practices are rather different from NDTV's imagined upper-class audience – in particular, they are much more tied to vicarious consumption suggesting the diverse nature of engagements with and articulations of "consumer culture" in India.

Vicarious consumption and the urban middle classes

In *Shoveling Smoke*, his brilliant ethnographic study of the advertising industry in India, William Mazzarella argues that transitions in the nature of Indian public life over the past couple of decades, especially the shift to a deregulated economy in 1991, have laid the foundations for a new "social ontology of global consumerism" (Mazzarella 2003, 12), a transition crucially mediated by television. Where once, Indian aspirations were tied to developmentalist images of nation building and raising up the poor, television and its associated commodity imagery have now ushered in a new conception of collectivity that, while spearheaded by a class elite, has legitimated itself via "the democratization of aspiration" (Mazzarella 2003, 98). Commercial TV has been key to this process, promoting through its aesthetics and "feel" a new focus on the sensory pleasures of life, rather than on purely working and saving.

Mazzarella's picture of an emerging middle class whose aspirations are increasingly tied to consumption-based imaginaries rings true in many ways with what I would call the steadfastly middling middle-class households that we interviewed in our Mumbai study. Certainly their TV consumption was often highly aspirational, although it was also often marked by a wide gap between their televisual tastes and pleasures and their actual lifestyle practices.

While the families we interviewed rarely watched shows like *Highway on my Plate*, generally they were regular viewers of food travel programming of some sort, as well as more conventional kitchen-based cooking shows. An example of the latter is the long-running Hindi-language Zee TV show *Khana Khazana* (meaning "an abundance of food"), hosted by celebrity chef Sanjeev Kapoor. While *Khana Khazana* is in certain ways an old-style "how to" cookery show, it also pitches itself to a modern aspirational audience. The opening credits offer glossy, highly aestheticized images of food, while specific episodes target the new savvy consumer with advice for a healthy lifestyle (tips might include how to use antioxidant-rich ingredients) or recipes for the busy bachelor who wants to whip up some quick and easy but impressive food, such as pizza (a food that would be seen as slightly exotic by many middle-class Indian viewers).

While many of our Mumbai interviewees were avid viewers of such shows, what was evident was the complex relationship between their viewing habits and their actual everyday practices, as well as the cross-generational differences around their engagement with television. Take Vidia's household, for example. Vidia is a busy radio producer and she and her husband (a business man), son (a law student) and brother (also in business) live in a small apartment in a solidly middle-class Mumbai neighborhood (we visited when her daughter, who was sitting postgraduate exams, and son-in-law were also staying). Spending time with Vidia and her family watching TV and discussing their viewing and lifestyle practices more broadly, it became evident that various members of the family saw lifestyle TV as an important space for learning about how to live. Like many of the middle-aged, middle-class viewers we spoke to, Vidia and her husband watched a range of lifestyle and advice-based programming and, in their daily viewing, would engage with a variety of lifestyle experts, from the religious gurus who feature on morning TV on many Indian channels, to health and well-being experts and celebrity chefs. As the main cook in the family, Vidia watched a lot of cooking shows, and described her pleasure in watching these shows as stemming largely from comparing the particular host's cooking skills and approaches with her own.

Much of Vidia's viewing with her husband, however, was linked to rather more vicarious pleasures; in particular, they talked about enjoying cookery-travel shows, seeing such shows as providing imaginative spaces where they were able to learn about the lifestyles and habits of others and to "travel" to places that they would never be able to visit themselves. While they exhibited a certain culinary literacy and served us "foreign" South Indian-style food they had bought especially for our visit, the couple laughed about the fact that they had never actually made "non-traditional" food and would very rarely eat it. This gap between people's televisual consumption (and knowledge) of food, which often stretched to various global cuisines, and their

Figure 10.1 The author watching TV with Vidia and her family, photograph by Kiran Mulenhalli

actual consumption, was a recurrent theme across our interviews with Mumbai householders. Vidia's son, the legal student, by contrast, was more adventurous in his taste and practices: enjoying shows like *Khana Khazana* with its tips for upwardly mobile bachelors and *MasterChef India*, he described even showing off his culinary skills from time to time to his family (this was often accompanied by much hilarity, given the still highly gendered associations of home cookery). For the son, however, cookery as a *practice* was clearly coded as an amusing leisure activity, with cosmopolitan associations, whereas for his mother it was a feminine-coded household duty that had to be managed alongside a full-time job.

While Vidia and her husband, as dual-income urban professionals, are clearly members of India's broadening middle class, discussing their lifestyle practices with them it was clear that the stresses of work and commuting and the rising costs of living in Mumbai meant that much of their consumption was mediated and imaginary rather than actual. Like those of many families we visited, their home was very modestly furnished, and they rarely ate out. Any travel they did was associated with familial duties rather than leisure. This was a common pattern across the families we talked to, though their children, as I have noted, were often markedly more cosmopolitan in their lifestyle practices, dress, taste and consumption patterns (Vidia's daughter, for instance, had attended a mediation and lifestyle course in Goa).

Despite these emergent trends among urban youth, a common theme in our study was the still largely aspirational quality of much middle-class consumption in India, with one TV producer pointing out that "everyone goes to the mall but no one shops." While consumption and lifestyle practices have shifted significantly compared with pre-1991 market reforms, the experiences of our middle-class Mumbai families suggest that one should be cautious about assumptions that Indians have embraced wide-scale commodity consumption. Estimated to be anywhere between 70 to 400 million by differing benchmarks, using the yardstick of a per capita daily income of above US$8–40, the middle class has grown from 5.7 percent of the population in 2001 to 12.8 percent in 2010 (153 million) (Shukla 2010). However, the middle classes are marked by significant precarity: data on the distribution of household incomes in Mumbai show that while the upper middle-income classes have grown relative to the total, lower middle-class incomes have shrunk, while much of the growth of consumption in the urban middle classes is credit based (Nijman 2006). Further, a study surveying high-income educated IT workers in Bangalore found that people's income first went on "household expenditure" and then on savings, rather than consumption (Upadhya 2009, 259). Given this context, Fernandes argues that the rise of a consumer middle class in India is perhaps best understood in discursive, rather than economic or material terms, as the production of a distinctive social and political identity that represents and lays claims to the benefits of economic liberalization (Fernandes 2006). Where the kinds of sensory and aesthetic modes of consumption foregrounded by Mazzarella have become increasingly normalized for the Indian middle classes, then, is in imaginary televisual practices, and in particular in lifestyle television.

"It is a competition, not really for learning": cookery shows and utilitarianism

As noted above, Indian TV producers in Mumbai and Delhi often commented on the fact that the majority of Indian TV viewers live lives far removed from the lifestyles depicted on NDTV Good Times or indeed the main general entertainment channels that air "popular" reality shows like *MasterChef India* and *Bigg Boss.* As the TV host of the hugely successful Indian reality show *MTV Roadies* (and CEO of a format production company), Rajiv Lakshman, put it: "lifestyle, the way it is defined globally, is not a big player in India [...] we have more existential issues than lifestyle issues."[5]

As discussed, while on the one hand the Indian media often trumpet the success of the new middle classes, the economic and material realities in India offer a salutatory challenge to this kind of triumphal discourse (Shukla 2010). Although the poverty rate in India is projected to fall to 22 percent in 2015 (from 51 percent in 1990), this impoverished section of the population is still a long way from reaching anything near middle-class status (*Times of India* 2011). Meanwhile, while urban centers like Mumbai are pictured as exuberant symbols of cosmopolitan media modernity, Mumbai's real estate boom in the 2000s has seen more than half the city's population now living in informal or "slum" housing (another 5–10 percent are pavement dwellers), characterized by a "huge infrastructure deficit" in terms of potable water, legally supplied electricity and sanitation (Echanove and Srivastava 2011). However, many slum-dwelling Mumbaikers are otherwise "connected" and technologically savvy, possessing cheap mobile phones, and direct-to-home (DTH) television (satellite provided direct to home via a small dish and set-top box), which has become a growing part of the market, particularly in rural areas not well served by technological infrastructure.

In our study of domestic TV practices, we conducted interviews with some poorer families who lived on the outskirts of Mumbai, including that of Ramesh, a taxi driver, and his wife. Ramesh, who self-identified as "middle class," and his wife and two children, live in a neighborhood consisting of very small houses that are "extralegally" constructed. Their television is situated in close proximity to their household shrine (shrines and TVs commonly occupy a central and sometimes shared space in Indian households) and in the same room in which they sleep, cook and eat. Ramesh and his wife are avid TV viewers and have DTH rather than cable TV, so that they can access a very wide range of channels, as well as multilingual channel options, so that they can switch languages from English to Hindi, Tamil or Bengali, and, importantly, given the temporary nature of their domestic situation, they can also easily move their TV connection if they are forced to move elsewhere.

Figure 10.2 The room housing Ramesh's family's TV and shrine serves as the main living and sleeping space for the family, with a small kitchen space cordoned off at one end, photograph by Kiran Mulenhalli

Ramesh and his family's viewing taste is in certain ways similar to that of many of the other Mumbai families we spent time with, ranging from serials to reality and lifestyle TV and also including astrology programs (Ramesh showed off an astrology ring he had bought from the Telebrand shopping channel). The multilingual channel options on DTH also enable Ramesh and his family to watch foreign popular documentaries, and reality and lifestyle shows on channels such as Discovery and Fox (which are often seen as "high-end" in the Indian market, and previously were only available via relatively costly subscriber fees). *Man Versus Wild* on the Discovery Channel, for instance, is a favorite show; interestingly, Ramesh reads the show primarily in terms of survival tips ("they show … how to survive. Say, if you are lost for four to five days, how do you save your life? How to deal with that situation?"), noting somewhat paradoxically that Bear Grylls (the show's presenter, a "survival expert") has taught him things he did not know about the healing properties of plants from his own home village. As he put it, "[w]e get to know Ayurveda-like information [via the show]. It is nice and informative show." Here we see a fascinating translation of a global entertainment format into a quite specific cultural and social context, marked by a rather utilitarian approach to televisual consumption. Ramesh read other entertainment-oriented genres in similarly educative terms ("one can learn"), interpreting the Indian version of *Fear Factor*, for instance, as an informative show about how to overcome phobias.

Like Vidia's family, Ramesh and his wife also watched a range of "tour-educative" travel-cookery shows, including an evening food show (*Food at 9*) on Fox Traveller, which introduces cuisines from around India and the world. While Fox Traveller describes its audience as including "people who are hungry for new, bigger, better, and varied experiences; open to trying out even challenging things and wanting to visit the places and ideas that they see on the channel," Ramesh and his wife's interest in the show was rather more pragmatic. As Ramesh put it, "[w]hat is nice about *Food at 9* is in one hour they would show at least seven to eight dishes. They also show dishes that could be made without using stove or gas … like green salad." Ramesh's wife often made dishes they had learned from television, although, given their extremely limited budget, they would substitute ingredients (such as Asian noodles) with cheaper, locally available products.

Ramesh's viewing habits and tastes were seemingly quite culturally omnivorous (few of the Mumbai families we interviewed regularly watched high-end cable channels like the Discovery Channel), and he had a technical knowledge of television that was superior to many of the other viewers and allowed him to engage with a far larger range of programs. His interest in lifestyle and food programming, however, was overwhelmingly informational in focus and there was little sense of engagement with the aspirational dimensions of some of the glossier lifestyle shows he watched, and in particular the model of adventurous, entrepreneurial selfhood promoted on many of the Discovery Channel shows. It is perhaps no surprise, then, that he and his wife were not fans of entertainment-style reality shows such as *MasterChef India*. As Ramesh put it:

> We cannot understand that show […] Because they have time limit to make a dish; someone like us who is interested in learning would find it difficult. It is a competition, not really for learning …

Patil and his wife, a 56-year-old government employee, who similarly live very modestly on the outskirts of Mumbai, were also interested in forms of advice television that offered information and useful life guidance. Like Ramesh, Patil and his wife appreciated cookery shows that offered everyday tips such as how to make tasty meals from leftover food. Like many Indian families, they also watched a lot of spiritual programming, seeing TV "*babas*" as providing helpful life guidance: "you learn to be happy with what you have." Patil, who suffered from heart disease, also talked extensively about the health benefits of the yoga he learned from watching and practicing the *asanas* demonstrated by gurus every day on morning TV.

Patil and Ramesh's viewing practices, then, represented something of a contrast to Vidia and her husband's engagement with television as a vehicle for vicarious pleasures and lifestyle tourism. Indeed, the poorer households we spoke to in general had a rather pragmatic approach to the forms of life guidance offered on TV, engaging in particular with advice programming that they either perceived as educational in some way or as being able to assist them with the daily struggles of pressured lives and making do with limited resources. With the privatization of many state-provided services, the poor in India are increasingly expected to manage and take responsibility for their own education and health. For instance, as in China (see Chapters 4 and 5 in this volume) in the area of health, state spending has declined over the past two decades as the sector is increasingly privatized (Varman and Vikas 2007). With the costs of health increasingly borne by Indian citizens, increasing numbers of poor urban and rural Indians are avoiding seeking healthcare (ibid.). In this context, television becomes a key site of access to advice, information and support for those with otherwise limited access to resources.

The dialectics of lifestyle television

This chapter has examined the kinds of social imaginaries and aspirational desires enacted in various types of Indian food television, and in particular how such programming might be seen to normalize Mazzarella's "ontology" of Indian middle-class consumerism. As we have seen, culinary TV is now widely available in India, with even families living in informal slum settlements being able to access a range of highly cosmopolitan programming. Such shows offer a kind of imaginary passport – a gateway to an adventurous mobile citizenship for viewers whose actual lives can be decidedly static, bound to household duties and routines and too often rigid gendered and caste-based social identities.

In my discussion of the TV viewing practices of Mumbai households, I have sought to highlight the negotiated relationship between commercial food television and people's often highly reflexive engagements with televisual culinary culture and with their own household habits and routines around cooking and consumption. The varied imaginary and material everyday life practices associated with culinary TV outlined in this chapter speak to the limits of an arguably dominant discourse of "one-size-fits-all" consumer middle-class identity and upward mobility at play in Indian public life, instead foregrounding the intense plurality of social identities found on the ground.

As Lakha has pointed out in relation to the Indian middle class:

> Consumerism and the consumption of global commodities are important in defining the *cultural* identity of the middle class. However, the existence of caste, religious and regional differentiation cautions against any homogenising attempts to characterise Indian middle-class identity in reference to consumption.
>
> (Lakha 1999, 264, emphasis added)

While Lakha's opposition between the cultural and the local or customary here is somewhat fraught, her comment does get at a central dialectic I have sought to highlight in this chapter vis-à-vis the normalizing rhetoric of the new middle class in India and the social "realities" of a nation characterized by multiple registers, scales, speeds and experiences of modernity. In the context of a post-liberalized India, commercial entertainment has undoubtedly come to play a central role in shaping the horizons of imagined social identities and national aspirations. At the same time, I would argue that it often does so in ways that enable a complex negotiation of difference – culinary TV providing a case in point. Culinary television on the one hand often takes its viewers into imaginary and affective spaces well beyond the household. At the same time, it engages with performances and practices that are embedded in and productive of ordinary, everyday socialities. In a media-cultural space where commercial entertainment is taking on an increasingly central role in shaping cultural identities (Turner 2009), food and lifestyle TV more broadly can be seen as a potentially powerful sites for the negotiation of identity and difference. In India, a nation marked by huge social diversity and fragmentation, the role of lifestyle media is perhaps even more potent, offering as it does a space of negotiated and localized forms of aspirationalism and modernity, albeit within a framework oriented towards marketized modes of lifestyle and consumption.

Acknowledgements

Parts of this chapter have been published in Tania Lewis, Fran Martin and Wanning Sun, *Telemodernities: Television and Transforming Lives in Asia* (Duke University Press, 2016).

Notes

1 Interview with Nilendu Sen, New Delhi, November 27, 2011.
2 Interview with Niret Alva, Mumbai, November 30, 2011.
3 Interview with Arati Singh, Mumbai, December 1, 2011.
4 Interview with TV executive, Mumbai, November 29, 2011.
5 Interview with Rajiv Lakshman, Mumbai, November 30, 2011.

References

Chua, Beng Huat. 2000. *Consumption in Asia: Lifestyles and Identities*. New York: Routledge.

Couldry, Nick. 2012. *Media, Society, World: Social Theory and Digital Media Practice*. Cambridge: Polity.

Derné, Steven. 2008. *Globalization on the Ground: New Media and the Transformation of Culture, Class, and Gender in India*. New Delhi: Sage.

Echanove, Matias, and Rahul Srivastava. 2011. "The High Rise & The Slum: Speculative Urban Development in Mumbai." In *Handbook of Urban Economics & Planning*, edited by Nancy Brooks, Kieran Donaghy, and Jan Knaap Gerrit, 789–813. Oxford: Oxford University Press.

Fernandes, Leela. 2006. *India's New Middle Class: Democratic Politics in An Era of Economic Reform*. Minneapolis, MN: University of Minnesota Press.

Kotwal, Ashok, Bharat Ramaswami, and Wilima Wadhwa. 2011. "Economic Liberalization and Indian Economic Growth: What's the Evidence?" *Journal of Economic Literature* 49(4): 1152–1199.

Lakha, Salim. 1999. "The State, Globalisation and Indian Middle Class Identity." In *Culture and Privilege in Capitalist Asia*, edited by Michael Pinches, 252–274. London and New York: Routledge.

Lewis, Tania. 2008. *Smart Living: Lifestyle Media and Popular Expertise*. New York: Peter Lang.

Lewis, Tania, Fran Martin, and Wanning Sun. 2012. "Lifestyling Asia? Shaping Modernity and Selfhood on Life Advice Programming." *International Journal of Cultural Studies* 15(6): 537–566.

Mazzarella, William. 2003. *Shoveling Smoke: Advertising and Globalization in Contemporary India*. Durham: Duke University Press.

NDTV Good Times. 2011. "NDTV Good Times Turns 4." Last modified September 8. www.indiantelevision.com/release/y2k11/sep/seprel11.php (accessed May 20, 2014).

Nijman, Jan. 2006. "Mumbai's Mysterious Middle Class." *International Journal of Urban and Regional Research* 30(4): 758–775.

Robison, Richard, and David S.G. Goodman, eds. 1995. *The New Rich in Asia: Mobile Phones, McDonald's and Middle-class Revolution*. London: Routledge.

Roy, Abhijit. 2008. "Bringing Up TV: Popular Culture and the Developmental Modern in India." *South Asian Popular Culture* 6(1): 29–43.

Shukla, Rajesh. 2010. *How India Earns, Spends and Saves: Unmasking the Real India*. New Delhi: SAGE and NCAERCMCR.

Strange, Niki. 1998. "Perform, Educate, Entertain: Ingredients of the Cookery Programme Genre." In *The Television Studies Book*, edited by Christine Geraghty and David Lusted, 301–312. London: Arnold.

Television Audience Measurement (TAM). 2011. *Television Audience Measurement Annual Universe Update*. www.tamindia.com/webview.php?web=ref_pdf/Overview_Universe_update_2011.pdf (accessed September 16, 2012).

Times of India. 2011. "India's Poverty will Fall from 51% to 22% by 2015: UN Report." Last modified July 8. timesofindia.indiatimes.com/home/environment/developmental-issues/indias-poverty-will-fall-from-51-to-22-by-2015-un-report/articleshow/9152344.cms (accessed October 16, 2011).

Turner, Graeme. 2009. *Ordinary People and the Media: The Demotic Turn*. London: Sage.

Upadhya, Carol. 2009. "India's 'New Middle Class' and the Globalising City: Software Professionals in Bangalore, India." In *The New Middle Classes: Globalizing Lifestyles, Consumerism and Environmental Concern*, edited by Hellmuth Lange and Lars Meier, 253–267. New York: Springer.

Varman, Rohit, and Ram Manohar Vikas. 2007. "Rising Markets and Failing Health: An Inquiry into Subaltern Health Care Consumption under Neoliberalism." *Journal of Macromarketing* 27(2): 162–171. doi: 10.1177/0276146707301333.

11 Islam's got talent

Television, performance and the Islamic public sphere in Malaysia

Bart Barendregt and Chris Hudson

Ordinary Malays and the Islamic public sphere

The proliferation of reality TV in the last couple of decades has had a profound impact on the potential for self-representation: identity production and management are now mediated spectacles, promoted extravagantly through social media, cinema and television. Islamic identity has always been partly constituted through the repetition of embodied practices such as fasting, praying, carrying out ablutions, wearing hijab, traveling to Mecca and so on, but reality TV has produced new embodied practices and opportunities for performing identity. In Malaysia, reality TV formats provide the structures for increasing possibilities for performance of Islam in a cultural and religious environment now characterized by commitment to orthodox Islam in the broader context of the blurring of boundaries between the modern and the traditional, the secular and the sacred, and the local and the global. This chapter is concerned with new forms of mediated performance of Malay-Muslim identity in Malaysia that have emerged in the spaces where such dichotomies have been challenged and where the global Muslim project can be imagined from a particularly Malaysian perspective.

The pivotal role of mass media in providing new resources and new disciplines for the construction of imagined selves and imagined worlds hardly needs reiterating (Appadurai 1996, 3). Certain globally dispersed television formats that seem to be multiplying on domestic screens are distinguished from many other programs by their requirement that contestants or participants carry out some sort of embodied performance. While forms of identity production are commonly expressed through the self-disclosure formats of talk shows, *Big Brother* and the like, a format of equal popularity is the talent show we know as the *Idol* model, now a global phenomenon. In this format, ordinary people can transform themselves into "celetoids," a term Chris Rojek coined to describe ordinary people who create moments of celebrity. Celetoids are "the accessories of culture organized around mass communications and staged authenticity" (Rojek 2001, 20–21). An important aspect of this development in the media's intervention into social life – and the apparently unquenchable thirst for fame graphically illustrated in the mania for "selfies" and YouTube uploads of the self – is that there has been a shift of focus from elites to a celebration of the ordinary. Paradoxically, as Graeme Turner, Frances Bonner and David Marshall point out, this shift has made it possible simultaneously to valorize the celebrity's elite status while celebrating their "intrinsic ordinariness" (Turner et al. 2000, 13). Turner has argued that performing ordinariness has become an end in itself (Turner 2006, 158), and is the result of attempts to construct desires, cultural identities and expectations of the real with no intrinsic content or necessary politics (ibid., 162). He adds that the forms of cultural identity that the media produce today are only loosely connected to the social conditions from which they emerge (ibid., 163).

Revisiting Turner's work from the position of a specific, non-Western site of cultural production might, however, reveal a different relationship between social conditions and cultural identity, and bring into focus "accessories of culture" whose "moment" has a more lasting effect than the lottery winners, one-hit wonders, have-a-go heroes and others Rojek identifies as celetoids (Rojek 2001, 1). In Malaysia, for example, the emergence of the ordinary Malay in talent competitions suggests that self-representation and the performance of the ordinary does not merely produce what Turner (2014, 36) have identified as a commercially constructed social identity, or "celebrity-commodity"; it appears that it also serves to construct a social identity at the site of the intersection of traditional Islam with Malay modernity, as well as modern Islam with Malaysian traditions. Our contention is that ephemeral Malay celetoids in the "famous today, gone tomorrow" mode, are, like their Western counterparts, expressions of intrinsic ordinariness, but are not without intrinsic content. The rise of celebrity populism has created new opportunities to enhance both "Malayness" and Islam. This development represents less a democratization of the media in the form of "democratainment" (Hartley 1999), and more a re-inscription and reimagining of Islam in the public sphere – a new Islamic social imaginary. Marwan Kraidy's work on reality television and Arab politics has illustrated the potential for reality TV to generate heated debates about Western cultural influence, gender relations, political participation and the role of Islam in public life in predominantly Muslim societies. His key point is that reality TV has profoundly altered the ways in which reality can be defined. Central to this is the struggle to define the terms of engagement with Western modernity (Kraidy 2009).

It should be noted that the ordinary celebrity and the reality TV format are both contested spaces that incite certain anxieties and tensions in the Malaysian context. We consider performance in the sense of an individual moment of theatricality, and examine how such a moment might reflect or animate an imagined Muslim world through the rehearsal of Islamic identity. Continuing rehearsal and reiteration of cultural and religious identities does not mean identities are free to be endlessly reimagined and reproduced at will. Certain constraints apply, as debates about the nature of performativity and identity highlight (see, for example, *Theory, Culture and Society* 16(2)). What must be considered is how identities can be embodied and reproduced under given historical, political and cultural conditions. With regard to representations and performance of Islamic identity on reality TV, questions arise around the overlaps between cultural and individual identity on the one hand, and between religious ritual and entertainment on the other. This may be considered with reference to the paradigm suggested by Richard Schechner that juxtaposes two domains of social life constituted by performance – that is, ritual and entertainment. His term, the "efficacy-entertainment braid" (Schechner 1988, 106–52), denotes a continuum at one pole of which are performances that are transformative, such as *rites de passage* and religious rituals, and at the other extreme are performances that are pure entertainment. Most performances are both efficacious in the sense of providing the means for transition from one state to another – such as, for example, becoming a better Muslim, or improving a society with the implementation of Islamic principles – and also entertainment for the purpose of pleasure. The performance of the celetoid as both an individual expression of self-representation and a reiteration of broader religious, national and communal identity is further complicated by its embodied performance as both ritual and entertainment.

This chapter also considers, then, two aspects of the performance of imagined selves and imagined worlds – that is, the nature of the performance and the space of the performance as the location of a new social imaginary. Charles Taylor defines the social imaginary as the common understanding that makes possible common practices and a widely shared sense of legitimacy (Taylor 2004, 23). Drawing on Taylor's work on an imagined collective arising from significations in the public sphere, Nilüfer Göle identifies a new Islamic social imaginary made possible by increased Muslim visibility in the public sphere (Göle 2002). The new public sphere characteristically allows Islamic social actors to accommodate forms of global cultural, economic and political modernity in their everyday lives, while still retaining and articulating a distinctively non-Western social imaginary with a commitment to religion as its reference point. Göle notes also that new ways of imagining the collective in an Islamic public space are underpinned by alternative corporeal and spatial practices (ibid., 174) that reflect local conditions and desires, and are facilitated through the dissemination and consumption of media. The social imaginary can be generated in electronic public spheres, such as those created by the use of mobile phones, information technologies and television. Media technologies have been used in Indonesia and Malaysia to reiterate religious principles and communicate with the faithful, but have also served as an important marker for Islamic modernity distinct from the Western form (Barendregt 2009, 77). In this chapter, we are specifically concerned with the performative dimension of this new Islamic social imaginary as it appears in the mediated spaces of popular culture, and with the role of the ordinary celebrity in its creation.

This chapter is structured accordingly. The first section provides an overview of local adaptations of global TV formats. The subsequent section examines the media as sites for articulation of the complexities and tensions inherent in the imagining of a Malay/Muslim modernity through performative practices. In the discussion that follows, we highlight two cases where modern Islamic identities are performed in a Muslim public sphere: the first is Mawi, a Malay village boy who became an instant Muslim celebrity after his successful participation in the Malaysian talent show *Akademi Fantasia*; our second case is the highly successful talent show *Imam Muda* (Young Imam). Already in its third season, it presents the spectacle of young men performing Islam by demonstrating their talent for reciting the Koran, marrying Muslim couples and singing Islamic songs as they compete for the title of the year's *Young Imam*. We end with some concluding remarks on the mediation of the Islamic public sphere.

Global formats and local identities

Televised talent contests are not new. The Eurovision Song Contest, for example, was first launched in 1956, but is predominantly a competition for professional songwriters and singers. It was with the advent of the *Idol* model that ordinariness became a key commodity. After *American Idol* appeared in 2002, *Idol*s proliferated, as did copy-cat talent shows such as *The X Factor* (2004), *Strictly Come Dancing* (2004), *Dancing with the Stars* (2004), *So You Think You Can Dance* (2005), *America's Got Talent* (2006) and so on. The *Idol* format is one of the most successful formats ever sold globally (Singh and Kretschmer 2012, 11). A significant amount of research on the adaptation of *Idol* to any number of national contexts shows that one of the key features of the reality TV/talent show format is the ease of its adaptability to local and national conditions (Moran and Keane 2004; Waisbord 2004; Moran 2007; Zwaan and de Bruin 2012a). An apparently universal feature of these adaptations is that local identities may emerge as predominant despite the global reach and similarities across instances of the format. Contestants on these shows can represent national, cultural and ethnic identities in constant negotiation of meanings from different sources (Zwaan and de Bruin 2012b, 4). Silvio Waisbord has argued that this feature reveals two developments in contemporary television: the globalization of the business model of television, and the efforts of international and domestic companies to deal with the resilience of national cultures (Waisbord 2004, 360). Format television shows, in effect, organize experiences of the national even if they are not specifically designed to articulate national narratives (Waisbord 2004, 372). Individual Asian nations have invented their own versions of *Idol*-style competitions with *Owarai Star Tanjō!* (1980) and *Asayan* (1995) in Japan, *Star Struck* (2003), *Philippine Idol* (2006) and *Pinoy Dream Academy* (2009) in the Philippines, *Super Star India* (2004), *Super StarK* (2009) in Korea and the *Voice of Indonesia* (2013), an Indonesian adaptation of *The Voice of Holland* (Netherlands, 2010), amongst others. Format shows have also been effective in animating a regional identity, most notably in *Asian Idol*. First launched in

Jakarta, it incorporated South and Southeast Asia. It was broadcast live and featured winners from *Idol* competitions in India, Indonesia, Malaysia, Philippines, Singapore and Vietnam.

In 2002, Mexico launched *La Academia*, a "reality musical talent show" in which contestants live together in a house while preparing for the competition. It has been extensively franchised in Southeast Asia, appearing in Malaysia as *Akademi Fantasia*, in Indonesia as *Akademi Fantasi Indosiar-Viva*, in Singapore as *Sunsilk Academy Fantasia*, and in Thailand as *True Academy Fantasia*. It has been argued that reality TV has been the single most influential phenomenon in the Malaysian TV industry in the last decade, and the success of locally produced programs owes a lot to the launch of *Akademi Fantasia* in 2003 (Shamshudeen and Morris 2014). Participation in such shows is regarded as a means for negotiating a global modernity and reconstructing a local modernity. As the work of Michael Keane, Anthony Fung and Albert Moran (2007) shows, television is a key site for the emergence of new forms of regional cultural imagination in the context of the global, and for the generation of rich re-imaginings of global forms.

Malay modernity, the media and the performance of Islam

The media in Malaysia have been important sites for navigating the social changes that were precipitated by the national project of modernization begun in Malaysia in the 1970s. These changes included rapid urbanization, the development of a burgeoning consumer culture and new forms of cosmopolitanism. Perhaps the most significant aspect of the social transformations in Asia, in particular Southeast Asia, of the last few decades has been the rise of the middle class and the generation of new tastes and desires (Robinson and Goodman 1996; Pinches 1999). Participation in a new public sphere – facilitated by the dissemination and consumption of mass media on a national scale – and a cosmopolitan outlook are prevalent characteristics of this class in Malaysia. Bart Barendregt has pointed out, however, that increasing secularity is not an inevitable outcome of transformed social stratification, improved economic conditions and an outward-looking populace (Barendregt 2006, 174). This new class may have extended its voice and colonized an enlarged public space, but it nevertheless remains deeply committed to religious values and traditions. Aihwa Ong has argued that one specifically Malaysian mode of modernity involves the interlocking of Islamic nationalism with modernity (Ong 2006, 47–8). Islam remains the spiritual and moral foundation of a secular state, despite a sizeable minority who are not Muslims. Muslim social imaginaries now have to be produced within a space that encompasses uncertain relationships between the sacred and the profane, secular time and religious time, non-Western and Western. It is also within that space that the ordinary celebrity as one version of the modern subject has emerged.

Shmuel Eisenstadt's seminal work on "multiple modernities" argues that Western modernity should not be understood as the "authentic" modernity.

Rather, the history of modernity is best understood as a "continual constitution and reconstitution of a multiplicity of cultural programs" (Eisenstadt 2000, 2). A recent volume of work on modernity and religion in Southeast Asia illustrates the extent to which the relationship between religion and modernity is a dynamic process that is played out in a range of sites and in multiple modes (Gottowik 2014). The media are not merely key sites for the struggle to define the terms of engagement with Western modernity, as Kraidy argues (Kraidy 2009), but are also sites for the constitution and reconstitution of culture-specific modernities. The mass media, in particular reality TV and soap opera, have been identified as ongoing sites for the imagining of a specifically Malaysian modernity (Hamzah and Md Syed 2013; Hudson and Md Azalanshah 2014). Furthermore, the constitution of Malaysian modernity through reality TV and soaps has not been confined to its engagement with Western versions, as the immense popularity of Korean soaps such as *Winter Sonata* (Iwabuchi 2004) and the multitude of *Idol*-type programs show.

As discussed above, Göle has argued that the new Islamic social imaginary that has emerged in non-Western public spheres provides the stage for the performance of modern subjects (Göle 2002, 177). Islam has a "new stage" (ibid., 190) for new subjects in the publics created by globalized TV formats, and it is on this stage that specifically Islamist performance has appeared. We understand Islamism as a modern era form of activism that sees Islam as providing answers to questions in all domains of life, not merely politics or spirituality but also economics and lifestyle issues (Calvert 2008, 4). Originally made popular by student activists and fundamentalist sects in the 1980s, the style of Islamist performances that express these commitments have increasingly been appropriated by the entertainment industry and strategically deployed in order to appeal to the emergent Muslim Malay middle class. Historical anxieties about ethnic and religious identities meant that televised talent shows were initially rejected in Malaysia and condemned by Muslim activists and intellectuals as hedonistic and idolatrous. In 2006, Indonesian writer Alwi Alatas pointed out in a booklet called *The Real Idol* that most "modern" youth have someone they adore, worship, or who simply turns them into a crazed fan, but questioned whether it is appropriate for a Muslim to idolize anyone (Alatas 2006). Using the language of new media he described the Prophet Muhammad as the only true idol. Malaysian TV celebrity and former rock star Ustaqz Akhil Hayy struck a similar chord when, in a motivational speech at the al-Firdous Mosque in Kota Damansara in 2008 entitled "Entertainment that leads astray" (Hayy 2008), he similarly maligned talent shows such as *Malaysian Idol* and *Akademi Fantasia*. Hayy warned his audience about the perils of entertainment imported from the West. His intention was to promote an Islamic form of "edutainment," which would both entertain and feed the soul. The quest to find appropriate forms of entertainment for an Islamic society continued, he said, and he lamented the fact that too little attention had been given to it by the Islamic clergy. It is important to note that Hayy's criticism not only employed the lexicon of popular culture, but also media technology. In a clear demonstration that tradition could be "modernized" without abandoning commitment to Islamic values, only two years after his public diatribe, Hayy performed the title song of what was dubbed the world's first truly Islamic talent show, *Young Imam* (Figure 11.1).

Entertainment with an Islamic message, or "intrinsic content," has since created new forms of Islamic publics made possible through media presentations of performances that are located somewhere along the ritual/entertainment spectrum described by Schechner (1988, 106–52). If edutainment has become popular, so too has "Islamotainment," illustrated by the success of Islamic entertainers in Muslim Southeast Asia in the finals of *Voice of Indonesia* and *Akademi Fantasia.* These appearances have been instrumental not only in "reinventing" Islam for a modern world in which so much social reality is mediatized, but also in encouraging the emergence of a modern subject and a performance of individuality that is at the same time an articulation of the spiritual and ethical values of Islam. The televisual story of a "simple lad" from a resettlement village is one such case.

Figure 11.1 Screenshot of the video clip "Hamba-mu" (Your Servant), performed by Akhil Hayy and pop singer Mawi, and featuring the contestants of *Young Imam*'s second season, Astro Oasis

From FELDA to the world

A defining moment for Malaysian talent shows and the Muslim social imaginary arrived in 2005 when Asmawi Ani auditioned for *Akademi Fantasia.* Asmawi, born in 1981 and popularly nicknamed "Mawi," was in many respects the ideal idol: simple, ordinary and a textbook example of "staged authenticity" (Rojek 2001, 20–21). The Malaysian media highlighted his humble origins as the son of a blacksmith born in Taib Andak, Johor – a district for resettlement of rural poor under the management of the Federal Land Development Authority, more commonly referred to as FELDA. While he was firmly positioned as an ordinary Malay, he was also heralded as a *qari*, a singer of recitations of the Quran and an exponent of Islamic songs known as *nasheeds.* Mawi reinforced his status as an ordinary, but decidedly pious, Muslim when he chose the song *Intifada* to perform in the selection process that preceded the contest. *Intifada* was originally performed by Rabbani, a popular *nasheed* boy band with its roots in Malaysia's Islamist movement. The song later became a symbol of the transformation of *nasheed* from a traditional genre into what is now widely considered to be the most global and modern of Islamic music. By performing *Intifada*, Mawi was able to position himself as simultaneously modern and assertively Islamic.

Perhaps the most interesting feature of Mawi in the context of the rise of the ordinary celebrity as an aspect of the modernizing of the Islamic public sphere is that he was not only considered to be not very good looking, but was also no better than an average singer. He was originally not selected for the finals. Despite his inherent mediocrity and early elimination, he was brought back onto the show by the jury the week following his initial failure; by week ten he had won the contest and his popularity was ensured. Constructed as the ultimate ordinary Muslim by the promotional "hype," the *tsu-mawi* – a combination of tsunami and Mawi – phenomenon quickly swept the nation. A new representation of the modern self as an amalgamation of local/ordinary and global/glamorous emerged when he was advised by his *Akademi Fantasia* mentors to portray himself as a "world-class entertainer," inserting the expression "world" as a tagline during his performances.[1] Within a mere three months he had become a national icon, performing with artists such as pop diva Siti Nurhaliza. Malaysian fans soon started referring to "Mawi World." Despite the performance of global selfhood, his elevation from village nobody to national pop icon, and the exploitation of media technologies for financial gain, he still promotes himself as a devout (*alim*) village boy. The performance of Islamic songs and Malay classics, coupled with his perceived connections in the global arena, proved a successful blending of the worldly and the parochial.

Following his *Akademi Fantasia* win, and with the triumph of the *tsu-mawi*, Mawi seemed to be omnipresent. By then he had begun to be associated in Malaysia with new forms of identity production that could be seen as both modern and traditional. In addition to starring in two major movies, producing his first album called *Best of Mawi World* (Figure 11.2), followed by a

Figure 11.2 A cassette version of Mawi's first album with songs he performed during the third season of the *Akademi Fantasia* contest

full album with prayer and Islamic chants (*Doa, Berzanji & Qasidah Berlagu*, 2006), he had a *tudung* (Islamic headscarf) named after him. The *Tudung ME World* ("Mawi World headscarf") signifies the combination of Islamic values demonstrated by restraint in the presentation of self, with a reach into the global. The appropriation of tradition by the modern, however, made him the target of criticism, especially from orthodox Muslims and Islamic media who looked to Mawi to uphold the Islamic cause without contamination by modern influences. The Malaysian media made much of him breaking up with his long-time fiancée Diana Naim, a singer of *nasheed* herself, fearing that fame and Western-style entertainment had after all corrupted the much-celebrated singer. Anxieties arising from Mawi's perceived un-Islamic behavior stemming from his high visibility on the national stage suggest that the talent show is still not entirely domesticated.

Mawi has since married and now presents a mature image, helped by his recordings of more traditional Islamic songs. He is no longer referred to as the "the king of texting" (*Raja SMS*), known for his fan base of predominantly young women. Talent shows may provide new platforms for the combined performance of individual and Islamic identity, but the promise of a more modern and popular Islam also calls forth other conservative forces that still demand that some aspects of modernizing Islam be contained and "forbidden" (see Göle 1996).

Young imams perform Islam

More recently, *Young Imam*, another Malaysian reality TV show that is even more compliant with religious traditions than *Akademi Fantasia*, has emerged. It has quickly become another important site for the packaging of local tradition in the framework of commercialization and the rise of the ordinary celebrity. Seen by some as an antidote to the perceived negative influences of modernity, the popularity of the show is an illustration of the extent to which the sustained commitment to Islamic values and the importance of correct behavior are still at the heart of the Muslim Malay social imaginary. Where the reality TV format was once considered to be too alien and a threat to Islamic values, with the appearance of *Young Imam*, it is now well adapted and domesticated, and able to play a significant role in reinforcing the normative culture with which most Malaysian Muslims are familiar.

Young Imam is a ten-episode TV series that was first broadcast from May to July 2010. Two further seasons followed in 2011 and 2012, and today it is one of the most successful shows in the history of Astro Oasis, the religious television channel that produces the show. In the show, ten young men, mostly aged in their twenties, compete for the sought-after position of imam in a Kuala Lumpur mosque. Participants are challenged to perform a series of written and practical tasks that test their religious skills and knowledge. Aspiring imams perform Islam by delivering sermons, providing spiritual advice to juvenile delinquents involved in some of Malaysia's notorious motorcycle gangs, counseling pregnant unmarried women and couples who are considering divorce, as well as overseeing the slaughter of animals in accordance with Islamic laws. One episode that particularly captured the imagination of the public had the contestants at a morgue washing and burying an unclaimed body of someone who reputedly had died of AIDS. The audience followed the young contenders as they then contemplated their own mortality on national television.

Apart from the glittering prize of appointment as imam, other prizes include modern consumer goods such as the latest model Proton, the much-loved national car. However, the rewards also recall Malay Muslims' spiritual ties to the history of Islam by offering a scholarship to Al-Azhar University – built in Cairo in the tenth century and one of the oldest universities in the world – or al-Madinah University in Saudi Arabia. Reaching out to the heartlands of a larger Islamic world and reinforcing tradition is also symbolized in the prize of a pilgrimage to Mecca. The promise of material rewards and celebrity combined with religious devotion not only engages the audience in a new sort of talent quest designed to satisfy both worldly and spiritual desires, but positions the Malays in the wider history of the Islamic world; it can also help re-inscribe tradition as an integral component of a modern social imaginary.

Another important aspect of the show where the boundaries between modernity and tradition are obscured is in the selection of contestants with the appropriate imam-like qualities. The producers want the quest for the best young imam of Malaysia to be exciting, but also to convey a certain legitimacy. The decisions are made by a panel of three rather than by the Religious Affairs Department or in the mosque, but are not without popular input. Wannabe imams engage with the public sphere to increase their store of populist celebrity by maintaining active blogs and Twitter accounts while they participate in the show. Being media savvy seems to be at least one criterion of success, since the audience complains if one of the imams appears to ignore his fellow Muslims in the Twitterverse. The show also demonstrates the centrality of popular culture for the new Islamic public sphere in other ways. In a spectacle of ordinariness modeled on *Big Brother*, throughout the ten weeks the program was recorded in a dormitory in a secluded mosque compound. To increase the isolation, the group of young imams was denied the use of computers, tablets or mobile phones, except for the purpose of counseling and providing spiritual advice.

While these men are arguably far too young to be accepted as true leaders of their communities, their youth and vaguely sexual allure is one of the main attractions of the program. Izelan Basar, the show's creator and manager of Astro Oasis, explained that the aim of the show was to entertain as well as to educate people in correct religious practices (Henderson 2010). Like television content everywhere, it is constrained by commercial imperatives, so the young imams are selected for their photogenic looks and media appeal to become Turner's "celebrity-commodity" (Turner 2014, 36). Rather than the standard Islamic dress of a typical elderly imam, they dress in elegant Western-style suits (see Figure 11.3), while also sporting well-trimmed, fashionable Muslim

Figure 11.3 Screenshot showing some of the first season's contestants of the Astro Oasis show *Young Imam*

beards. It should come as no surprise, then, that the show appeals to young women who imagine them not only as candidates for young imam, but also as eligible bachelors and candidates for marriage.[2] The show is presented as a televised ritual consisting of a series of small, stylized acts. These performative moments, called "tests," put the spotlight on the way the contestants greet others, speak or dress. While tests that participants must pass are central to many reality TV shows, for competitors on *Young Imam* such acts of embodied performance must be meticulously executed in compliance with guidelines set by ritual authorities.

If *Young Imam*'s intention is to repackage Islamic authority in line with the modernizing agenda of Islamic nationalism alluded to by Ong (2006, 47–8), the show must also find a middle ground that falls short of disrupting that authority. Astro Oasis channel manager Izelan Basar is reported as saying: "We have been very careful not to cross any lines or offend anyone and to take a middle path" (Henderson 2010). To ensure that there was no inadvertent violation of Islamic sensibilities or orthodoxy, the program was co-produced with the Federal Department of Islamic Religion (*Jabatan Agama Islam Wilayah Persekutuan*), a government body that oversees Islamic religious activities and is legally responsible for the appointment of imams to mosques and for providing guidance on the content of sermons. The show was launched during a ceremony that saw Minister for Religious Affairs Jamil Khir Baharom voicing his hope that *Young Imam* would "push a younger generation into the direction of good behavior and a righteous character" (Bernama 2010). From its inception, it has been a vehicle for governmental interpretations of what public Islam should look like. The final spectacle to select the winning imam did not take place in a Kuala Lumpur TV studio, where other episodes had been staged, but was televised live from the national mosque. An important part of the media extravaganza was the appearance of the country's most respected Muslim authorities, including the minister for religious affairs. It probably does not need reiterating that this is a particularly compelling example of state strategies to conflate Islamic nationalism with modernity and to ensure their continued high visibility in a mediated public sphere.

Concluding remarks

Digital and other global communications technologies have for some time been instrumental in the emergence of new Islamic publics. As Göle (2002) argues, these publics are characterized by Islamic vocabulary, specifically Islamic corporeal rituals and spatial practices, and public debates transformed by religious issues. A major contributing factor of this development is the rise of a middle class (ibid., 173). It is in the context of concerted efforts by the Malaysian government to generate new public understandings of a national Islamic modernity with its origins in the 1970s that Mawi, humble origins notwithstanding, becomes the quintessential Malay celetoid. Reality

TV has been one of the most powerful platforms for offering alternatives to the ways Islamic modernity can be defined. It can also be one vehicle for negotiating engagements with Western modernity, but this has not been without its tensions and the ability to generate anxieties around potential challenges to Islamic authority.

Astro Oasis promotes *Young Imam* as the "first program to document the Islamic journey" as it turns ordinary Malays into glamorous religious role models and makes a televised spectacle out of worship and other forms of embodied expressions of Islam. *Akademi Fantasia* and *Young Imam* have borrowed liberally from the *Idol, X Factor* and *Big Brother* formats, and have adapted them to localized conditions and audiences. Specifically Malay-Muslim identities are reconstructed with "intrinsic content" that will satisfy the requirements of Islamic spiritual values and ethics. The creation of expectations and the reinforcement of normative cultural values that are seen in *Akademi Fantasia* and *Young Imam* are common to popular talent shows worldwide. They also promote the idea that despite being too fat, too queer, too ugly, too young or too old, an ordinary person can "against all odds" become a celebrity in their own right. What is distinctive about these Malay shows is that they not only signal Turner's (2010) "demotic turn," demonstrated by the elevation of the ordinary as a desired commodity, but *Young Imam*, in particular, also points to a Malaysian "spiritual turn" that has opened up new possibilities for the media to operate not merely as a mediator of cultural identities. As Turner argues, its contemporary function is closer to that of translator or even an author of identities (ibid., 5). Performances that fall into the category of "edutainment" or "Islamotainment" can fuse the entertainment value of the ordinary individual with the transformative potential of ritual, in the way suggested by Schechner (1988). Its genius lies in its potential to be both.

The focus on TV talent contests as adaptations of Western formats should be seen in the context of a tradition of Muslim entertainment that reaches back to popular *nasheeds* of the 1970s and 1980s and the International Quran recital competitions, first begun in 1961 by then Prime Minister Tunku Abdul Rahman and later televised. More recent formats, however, have been very successful in imagining the global Muslim project from a particular Malaysian perspective. Such formats have led to even more overtly religious shows such as *Akademi al-Quran* (2006) and *Solehah* (*Pious Woman*, 2011), a talent show for women competing for the title of most charismatic preacher.[3] If, as Nick Couldry has pointed out, ordinary people have never been more desired by or more visible within the media (Couldry 2003, 102), perhaps it is fair to say that in the Malaysian case, pious people have never been more desired by or more visible within the media.

Notes

1 Facebook correspondence with Shazlin Amir Hamzah (UKM) and Frizdan Fizarahman (Inteam Records), October 2013.

2 Nonetheless, viewers are cautiously aware of the inappropriateness of such worldly attraction, as a comment by a user called Etykus on her own weblog demonstrates: "… it is important to remember that the *nawaitu* [intentions] must always be because of Him and for Him … lets [sic] take the lessons available and learn and our nawaitu must be straight too […] not to watch because they are potentially eligible husbands *though they indeed are. ehem*." To which another visitor, Pikasya, more bluntly adds: "choose choose, a candidate husband, hehehe" (*pilih plih. calon suami. hehehe*). Both quotes are at etykus.blogspot.nl/2011/04/imam-muda-2.html (accessed April 26, 2011).

3 *Liga Ilmu: Debat Imam Muda Vs Ustazah Pilihan* (Knowledge League: Debate between the Young Imam and the Elected Ustazah), a show which in 2012 was similarly launched by Astro Oasis, seems to combine several of the elements of these programs, with female and male youngsters now challenging each other in debate and thus both exposing and sharing their religious knowledge and skills with a larger audience. Like its predecessors, the program is strongly normative and overall affirmative of existing gender roles within Malaysian Islam.

References

Alatas, Alwi. 2006. *The Real Idol*. Bandung: Syaamil Cipta Media.

Appadurai, Arjun. 1996. *Modernity at Large: Cultural Dimensions of Globalization*. Minneapolis, MN: University of Minnesota Press.

Barendregt, Bart. 2006. "Cyber-nasyid: Transnational Soundscapes in Muslim Southeast Asia." In *media@sia: Global Media/tion in and out of Context*, edited Todd Joseph, Miles Holden and Timothy J. Scrase, 170–187. London: Routledge.

Barendregt, Bart. 2009. "Mobile Religiosity in Indonesia. Mobilized Islam, Islamized Modernity and the Potential of Islamic TechnoNationalism." In *Living the Information Society in Indonesia*, edited by Erwin Alampay, 73–92. Singapore: ISEAS Publishing.

Bernama. 2010. "Perkahwinan Dengan Kanak-kanak Tidak Ikut Sunnah – Jamil Khir." *Bernama*, March 2. www.bernama.com/bernama/v3/bm/news_lite.php?id=481852 (accessed May 29, 2015).

Calvert, John C. 2008. *Islamism: A Documentary and Reference Guide*. Westport, CT: Greenwood Press.

Couldry, Nick. 2003. *Media Rituals: A Critical Approach*. London: Routledge.

Eisenstadt, Shmuel N. 2000. "Multiple Modernities." *Daedalus* 129(1): 1–27.

Göle, Nilüfer. 1996. *The Forbidden Modern: Civilization and Veiling*. Ann Arbor, MI: University of Michigan Press.

Göle, Nilüfer. 2002. "Islam in Public: New Visibilities and New Imaginaries." *Public Culture* 14(1): 173–190.

Gottowik, Volker, ed. 2014. *Dynamics of Religion in Southeast Asia: Magic and Modernity*. Amsterdam: Amsterdam University Press.

Hamzah, Azizah, and Md Azalanshah Md Syed. 2013. "Imagining Modernity in Contemporary Malaysia: Non-Western Soap Opera and the Negative Urban." In *Popular Culture in Asia: Memory, City, Celebrity*, edited by Lorna Fitzsimons and John A. Lent, 142–159. London: Palgrave Macmillan.

Hartley, John. 1999. *Uses of Television*. London: Routledge.

Hayy, Ustaqz Akhil. 2008. *Motivasi Perdana Badak Sumbu*. Kuala Lumpur: ALIAS-Salam Enterprise. VCD.

Henderson, Barney. 2010. "X Factor for Muslim Preachers in Malaysia Wows Television Audience." *The Telegraph*, June 25. www.telegraph.co.uk/news/worldnews/a

sia/malaysia/7855062/X-factor-for-Muslim-preachers-in-Malaysia-wows-television-audience.html (accessed May 29, 2015).

Hudson, Chris and Md Azalanshah. 2014. "Women and Television in Malaysia: Soaps, Transnational Pleasure and Modernity" In *Reading Asian Television Drama: Crossing Borders and Breaking Boundaries*, edited by Jeongmee Kim, 125–145. London: I.B. Tauris.

Iwabuchi, Koichi, ed. 2004. *Feeling Asian Modernities: Transnational Consumption of Japanese TV Dramas.* Hong Kong: Hong Kong University Press.

Keane, Michael, Anthony Y.H. Fung, and Albert Moran. 2007. *New Television, Globalisation and the East Asian Cultural Imagination.* Hong Kong: Hong Kong University Press.

Kraidy, Marwan M. 2009. *Reality Television and Arab Politics: Contention in Public Life.* New York: Cambridge University Press.

Mawi. 2006. *Doa, Berzanji & Qasidah Berlagu.* Maestro Records 2071–2072. CD-ROM.

Moran, Albert. 2007. "Localising Global Television." *Media International Australia* 124: 145–155.

Moran, Albert, and Michael Keane, eds. 2004. *Television Across Asia: Television Industries, Programme Formats and Globalisation.* London and New York: RoutledgeCurzon.

Ong, Aihwa. 2006. *Neoliberalism as Exception: Mutations in Citizenship and Sovereignty.* Durham and London: Duke University Press.

Pinches, Michael, ed. 1999. *Culture and Privilege in Capitalist Asia.* London: Routledge.

Robinson, Richard, and David S.G. Goodman, eds. 1996. *The New Rich in Asia: Mobile Phones, McDonald's and Middle-Class Revolution.* London: Routledge.

Rojek, Chris. 2001. *Celebrity.* London: Reaktion.

Schechner, Richard. 1988. *Performance Theory.* New York and London: Routledge.

Shamshudeen, Rosya Izyanie, and Brian Morris. 2014. "'No hugging please, we are Muslims': Akademi Fantasia, Malay Television Audiences and the Negotiation of Global Popular Cultural Forms." *Asian Journal of Communication* 24(2): 142–157.

Singh, Sukhpreet, and Nartin Kretschmer. 2012. "Strategic Behaviour in the International Exploitation of TV Formats: A Case Study of the Idols Format." In *Adapting Idols: Authenticity, Identity and Performance in a Global Television Format*, edited by Koos Zwaan and Joost de Bruin, 11–26. Farnham, Surrey: Ashgate Publishing.

Taylor, Charles. 2004. *Modern Social Imaginaries.* Durham, NC and London: Duke University Press.

Turner, Graeme. 2006. "The Mass Production of Celebrity: 'Celetoids', Reality TV and the 'Demotic Turn'." *International Journal of Cultural Studies* 9(2): 153–165.

Turner, Graeme. 2010. *Ordinary People and the Media: The Demotic Turn.* London: Sage

Turner, Graeme. 2014. *Understanding Celebrity.* London: Sage.

Turner, Graeme, Frances Bonner, and P. David Marshall. 2000. *Fame Games: The Production of Celebrity in Australia.* Cambridge: University of Cambridge.

Waisbord, Silvio. 2004. "McTV: Understanding the Global Popularity of Television Formats." *Television and New Media* 5(4): 359–383.

Zwaan, Koos, and Joost de Bruin, eds. 2012a. *Adapting Idols: Authenticity, Identity and Performance in a Global Television Format.* Farnham: Ashgate Publishing.

Zwaan, Koos, and Joost de Bruin, eds. 2012b. "Introduction: Adapting Idols." In *Adapting Idols: Authenticity, Identity and Performance in a Global Television Format*, edited by Koos Zwaan and Joost de Bruin, 1–10. Farnham: Ashgate Publishing.

Index

For Product Safety Concerns and Information please contact our EU
representative GPSR@taylorandfrancis.com
Taylor & Francis Verlag GmbH, Kaufingerstraße 24, 80331 München, Germany

www.ingramcontent.com/pod-product-compliance
Ingram Content Group UK Ltd.
Pitfield, Milton Keynes, MK11 3LW, UK
UKHW021303190926
475701UK00009B/631

* 9 7 8 1 1 3 8 4 7 7 4 1 4 *